ABOUT THE AUTHORS

CESAR MILLAN, star of *Dog Whisperer with Cesar Millan*, founded the Dog Psychology Center in Los Angeles. In addition to Cesar's educational seminars and work with unstable dogs, he and his wife have founded the Cesar and Ilusion Millan Foundation, a non-profit organization dedicated to providing financial support and rehabilitation expertise to shelters. A native of Culican, Mexico, Cesar lives in Los Angeles with his wife, Ilusion, and their two sons, Andre and Calvin.

MELISSA JO PELTIER, an executive producer and writer of *Dog Whisperer with Cesar Millan*, has been honored for her film and television writing and directing with an Emmy, a Peabody, and more than fifty other awards. She lives in Nyack, New York, with her husband, writer-director John Gray, and stepdaughter, Caitlin.

CESAR MILLAN

with Melissa Jo Peltier

A MEMBER *of the* FAMILY

Cesar Millan's Guide to a Lifetime of Fulfillment with Your Dog

HODDER

The techniques presented in this book are for informational purposes only. As each individual situation is unique, you should use proper discretion, in consultation with a professional dog expert, before utilizing the information contained in this book. The author and publisher expressly disclaim responsibility for any adverse effects that may result from the use or application of the information contained in this book.

First published in Great Britain in 2009 by Hodder & Stoughton
An Hachette UK company

Offset by arrangement with Harmony Books, an imprint of the
Crown Publishing Group, a division of Random House, Inc., New York.

First published in paperback in 2009

A CIP catalogue record for this title is available from the British Library

ISBN 978 0 340 97856 6

Printed and bound in the UK by CPI Mackays, Chatham ME5 8TD

Hodder & Stoughton policy is to use papers that are natural, renewable and recyclable products and made from wood grown in sustainable forests. The logging and manufacturing processes are expected to conform to the environmental regulations of the country of origin.

Hodder & Stoughton Ltd
338 Euston Road
London NW1 3BH

www.hodder.co.uk

First and foremost, I'd like to dedicate this book to my human family members—my parents, my brother and sisters, my wife and my two sons. Second, I want to remember all the amazing dogs in my life that have been loyal family members to me.

I'd also like to give an individual acknowledgment to one very special dog, my pit bull, Daddy. I have loved many dogs in my life, but Daddy really takes the cake. He has helped me to raise my kids, taught me how to be a calm-assertive parent, and helped me to rehabilitate hundreds of troubled dogs. Most important of all, Daddy has shown me what it really means to give for the good of the pack, expecting nothing in return, but knowing that good will eventually come. Daddy is one of the wisest beings (of any species!) I have ever known, and it has been an honor to work with, live with, and love him for these fourteen amazing years.

CONTENTS

ACKNOWLEDGMENTS

This book would not have been possible were it not for the invaluable contributions of some of the finest veterinarians in the profession. Graciously adding their wisdom, advice, and tips were Dr. Sherry Weaver of the Animal Hospital of Towne Lake in Woodstock, Georgia; Debbie Oliver, DVM, of the Blue Cross Pet Hospital in Pacific Palisades, California; Charles Rinehimer, VMD, of Northampton University in Pennsylvania (who also contributed greatly to our last book); and Paula Terifaj, DVM, of Founders Veterinary Clinic in Brea, California.

Others have helped me quench my thirst for more knowledge about canine wellness: Dr. Brij Rawat, DVM, of Hollypark Pet Clinic in Gardena, has generously supported my mission to help dogs since I was a struggling young trainer newly arrived in Los Angeles. Dr. Rick Garcia and his mobile veterinary hospital, Paws 'n Claws, have rushed to many emergencies where pack members or clients' dogs have needed special care.

Most recently, Dr. Marty Goldstein of the Smith Ridge clinic in South Salem, New York, the premier integrative veterinary medicine clinic in the country, has had a great influence on me as I continue to explore the areas of homeopathic and naturopathic medicine for dogs, as well as tools such as acupuncture, acupressure, and massage. Also instrumental in these efforts are homeopathic doctor Dahlia

Shemtob and acupuncturist Vivian Engelson. All these dedicated health professionals have been part of a solid support system—not just for this book, but also for the Dog Psychology Center, the *Dog Whisperer* television series, and for all of our questions, fact checks, and emergencies throughout the years. We truly are blessed to have such a diverse and talented pool of professionals as our role models and trusted references.

The authors would also like to thank our literary agent, Scott Miller of Trident Media Group; Julia Pastore, Shaye Areheart, Kira Stevens, and Tara Gilbride at Random House; Steve Schiffman, Steve Burns, Michael Cascio, Char Serwa, Mike Beller, Chris Albert, and Russell Howard at the National Geographic Channel; Fred Fierst, Esq.; Michael Gottsagen and company at IMG; and Neil Stearns and Damon Frank at Venture IAB.

At MPH, thanks to Bonnie Peterson, George Gomez, Nicholas Ellingsworth, Todd Carney, Christine Lochman, Cherise Paluso, and especially to Crystal Cupp for her fact-checking, research, and consistently upbeat attitude. We are indebted to Cynthia "CJ" Anderson, moderator of the Dog Whisperer Yahoo.com fan group and coordinator of the "Cesar Ambassadors" program, for her help in finding our success stories.

On the *Dog Whisperer* series, Kay Bachman Sumner, Sheila Possner Emery, and SueAnn Fincke keep the show running smoothly, with the help of our peerless field crew and editorial staff. Special gratitude goes to the woman behind the scenes who keeps all of us at the *Dog Whisperer* television show looking beautiful—makeup and hair artist Rita Montanez.

Finally, Cesar Millan wants to extend his special appreciation and gratitude to Oprah Winfrey: "Thank you for giving me a dream opportunity to be able to work with you and your sweet Sophie. God rest her soul; I will always value our experience together dearly"; and to IMG: "Thank you all for believing in me and helping the world to become a better place for dogs and humans. I am so proud to be on such a dedicated and committed team."

Melissa Jo Peltier wishes to thank her MPH partners, Jim Milio and Mark Hufnail, for their consistent and immeasurable support; and Ilusion Millan for her friendship and inspiration. Gratitude also goes to her dear friend Victoria A.; her dad, Ed Peltier; her stepdaughter, Caitlin Gray; and her husband, John Gray, who is as much her muse as she is his.

INTRODUCTION

Biologists, historians, anthropologists, and archaeologists have spent years arguing over how the bond between humans and dogs—now many thousands of years old—came to be. But since dogs live in the moment—and I try to follow their example—I'd like to put forth a theory of my own that relates only to dogs as they are today. Dogs and humans are alike in one way that is so fundamental to our being, neither species can survive without it. Like human beings, dogs are eternally attracted to the concept of *family*.

When they live in the wild, most canids naturally arrange themselves into family-based packs. Even if the dogs aren't related to one another by blood, the bonds of living and surviving together turn them into a smoothly functioning unit. Within that unit, there forms a loyalty, a trust, and an understanding so deep, we as humans can only look on with awe. These are the qualities we dream of having in our own relationships with the families that we are born into and the families we create, but being "only human," we often fall short. But when we bring dogs into our lives, we have access to their inborn integrity. By making dogs full-fledged members of our families, we have the ability to make those human families stronger.

In our human society, the definitions of family are always adapting and changing. In some parts of the world, families consist of many generations of related members, still bound together in tribal groups or clans in the struggle to survive. Here in America, the concept of the "average" household being a mom, a dad, and two-point-five kids has shifted to include blended families from various marriages and divorces, as well as single-sex couples living together, with or without kids. We have aunts and uncles and cousins; godfathers and godmothers; in-laws; stepsiblings and foster siblings. To me, even all these titles limit the true definition of *family*. When an owner calls me in to help a dog, what I am really there to do is to create an orderly, functioning pack out of what appears to the owner as chaos. That pack can be anything from a single woman and her one dog living in a small apartment, to a monastery filled with twenty candidates for the priesthood and their watchdog, to a college sorority house and their canine mascot, to a senior citizens' home and the therapy dogs that regularly visit there. To me, a pack *is* a family; they are one and the same. And wherever you have a dog that needs a home, you have the potential for a fantastic pack.

But although we yearn to include dogs as members of our families, we often don't work together as families to welcome them into our human world. Just as it takes a village to raise a child, it takes a whole family to create a smoothly running pack. My intent with this book is to invite myself into your family throughout these pages. I want to stand by your side and guide you and your family through every phase of your dog's life, from the day you bring her home, to the day you say good-bye and celebrate her life and death. I hope this book will reach out to every member of your family—from youngest to oldest—and invite each of them to participate in a way of connecting with dogs that creates balance for dogs and humans alike. This connection doesn't really require money, and it doesn't really require any great level of education or intelligence. What it does require is putting common sense and instinct first, and understanding that sometimes what seems best for the human is not the best thing for the dog.

I believe a strong family is the foundation of all achievement. If we have a family behind us cheering us on—whether that means just one dog or one human, or ten people or fifty dogs—we have a springboard of support to reach any dreams to which we dare aspire. Since my own human family is such a big part of my own mission, I have enlisted their help in the writing of this book. My wife, Ilusion, speaks to women in Chapter 9, and my sons, Calvin and Andre, offer their advice to kids in Chapter 10. I also include the wisdom of the dogs that are always members of our family, especially Daddy, the oldest member of my pack, and Junior, the youngest. Ilusion, Calvin, Andre, and I are always learning from the wisdom our dogs share with us. Dogs teach us to live in the now. They teach us that the trappings of our human existence don't matter so much in the long run—as long as we celebrate the moment, and never forget to appreciate one another.

If we remember to fulfill their needs first, dogs can add so much to our human families. A dog will always have your back, no matter what. With a dog in your life, you will never feel alone. And if you do, just go to a shelter. There is always a dog there, waiting, just looking forward to becoming a member of a family.

1

A Match Made in Heaven:

Determining the Right Dog
for You and Your Family

Cesar and Molly

When eleven-year-old Jack Sabato first spotted the little male Pomeranian-papillon mix, his eyes lit up. "This one looks like Dixie!" he excitedly called out to his mother, the Academy Award–nominated actress Virginia Madsen. The little dog in the cage in the back of the van clearly reminded Jack of his adored but recently departed shepherd mix.

Virginia is a valued client of mine. Several years ago, she called me in to help with Dixie's issues of constantly bolting from the yard. Virginia was an ideal client who picked up on the concept of leadership right away, and Dixie turned out to be a dream-come-true as a family dog for thirteen happy years. Now that Dixie had passed away at the age of fourteen, Virginia called for my advice again in selecting the right new dog to add to her pack—which consisted of her, her son, and their aging French bulldog, Spike. This was going to be an interesting and important case for me. What if the family's choice for a dog went against my own instincts? I could give advice, but it was, after all, ultimately their decision.

Virginia told me she wanted a small dog. United Hope for Animals, a group that rescues death-row cases from both Mexico and Southern California, had kindly answered my call to bring up a van full of possible candidates for Virginia and her son to choose from. Jack immediately gravitated toward Foxy, the two-year-old male that reminded him of Dixie. Virginia preferred Belle, a female Chihuahua mix. I showed Jack how to present Spike—rear first—to the other dogs while they were in their kennels in the back of the van, to help smooth the way for an off-leash meeting. Then mother and son took their respective choices into the backyard, to observe their off-leash behavior, and to see how well they interacted with Spike.

From the first moment in the backyard, Foxy's energy became clear. Though he looked adorable—with bright, dark eyes, a foxlike muzzle, and soft, fluffy, reddish fur—his behavior betrayed him as an insecure, dominating male. Foxy's first order of business was to take a thorough tour of the yard, marking his territory everywhere he went. For me, that was a red flag right off the bat, especially considering the new dog would be sharing his home with another male, Spike. If Foxy was to be the family's choice, there were going to be dominance issues; and for ten-year-old Spike—a laid-back guy who had enjoyed calm, mellow golden years while living with Dixie—that would no doubt be a very stressful experience. Belle the Chihuahua mix, on the other hand, was curious yet respectful of her new environment. When Foxy spotted Spike's dog bed on the patio, he headed for it and lay on it, wriggling on his back to cover it with his scent. Spike approached to become a part of the action, and Foxy snapped at him to drive him away. When Jack reached out for Foxy, Foxy nipped at Jack as well.

But Jack was clearly enamored with Foxy. "I love the way he's so affectionate with me," he said. "She's affectionate, too," his mother said of Belle, "whereas he kind of bit you." "Yeah, but that's cool!" Jack protested. Foxy's physical appeal and resemblance to Dixie were powerful forces in driving his choices. Jack was like most potential dog owners—deep, often unconscious personal needs were driving his instant attachment to this particular dog. "I like that he's so active," he said to his mother. "But is that right for Spike?" she asked him cautiously. "Are we getting a dog for you, or for all of us?" Ms. Madsen had zeroed in on exactly the right question. Getting a family dog should always be a pack—and not an individual—decision.

Selecting the right dog is the first and perhaps most important step in creating the wonderful family experience of adding a new canine member to your household pack. Of course, many of you who own a dog have already gone through this process—some of you with great results; others, disappointing ones. Never fear; I maintain that nearly all common dog problems can be fixed—or at least, greatly improved—by those honest and dedicated owners who are willing to do the work to rehabilitate their dogs, and retrain themselves. In fact, if you do own a dog, you may be tempted to skip this chapter, but I suggest you buckle down and get everyone in the family to read it. First, it will contain reviews of basic skills and procedures I outlined in my two previous books and about which I talk often in my television show. Second, it will be useful for you in your attempt to get honest with yourself about the current state of your relationship with your dog. You can begin to assess which methods that you've been using have worked with your dog, and which methods have not. And you can begin to look honestly at your own family and family dynamics as part of the problem with your dog—but also, as the biggest part of the solution!

After spending some time with Belle in the backyard and seeing how effortlessly she brought out the young pup in Spike, Virginia Madsen's son, Jack, put his emotions aside and agreed that Belle rather than Foxy would be the best match for their whole family. I was impressed. It takes a lot of maturity and wisdom for an eleven-year-old boy to do what's best for everybody, not just himself. I left the adoption certain that the Madsen pack was going to be just fine.

Mortgages and Dogs

One of the things I've learned in America is that when people are getting ready to buy a house for the first time, they make sure to educate themselves thoroughly about real estate. From knowing nothing one day, suddenly, potential home buyers will learn everything about mortgages, loans, percentages, APRs, taxes, and how much they'll end up paying over twenty or thirty years. The adults, or whoever happens to be the pack leaders who will be paying the mortgage, usually make a very careful decision based on where they need to be, what they can afford, and what will have the best long-term value. Of course, there is always an emotional component to buying a house—but the practical aspects of it overrule the emotional. If the new homeowners make the wrong decision and get in over their heads, the consequences are dire for them, so they do everything in their power to avoid long-term disaster. When it comes to buying a home, most Americans truly understand commitment. But when it comes to adopting a dog that will likely be a member of their family from nine to sixteen years, it's another story. More often than not, people choose their dogs on an impulse with no planning or logic. If they become unhappy with their decision, they know the Humane

Society will always be there to bail them out—even if it is ultimately at the cost of the dog's life.

When people buy homes, they hire knowledgeable Realtors to help them navigate the complex housing market. I would like to be your "Realtor" in the dog world, to help educate you and your family so that you make a solid, conscious decision about the dog you want to bring into your life.

BE HONEST WITH YOURSELF

Making the right decision from the start may seem daunting. The best way to start is to make an honest assessment of your family's lifestyle and energy level . . . even if that "family" will only be composed of you and your dog. Without an idea of who you are and what your own energy is, you run the risk of bringing an incompatible energy into your home. Why is unflinching honesty so important? Because you can fool many people about who you really are inside, but you'll never be able to fool a dog. That's because a dog doesn't care about your clothes or your hair, how much money you make, or what kind of car you drive. All the dog cares about is what kind of energy you are projecting. Your energy—that is, your essence, your true self—will determine for that dog how to be around you. For a dog, there are only two positions in any situation: leader or follower. If you are showing your dog that you have what is considered "weak energy"—for example, if you're tense, anxious, overly emotional, or insecure as a person—then your dog will automatically feel that he has to fill in the gaps for you in those areas. It's in a dog's DNA to try to keep the pack stable. Unfortunately for both dog and human, this approach usually backfires when a dog tries to take over and run the show in the human world. In my work, I see again and again how dogs form issues because of their reaction to their owners' energy—and yet the owners have no clue how their own be-havior is affecting their dogs. You can avoid this problem altogether by starting the whole process from an unflinchingly honest place. But self-honesty cannot take place without good information, and many of my clients have either no information about how to choose a dog, or they have the wrong information. And sometimes, the re-sults of a "bad match" between human and dog can have devastating consequences.

SELF-ASSESSMENT GUIDELINES

The first step in creating a match made in heaven is to call a "family meeting" of all pack members. If it's just you, call in the help of a friend or family member who knows you well and isn't afraid to be honest. Whatever your situation, please ask these three basic ques-tions before you embark on the major commitment of bringing a dog home:

1. What are our real reasons for wanting to bring a dog into our lives?

The dog you choose will figure out those reasons, even if you aren't consciously aware of them. For example, if two parents want to get a dog to keep a lonely child company, the dog may become so protective of that child, it causes problems. If a mom wants a dog be-cause her kids are leaving the nest, the dog may pick up on her need-iness, as well as her resentments toward the rest of her family members, and make them targets. When we make animals totally responsible for fulfilling our own unspoken needs, we place too much weight on their shoulders. Avoiding such a situation starts with a family meeting in which all these issues are laid out on the table . . . before the dog comes home with you.

2. Is everybody in the family on the same page when it comes to wanting a dog?

If the kids beg and plead and persuade Dad to bring a dog home, but Mom is resentful because she knows she'll end up taking care of it, the dog is going to pick up on her anger and react accordingly. If a group of roommates bring a dog home but one of the roommates wants nothing to do with the dog, that may be a recipe for some aggression problems toward the "unfriendly" roommate. No matter what the makeup of your family "pack"—be it a frat house at a college looking for a mascot, or a retired couple looking for a late-life "child"—every member of that pack needs to be equally committed to adding a canine companion to the mix.

3. Is everyone in the family aware of and prepared to take on the very real responsibilities—including the financial burdens—involved in caring for a dog? Is everyone willing to pitch in and take part in leadership as well as affection?

Everyone in the family must be aware of the realities of dog ownership. That means everyone needs to be familiar with my three-part fulfillment formula for creating a balanced dog.

BASICS REFRESHER

Cesar's Fulfillment Formula

Every dog needs . . .

1. Exercise (in the form of a minimum of two thirty-minute structured walks with a pack leader, twice a day)
2. Discipline (clearly communicated and consistently enforced rules, boundaries, and limitations)
3. Affection (in the form of physical affection, treats, playtime)

(continued)

...but in *that* order! Though you may be adopting a dog in order to give it love, the reality is dogs need a lot more than love to keep them balanced. A good pack leader shows love by fulfilling the dog in all three areas—in the right sequence.

ARE THE KIDS READY FOR A DOG?

I don't believe any child is ever too young to have a dog. Raising a baby around dogs is a fantastic way to communicate a love and respect for Mother Nature from the start, because babies have no issues, and they are very connected to nature. With older children, in my opinion, there is no best age to bring a dog into a family, but if you are going to try to make the dog a child's responsibility, you had better know your child well . . . because even if you don't, the dog will have his or her number.

If your family includes a parent or guardian and children, you are likely to wake up one day and hear your kids tell you they just *have* to have a dog. It's up to you as a parent to figure out if they're asking as a whim, or if they are really serious. When a child sees a puppy in a window and simply must have that puppy, that is a child who needs leadership and guidance. It's a classic "teaching moment." Perhaps that first whim will eventually turn into a true commitment, but countless parents have paid the price for giving in to their kids' "please" without carefully considering their decision—and its consequences.

It's very easy for children to fall in love with the way a dog looks on the outside. A child might say he is serious about having a dog and use as an argument that he knows what kind of fur he wants, what size dog he wants, what kind of breed he is attracted to. Of course, liking a dog's physical appearance can be important to the process of bonding a child to a dog, but as parents, we need to teach kids about the next level of commitment. If you adopt a dog for your kids, but no one in the household is really committed to that dog on a deep, lifelong level, the dog is going to know. Dogs are the best lie detectors in the world.

ENERGY LEVELS

As human beings, we tend to look at the world through a very self-centered lens. Because we think the way we think and communicate the way we communicate, we assume somehow the rest of the earth's beings either do as we do—or are somehow inferior. The truth is that for all the advantages that language affords our species, in the grand scheme of life, it is a secondary means of communication. The universal language of nature is *energy*—the way all animals transmit their feelings and intentions to one another.

Every animal on earth is born with a particular level of energy. Energy transcends breed and bloodline, race and nationality. When choosing our friends, lovers, husbands, and wives, we usually unconsciously seek out an energy level that in some way complements our own. When selecting a dog, making sure your energy levels are compatible is the most important thing you can do, right from the beginning, to help predict a happy companionship down the line.

BASICS REFRESHER

Energy Levels

When selecting a dog, keep these energy levels in mind:

1. Very High: Constantly on the move, from dawn to dusk. Can walk or run for hours on end and still have energy to spare.

(continued)

2. High: Very athletic, prefers very vigorous activities, but tires normally and is ready for sleep at the end of the day.
3. Medium: Seeks out normal physical activities, sometimes vigorous ones, but balances them with equal periods of rest.
4. Low: Your basic couch potato dog. Prefers rest to activity. A couple of regular walks a day will be plenty of exercise for him.

Humans selected dogs over generations for certain characteristics to create the breeds we have today. That's why some breeds tend toward higher or lower athleticism, or other skills that require strength and stamina. Still, all dogs of a certain breed aren't necessarily one energy or another. I've worked with mellow, low-energy Labradors and anxious, very-high-energy bulldogs. In the same litter, energy levels can vary wildly. ***Your goal as a successful dog owner is to find a dog with a lower energy level or the same energy level that you and your family (including any current dogs or pets you might have) possess.*** That's why, even before you seek out your new dog, you need to know yourself. When people choose a dog with a higher energy level than themselves, it often results in frustration for both the humans and the dogs.

PETE AND CURLY: IRRECONCILABLE DIFFERENCES

The case of Pete Spano and his dog, Curly, is a perfect example of the heartache that can arise from choosing a dog with the wrong energy level. I met Pete in September of 2006, on the *Dog Whisperer* series' first trip to New York City. He's the real deal, a genuine Brooklynite, with a tough exterior and a heart of gold, and I liked him right away. Pete told me that a year earlier, he had headed down to the shelter to look for a dog to adopt. Once there, his hard-boiled New Yorker's heart just melted for a hyperenergetic, short-haired Lab mix that rushed up to him, licked his hands, and looked up at him with pleading, soulful brown eyes. "That was it right there," Pete told me. "He was the one." Because of the dog's goofy, playful demeanor, Pete named him Curly after the hyperactive Curly of the Three Stooges.

Pete described walking the thirty blocks back to his apartment with Curly as "like tuna fishing." Curly pulled him all over the sidewalk, went crazy chasing every squirrel and every other dog that passed by, and stayed at a level-ten excitement all the way home. Pete saw a chance for a break when he came to a public dog park near the Museum of Natural History. He let Curly off his leash and—boom! Curly got into his first fight with another dog.

Over the next year, Curly's aggressive, hyperactive behavior only escalated after living in Pete's small one-bedroom Central Park apartment. Pete's apartment building was dog friendly, but some of the other dogs in the building were equally as unstable as Curly, so fights in the hallways and elevator broke out all the time. Pete, who worked as the sexton for a historic and very busy Manhattan church, eventually resorted to taking Curly to the park at dawn or late at night, when he knew there wouldn't be many other dogs around. He hired several dog trainers and tried every leash and collar known to man, but nothing made a difference. Pete was becoming exhausted, stressed out, and despondent, as Curly got involved in incident after incident. People in Pete's life were suggesting he get rid of Curly, but he didn't have the heart to take him back to the shelter and leave him to his fate. "People keep telling me, 'Take him out to the country.' What country?" Pete despaired. "I'm from Manhattan. I don't know anyone in the country."

The first thing I noticed about Pete during our consultation was his energy level. It was low. Pete was a kindhearted guy, hardworking and dedicated to his job, but very laid-back. Even his speech cadence was slow and deliberate. He was a smoker and not at all athletic. On the other hand, the first thing I noticed about Curly was his very, very high energy. From the moment Pete's friends brought Curly into the room, he was all hyped up, pushing against and jumping on and trying to dominate everyone. While Curly was barging around the small apartment like a bull in a china shop, Pete was petting him and talking sweetly to him. "Do you see what you're doing?" I asked Pete. Pete had no clue at all. He didn't realize that he was feeding Curly's hyperactive energy—and frustration— by giving him affection when the dog was all revved up at a level ten. During the consultation, Pete shared with me all of Curly's recent transgressions. "He *hates* other dogs," he told me. He had hurt at least two dogs so far and caused a nearby dog walker to be bitten by one of Curly's "enemies" in a fit of redirected aggression. Pete described Curly as if he were a serious red-zone case . . . but that was not the vibe I was getting from this sleek, lanky guy. I was picking up anxiety, and a lot of frustration.

Without Pete, I took Curly into the mobile home that *Dog Whisperer* personnel use when we travel, and let him sit for a while with the balanced pack I had with me—Coco the Chihuahua, Sid the French bulldog, and Luigi the Chinese crested. It only took a moment for Curly to relax around the little dogs. Curly didn't "hate" other dogs, and he didn't even have a bad dog-aggression problem— not with balanced dogs, at least. But Pete clearly wasn't giving Curly the kind of strong leadership he needed. He also wasn't giving him enough exercise.

It was an unseasonably warm, clear September day. I put on my skates, took Curly into Central Park, and we started to run. At first, Curly had trouble keeping an even pace. He was used to controlling Pete, dragging him all over. Every time he saw a squirrel, he'd start to veer off. But eventually, he got into the zone. Then, he took off running! It was like taking a brand-new sports car out for its first spin on an open road! The fact that Curly wanted to chase the small animals he saw, plus the way he opened up at high speed, made me believe he was a Lab-greyhound mix. Although he was blond and muscular like a yellow Lab, his face had the long, narrow nose of a sight hound, and his body was tall and lean. And did he love to run! This was one of those cases where I was much more tired out than the dog at the end. It was a magical experience. I'm not a city guy by nature, but I think everyone should have the experience of Rollerblading with a beautiful dog through Central Park, at least once in his or her life!

After the blading session, Curly was much mellower, and I was able to work with him and Pete in the park, on the street, and in the apartment. Pete really stepped up to the plate and worked hard. We even succeeded in walking Curly next to his sworn enemy, a huge Akita named Razor. At the end of a long, exhausting day, Pete and I

Cesar, LandRollers, and Curly

sat down for a heart-to-heart. I talked about Curly's needs as a high-energy dog, and the fact that Pete would not only need to be a better pack leader to Curly, but would also really need to up the vigorous exercise. Without the outlet to drain his abundant energy, Curly would never be able to shake the frustration and anxiety that was driving him to get into conflicts with other dogs. Pete listened hard to what I said to him, seeming a little overwhelmed by it all. As he put it, this was a "reality check" for him. Pete told me he really wanted to make the changes in his life that Curly would need to be a happy, fulfilled dog. But he worried that his job, his lifestyle, and his energy level would get in the way.

After we returned to California, our *Dog Whisperer* team kept in close touch with Pete, checking on his progress with Curly. I was so excited to hear that Pete had bought a bicycle so he could take Curly on fast rides through the park, and I cheered when he began wearing the nicotine patch to try to quit smoking. For a while there, it seemed as if Curly was really improving. But they had a big setback when Pete had to work long hours at his church during several weeks of special events and had to cut way back on his exercise time with Curly. Pete didn't give up—that's what I was most proud of. He loved Curly so much; he was actually working to change his whole life in order to make his dog's life better. My philosophy is that sometimes we get the dogs we need, not the dogs we want. Pete was clinging to that philosophy—but by the end of January, he was very downhearted. Curly's aggression had returned, and there had been another incident with a dog. Curly was a lawsuit waiting to happen. Both Curly and Pete were once again as miserable as they had been before my visit. Pete told our producers he didn't think he could change his lifestyle enough to make Curly balanced. He didn't want to give Curly back to the shelter, but he didn't know what else to do.

Fortunately, my wife had a brainstorm. Curly was the perfect dog to come live at the Dog Psychology Center with the pack. He was a super-high-energy guy who would really thrive with all the hiking, swimming, and Rollerblading we do. Plus, living among the pack would help cure his dog aggression. Eventually, Curly might make a great dog for a really athletic California woman or man. And we had another New York trip planned for the near future.

On a painfully cold January morning, I met Pete and Curly on the street outside his Central Park West apartment building. Curly recognized me right away, which was helpful, since it was important for him not to think that going away with me was a "big deal," just a new adventure. Even though Pete thanked me and said he knew this was the right thing for everyone, he was truly choked up as he watched us walk away. Pete tried his luck fostering another, lower-energy dog from the Dog Psychology Center, but finally admitted to himself that his current lifestyle just could not handle caring for a dog.

Despite its heartbreak, many situations like Pete's don't end as happily for the dog. Had we not come into Pete's life, chances are a bite or a lawsuit would have forced him to give Curly away or take him back to the shelter. The National Council on Pet Population Study and Policy estimates that 40 percent of dogs are returned to shelters because of behavioral incompatibility.[1] Being returned multiple times greatly increases the chances that a dog will be euthanized. Learning to recognize a dog's energy—and understanding your own energy needs—is the key to preventing such extreme situations from happening at all. Curly had shown Pete many signs of his energy level at their first meeting in the shelter, but Pete interpreted the dog's bouncing around in the cage, licking his hand, and "goofy" antics as "happiness." And as Pete later admitted, he didn't think at all about his own energy level and lifestyle when he brought Curly home with him.

ASSESSING YOUR FAMILY'S ENERGY

Evaluating a family's energy can be tricky, because families are made up of individuals, all of whom may have different energy levels. But in general, every "pack" develops its own internal set of rituals and rules, even if those are unspoken. Here are some questions to help you discover your own family's energy style.

1. What is your overall lifestyle?

Do the people in your pack have an active lifestyle? Is someone up every morning at six to run around the neighborhood track? Do the activities you enjoy together involve outdoor activities like camping, hiking, going to the beach, or skiing? An active family will have better luck with a higher-energy dog that can join in those activities than would, say, a family whose shared activities tend more toward lazy Sundays spent doing crossword puzzles or playing Scrabble. The second kind of family would definitely do better with a low- to medium-energy dog that enjoys relaxing next to them during their less physical pursuits, rather than a high-energy dog that will be pacing and whining with frustration.

2. What is your conflict-resolution style?

We all know families in which loud arguments, dramatic displays of emotions, and door slamming seem to be the norm when there's a disagreement to be resolved or an opinion to be expressed. For some groups of people, this style of conflict resolution seems to work just fine among the humans—but it's important to realize right off the bat that yelling at a dog will get you absolutely nowhere. Learning how to create calm-assertive energy among one another should be the first assignment for this style of human pack, even if they only practice it around the dog. Other packs seem to behave exactly the opposite when it comes to conflicts—there is no outward disagreement, but beneath the surface, anger and resentments are seething. These hidden emotions will be all too apparent to a dog and can contribute to his instability. Learning how to communicate more directly among one another should be a goal for this type of family . . . especially where the dog is concerned.

3. Are you a group of people who works together, functioning best as a unit, or do you seem to be sharing the same living space while everyone does his or her thing?

This is an important question to ask yourselves, because while human societies often function just fine when everyone seems to be going in separate directions, dog societies are always all about the group. There is no such thing as an "independent-minded" dog in a pack. A family that never connects on anything can be distressing for a dog, whose very instincts make him long for everyone to be on the same page. This isn't to say your family needs to change its style completely, but when it comes to behavior and making major decisions *regarding the dog,* it's essential that everybody rally and do the right thing *together.*

YOUR DOG AND THE COMMUNITY

Although the nuclear family is often seen as an island unto itself in American society, the truth is that when you adopt a new dog, you are also going to be affecting your friends, your neighbors, and the immediate community. Not only that, but the lifestyle of the area around you will also have a profound impact on your dog. This will become immediately apparent to you when you take your dog for his first walk through your neighborhood and have to contend with the various dogs and cats owned by your neighbors. Most of my clients have more problems with their dogs in the outside world than they do when their dog is in the house, and this often prompts them to isolate their dogs or deprive them of exercise, just to avoid the hassle. Long before this happens, you and your pack need to honestly weigh the needs and desires of your own group with the general welfare of the environment in which you live.

Let me give you an example from my own life. When I opened my Dog Psychology Center in South Los Angeles, the land I rented was a large lot in the middle of an industrial district. I soon discovered that many of the warehouse owners in the area keep fenced dogs as guards, and some even let off-leash dogs wander around outside to patrol their property! To make matters worse, many Los Angeles gangs have their "turf" on the periphery of my area. I often encounter dogs that gangs involve in their unlawful activities—from drug dealing to actual illegal dogfighting—either protecting property or wandering around, having either escaped or been abandoned. It became clear to me early on that I would have to keep all those factors in mind when creating an area in which my pack would live. That's why there are double gates around the center—to keep my dogs from escaping, as well as to keep any unwanted neighborhood visitors out. In addition, I consider every dog's temperament when I take him or her for a walk, bike, or Rollerblade in the area. It goes without saying that certain fearful, anxious, or nervous dogs, and especially dogs suffering with red-zone aggression, shouldn't be around unpredictable, off-leash dogs until they are further along in their rehabilitation. Now that I am building a new Dog Psychology Center in a less-populated area in the Santa Clarita Valley, I will have to adapt both my facility and practices to the rules and realities of that new neighborhood. My dogs don't exist in a vacuum—once I bring them into the local community, I have to take all those new factors into account, for both the sake of the dogs and the sake of all the rest of the people and animals living around us.

The community can have subtle and not-so-subtle influences on your dog. If your neighbors' attitude toward your dog is "How dare you bring that beast into our space!" it's very likely your dog is going to sense that negativity every time you're out walking and encounter those neighbors, and their attitude will become a self-fulfilling prophecy. Dogs always reflect our energy right back to us, and if an acquaintance of yours looks at your dog with murder in her eyes, chances are the dog will dislike her right back.

Make sure you are totally familiar with the rules of your neighborhood association or apartment complex when it comes to pets, and fill out any necessary forms or applications. Do this far in advance; you don't want to become attached to a pet that a landlord has the power to take away. If you live in a condo or apartment, you want to make sure all the neighbors on your floor or in your area know your plans. Even if they don't like dogs, they will appreciate your concern for their feelings ahead of time more than if you just spring the dog on them without notice. These may seem like obvious suggestions, but you'd be surprised at the number of cases I'm called in to help where a dog has caused serious bad blood between owners and their neighbors.

HOOTIE AND THE NEIGHBORS

Pam Marks's case is a good example of what can happen when someone moves into a neighborhood without considering the effect her dogs could have on the dynamics of the surrounding community. Pam owns four gorgeous, award-winning Australian shepherds. Two years ago, she called me in to help her with Hootie, her five-year-old

agility-course "star," which had developed a fear of kids after a traumatic incident. Pam says that now Hootie is 85 percent better during
his tournaments—but shortly after our first consultation, she contacted me about another problem. Ever since Pam moved into her
Woodland Hills neighborhood two years earlier, her next-door neighbors had taken issue with her dogs and had recently reported Hootie
to animal control. What would prompt them to take such a drastic
step? "When Pam first moved in, I came over to the fence to say hi to
the dogs, and they must have been too excited, because he [Hootie]
bit me," Tim Bryson, Pam's neighbor, told me. "From that day on, I
was concerned, because I have three small children," his wife, Carrie,
added. Then, the week before my visit, Hootie had jumped the fence
and chased after the kids for the second time since Pam moved in,
sending Carrie Bryson into full-blown protective-mom mode. "That
was really the final upset," she said. "All of a sudden the dog just flew
over the fence—again—and I just blew up. I was so afraid."

The incident and the Brysons' response to it had inflamed the
simmering hostility between Pam's pack of five (Pam plus her four
dogs) and the Brysons' pack of five. "It's really difficult being right
next door to someone when there's tension like that. It's really difficult," Pam admitted. When I arrived on the scene, I learned that even
when not jumping the fence, Hootie would hear the sounds of the
kids playing in their own backyard and start to rush the fence, barking anxiously. His unstable behavior would agitate the other three
dogs, which also became hyperactive. The cause of Hootie's behavior was clear to me when I asked Pam to greet me at the door. The
moment the doorbell rang, Pam's pack became frantic, barking and
rushing all over the home and furniture. Pam halfheartedly removed
them from the door, but she clearly was not in control inside her
own house! Here is a decorated agility-dog trainer, and four highly
skilled dogs, yet there was no structure in the pack at all. In the yard,
Hootie was the instigator. With no structure at all, Hootie was re-

leasing his anxiety through his Australian shepherd genes—and trying to herd the neighborhood kids!

We were able to make amazing progress within one day, by just providing some basic boundaries for the dogs. These dogs were already conditioned to respond to Pam—but she hadn't been transferring her leadership in the agility ring to leadership in her own home. I told the Brysons and their kids about my no-touch, no-talk, no-eye-contact rule, and by the end of the day, we had both packs standing together calmly by the fence. The Brysons were relieved and excited about participating in helping Pam in her quest to improve Hootie's behavior—all they wanted was peace. But the truth is, this situation didn't have to happen at all. When Pam first realized she was moving in next to a houseful of kids, she should have come up with a strategy to introduce the family to her dogs right away, perhaps even enlisting the kids to go on a pack walk with them. I

Andre works with Hootie

applaud Pam for stepping up to the plate yet again and asking for help . . . because living next door to hostile neighbors wasn't only bad for Pam. It was bad for her already anxious, high-energy dogs.

Before you make the decision to adopt a dog, ask yourself whether or not your neighborhood contains children or senior citizens, potentially aggressive dogs (and their irresponsible owners), cats, dangerous street traffic—or any conditions that will need to be addressed before you bring the dog home.

What's in a Breed?

Now that you and the members of your group or family have had your heart-to-heart talks and identified what your individual needs, energy levels, and lifestyles are, it's time to go to the library, Internet, or local breed rescue group and do some serious research about dog behavior in general, and breed characteristics in particular. If you are familiar with my television show and my other books, you will already know that I don't believe for a minute that "breed is destiny" for a dog. I believe that a dog's inborn energy level is far more important than breed when it comes to compatibility with an owner or family. Though certain breeds may be much more inclined to be higher or lower energy than others, the fact is that many dogs of the same breed—indeed, many dogs in the same litter—can have wildly varying energy levels or what most people call "personalities." But having at least a basic education on the special needs of your favorite breed should be the goal of any dog owner. I find that many people fall in love with a breed—perhaps they are attached to the breed of dog they remember from their childhood, or a particular breed of dog appeals to them as cute, or elegant, or tough. Often, people choose breeds of dogs the way they would choose an outfit, as something that reflects a certain image of themselves they would like to convey to others. But a dog is not a suit of clothes; it is a part of Mother Nature, a living, feeling being with a full set of needs—and rights—all its own.

BASICS REFRESHER

Your Dog's Identity

Many dog owners think of their dog as name first. "Oh, Smokey doesn't like men," or "Smokey's always been impossible on walks." Referring to a dog as name first implies that your dog has some conscious, logical control over his behavior likes and dislikes in the same way that a human does. This way of thinking prevents you from relating to your dog as who he really is, and having influence over his whole being.

I recommend you relate to your dog in this order, particularly when setting rules, boundaries, and limitations, and when dealing with any issues your dog may have.

1. Animal
2. Species: Dog (*Canis familiaris*)
3. Breed
4. Name

Once you have fulfilled your dog's need as animal, dog, then breed, only then should you relate to your dog as name, in the way you would relate to another human.

Thinking of a dog as name or breed first can get you into trouble when it comes to generalizing about breed behavior. For example, if a woman had Labrador retrievers growing up and they were always calm and well behaved, then she will tend to think of all Labs as having those characteristics. When she adopts a Lab that turns aggressive, she will automatically blame it on the name—or that particular dog. Instead, she should consider who in her family was the pack leader of the previous Labs, what the dogs' roles were in the household, what kind of exercise and discipline the family provided for them, and what the family's overall lifestyle was like. Chances are, she didn't just happen to get the world's only "faulty" Labrador! She may be a weaker pack leader than her mother or the person in her childhood who was responsible for the dogs she remembers. She may not be providing the kind of structure or exercise the dog needs. Or perhaps she just adopted a very high-energy Labrador—with more energy than the dogs of her childhood, and more needs than her lifestyle can fulfill. This dog may be frustrated and turning that frustration into aggression. This is a good example of the fact that a dog's breed doesn't necessarily determine what kind of pet he will be.

I like to think of breed as kind of a "booster shot" to a dog's inborn energy level. The more purebred the dog, the more likely he is to be driven by the needs and impulses that are hardwired into his breed. Remember, we humans created breeds for our own selfish reasons! We "manufactured" dogs to help with herding livestock or hunting or tracking prey across long distances. We are the culprits who put those powerful genes into these dogs; so in my mind, we are the ones who should be responsible for fulfilling those breed-related needs. Don't just think of a purebred dog as the "pretty face" of his lineage! Remember what that lineage was originally created for.

There are many ways to think about breed. Internationally, there are approximately four hundred breeds that are listed with registry organizations in other countries, but the American Kennel Club, founded in 1884, does not register all of these breeds, either because there are too few dogs (of that breed) in this country or there is too little interest among owners of these breeds to obtain AKC registered status. The AKC maintains the largest registry of purebred dogs in the world and currently registers 157 breeds.[2] Fortunately, the AKC also breaks down these breeds into helpful general groupings, which I'll review here in terms of behavioral needs and general characteristics.

THE SPORTING GROUP

These are the dogs originally bred to help hunters locate, flush out, or retrieve game—both on land and in water. Early humans discovered they could take the prey instinct of the dog's wolf ancestors and stop it short of actually killing the prey. Dogs in this group include pointers, retrievers, setters, and spaniels.

THE HOUND GROUP

Hounds were bred to help early humans track prey on the hunt. This group is a large one but generally breaks down into two larger categories. Sight hounds, such as greyhounds, Afghan hounds, basenjis, and salukis, use their vision to track prey's movement. Scent hounds, including beagles, foxhounds, dachshunds, and bloodhounds, use their amazingly acute scenting abilities. Many hounds were bred to run in packs. Some were created for short sprints of intense pursuits, while others have the ability to track for hours on end without tiring.

THE WORKING GROUP

Dogs of the working group came into being when early humans stopped their nomadic hunter-gatherer lives and began to settle into villages. These newer breeds were designed for more domestic tasks such as guarding, pulling, and rescuing.

This is also a diverse group, and many were selected for body size, strength, and, sometimes, aggressiveness. The Doberman pinscher, Siberian husky, boxer, Great Dane, mastiff, and rottweiler are included in this group. Many of these dogs are what I refer to as "powerful breed dogs." The more purebred they are, the more likely they are to be driven by the needs of their breeding. I often don't recommend that a "beginning" dog owner take on very powerful breed dogs in their purebred form, unless he is willing to put an enormous amount of his own time and energy into fulfilling the dog's working nature.

THE HERDING GROUP

The AKC used to include the herding group dogs in with the working group, since both groups were created to help early humans with the tasks of a domesticated—as opposed to a hunting—lifestyle. The creators of these breeds were able to adapt the ability of wolves to use coordinated movement to "corral" the animals they hunt but remove the final prey drive that led to a kill. As a result, herding dogs share the amazing ability to control the movement of other animals. These are tasks that take energy, patience, and focus . . . and those traits will often shine through in the modern incarnations of herders—including sheepdogs, corgis, Bouviers, Australian shepherds, and collies. Some working group dogs cross over into herding as well, such as the rottweiler, which was once used to herd large groups of cattle.

THE TERRIER GROUP

Terriers' ancestors were originally intended to hunt and kill vermin. They range from very small in size, as in the Norfolk, cairn, or West Highland white terrier, to much larger, as in the Grand Airedale terrier. As you can imagine, flushing rats from burrows and bushes required the original creators of these breeds to select for qualities of high energy, focus, and perseverance, or what some terrier owners tend to humanize as "feistiness" or "stubbornness."

THE TOY GROUP

Chihuahuas, Maltese, toy poodles, King Charles spaniels, Yorkshire terriers, Pekingese, pugs . . . there's no better historical proof of the timeless love affair between humans and canines than the toy group, many of which were created simply to be their owners' devoted companions. Some were also bred to be bird dogs and ratters, but all were selected for their small size. While many first-time dog owners choose toys assuming they will be "easy," I'm called in on just as many cases of small dogs out of control as more powerful breeds. That's because the "cuteness" factor of toys often gets in the way of their owners seeing them as animal-dog first. I often counsel owners to imagine their tiny toy wearing a different outfit— say, that of a German shepherd. Would they still think that his nipping and growling is "adorable"?

THE NONSPORTING GROUP

This group includes dogs that were bred for variations of the purposes of all the previous categories, but which don't fit perfectly into any single one. It's much too broad a category to be useful for guidelines in selecting a dog, which is unfortunate, since it includes some of America's most popular breeds, including the poodle, the bulldog, the Boston terrier,

the bichon frise, the French bulldog, the Lhasa apso, the shar-
pei, the chow chow, the Shiba Inu, and the dalmatian. If you
are interested in learning about any of the dogs that fit into
this group, I recommend you do very specific research on
each breed's history and general characteristics.

One of the smartest things you can do for your family if all or some
of you are dead set on a particular breed of dog but haven't experienced it firsthand is to locate a local rescue group that specializes in
that breed alone. Then take everyone out to visit the rescue facility
and spend at least an hour among a whole pack of dogs of that breed.
You may believe you are destined to have a basset hound because of
the breed's winsome brown eyes, sad expression, and soft floppy
ears, but find yourself in for a shock when you hear a group of them
baying and howling whenever a new person enters the pen. Your
husband may like the concept of a compact, tiny min-pin, but can't
take the energy of half a dozen of them bouncing up and down all at
once in a shelter.

   Volunteers at reputable breed-specific rescue organizations will
often be extremely well informed as to the quirks and requirements
of the breed they handle, and they are usually happy to answer any
questions you may have and provide you with excellent reading ma-
terials and references. They are motivated for you to make the right
decision when adopting one of their dogs—because if the fit isn't
right, the dog is likely to be returned to them, usually in worse condition than when it left.

Taking Your Time

Once a group of people make the shared decision to bring a dog
into their lives, impatience can easily set in. Everybody has the pic-

ture of the dog in their mind's eye and they want it *now*! Many prospective adoptive families will simply visit a shelter, breeder, or rescue group and rush to bring home whichever dog they think is "cutest." They make the choice using their emotions without stopping to consider the problems that can come later from failing to consider the different energy levels. Adopting a dog is a life-changing decision for you, the dog, and your entire family. Rushing the process can result in mistakes that will have long-lasting consequences. If you don't find the dog you feel is perfect for your family the first time out, then wait a week and try again. It's more important that you find the dog that's the right "fit," as opposed to the dog that's available at that very moment.

Taking the time to find the right dog at the right time can be the best thing that ever happens to a person—or a dog. Remember Curly from Central Park? Well, our *Dog Whisperer* production assistant Todd Henderson drove Curly from New York to California, and the two of them really bonded on their cross-country trip. Todd is in his twenties and a real athlete, a long-distance runner. He's got a very high level of energy and also knows all the dos and don'ts of how to handle a dog, after working on the show for three seasons. During their long drive, Curly and Todd ran wind sprints and took long runs and walks together. But when Todd came back to L.A., his living situation at the time plus his schedule traveling with the show didn't allow him to adopt our New York transplant. This turned out to be a good thing for Curly, who had the chance to live at the Center for a year and improve his social skills. He adapted right away to living among the pack and, as I'd predicted, not only got along fine with the other dogs, but also became incredibly popular among them! Curly was one of our most active guys and loved our Rollerblade sessions, runs in the mountains, and days on the beach. He also helped several other unstable dogs achieve balance. Whenever he could, Todd would foster Curly on weekends, and their relationship got stronger and stronger.

Todd recently moved into a house with his girlfriend and was able to have Curly full-time at last. Curly sometimes comes to the production office with him, peacefully resting under his desk while he logs footage and makes phone calls. No one would ever recognize Curly as the same monster we met in Manhattan a year and a half earlier. And Todd can't imagine life without him. "From the moment we hit the road, I knew this was a special dog," Todd muses. "He brings so much love, excitement, and flat-out goofiness wherever he goes. Finally being able to adopt him for good was a great day, and he's loving his new life with me, my girlfriend, and her two dogs."

I have absolutely no doubt that the right dog is out there, waiting for your family as well.

Gimme Shelter

Navigating Shelters, Rescue Organizations, and Breeders

Shelter dogs from Tijuana

You've had your family meeting, and you've done so much research on dog breeds and behavior you could give a lecture. Now, where do you go to get your dream dog?

ADOPTING A SHELTER DOG

I greatly respect people who choose to adopt animals from their local shelters and pounds. There is no shortage of dogs in the world that need homes—as of this writing, at least six to eight million dogs and cats enter shelters every year according to the Humane Society—so these people are helping to make a dent in the huge problem of dog overpopulation in our nation. Shelters also have the added advantage of much cheaper adoption fees than breeders, pet stores, and even some breed-specific rescue organizations. A pet from a reputable shelter is also more likely to be vaccinated, wormed, and spayed or neutered. But keep in mind that one of the reasons there are so many animals in our local shelters in the first place is that people often take home dogs on a whim or for superficial reasons. Their unrealistic expectations of the actual commitment it takes to care for and share one's life with a pet causes them to abandon or return the animal, often resulting in a death sentence. The Humane Society of the United States estimates that about half the animals in shelters will eventually be euthanized, simply because there aren't enough homes for them.[1] So remember that choosing a shelter or pound as a place to find your new dog is an admirable gesture, but it can backfire on you, your dog, and even the community if you go into the process uninformed, or make your selection for the wrong reasons.

What are those misguided reasons? We humans have an important set of emotions that trigger our feelings of empathy, sympathy, and pity for other animals in need. But in the animal world, those very important emotions can be our downfall! Feeling sorry is always a weak energy in the animal kingdom, and when any dog is face-to-face with weak energy, it makes him or her more powerful than the human projecting it. If your dog starts your relationship as the dominant one, its behavior is more likely to be unruly, and it is also more likely to develop issues. These are all reasons owners have buyers' remorse and return dogs to shelters after "failed" adoptions. The more times a dog is returned to a shelter, the more likely it is to be given a death sentence. So if you and your family decide adopting a dog from a shelter is the right thing to do, then spend some time talking about your sadness and frustration over dog overpopulation and homelessness beforehand. Once everybody has fully aired their emotions, then ask them all to make a conscious decision to leave those feelings at the door before they enter the shelter itself. Look at it this way—you are rescuing a dog in order to help it. And you can't help any dog if it perceives you as weak.

I recommend you choose a shelter within a reasonable distance from your home. That way, if you need a day or two to make up your mind and decide to return a second time, you won't have to make a long journey to do so. You'll also be less likely to make a spur-of-the-moment decision. Some of these shelters are joining the computer age and have websites displaying the photos and descriptions of the animals they have up for adoption. If the type of dog you are seeking isn't available when you visit, many shelters will put your name on a waiting list and notify you if such an animal arrives. Sadly, there are no shortages of animals arriving at most shelters. To locate your local animal shelter, check online or in the Yellow Pages under "Animal Shelter," "Animal Control," or "Humane Society." Petfinders.com or Pets911.com are also useful websites. Additional suggestions are included in the resource guide at the back of the book.

Before you enter any shelter, take a deep breath and summon your best calm-assertive energy. You will be face-to-face with dozens of adorable dogs that all need homes . . . but right now, you can't afford to let that influence you. You need to take a businesslike attitude in order to choose the right dog for you.

For my video series *Mastering Leadership,* my team and I put together an in-depth program called *Your New Dog, First Day and Beyond.* In this video, I met with an upbeat and active single woman, Sylvia Ellis, who wanted to adopt a shelter dog that would fit some very specific requirements for her lifestyle. First, the dog had to be less than twelve pounds, to comply with the rules of pet ownership in her condo complex. Those rules also specified the dog had to be well behaved and quiet—any complaints about a pet in the complex would result in its immediate expulsion. Finally, the dog had to have a high enough energy level to be able to join Sylvia in her athletic lifestyle, which included daily racewalking and regular hiking and biking excursions.

Sylvia and I went to the Downey Animal Shelter in Los Angeles, where I showed her the correct way to approach a caged dog in a shelter—not face-to-face, engaging in eye contact or talk, but using the no-touch, no-talk, no-eye-contact rule, and approaching the dog *sideways.* If you face the dog or try and talk with it or pet it, you will be forcing the dog to alter its behavior in order to *react* to you. Any interaction you have with an animal is a conversation, except you are conversing with energy, which is much more subtle than language. By ignoring the dog but standing, kneeling, or sitting next to it, you are allowing the dog to come to you, check out your scent and energy on its own terms, and show you his or her true self.

Just like humans, dogs have a very clear concept of personal space among one another. In America, the usual practice is to invade a dog's personal space at will. In fact, dog owners will often act insulted if, upon meeting a new dog, you don't immediately kneel down and pet him! In teaching our children to follow us in this practice, however, we are making them potential targets for bites. Just like you don't rush up and kiss an acquaintance on the cheek until you and she are comfortable with each other, a dog wants to get a sense of your scent and energy before he decides whether or not he wants anything to do with you.

Cesar and Sylvia Ellis at the shelter

BASICS REFRESHER

Meeting a Dog for the First Time

1. Do not approach the dog. Pack leaders don't go to followers; followers pursue pack leaders. If you want to earn a dog's respect and trust right away, allow the dog to come to you.

2. Stand still (but relaxed), and apply my rule: *No-touch, no-talk, no-eye contact,* until the dog signals it wants to meet you. A dog will do this by rubbing up against you, looking at you, licking you, or in a number of other ways.

3. Observe the dog's energy and body language. If the dog has its ears perked up and tail high, it may be in an excited, dominant state. Don't reward this state of being

(continued)

with attention or affection, because that can also label you as "follower" in the dog's mind. Instead, give affection to a dog when its head is slightly down, tail wagging but in the middle, and its ears are back and relaxed. This signals a calm-submissive state of mind.

4. If the dog walks away or otherwise indicates it's not interested in you, don't chase after it! Respecting a dog's boundaries is the best thing you can do to encourage that same dog to respect you.

Being in the shelter right next to Sylvia, I was able point out to her some common signs of behavior that indicated a bad match for the kind of dog she was looking for. Some of the dogs rushed to the front of the cage, jumping toward her and trying to paw her. I told her it was common for many people to interpret this as the dog saying, "I'm happy!" or "I like you!"—remember Pete and Curly—when in actuality, it can be an indication of overexcitement, anxiety, frustration, or dominance. At the same time, other dogs cowered from her or ignored her, showing no curiosity about her at all. Those dogs might have shyness issues that, in a small condo complex, could escalate into fear-related aggression. Now, if Sylvia had a lifestyle or living situation that would allow her the time, room, and freedom to rehabilitate any mild negative behavior in an otherwise healthy dog, then maybe those responses would have been acceptable. But Sylvia had little leeway. Her dog *had* to fit into her condo environment right off the bat, or the match wouldn't work. She couldn't risk any trial and error; she needed to find a dog whose state of mind was one she only had to maintain, not rehabilitate.

After spending an hour and a half meeting dogs at the shelter, Sylvia and I narrowed it down to three choices, all of which were dogs that showed curiosity and mild excitement about her presence, but were also submissive and respectful, not forcing themselves into her space. The dog she was most attracted to was a sweet little Chihuahua mix that locked right onto her eyes in an expectant manner. "That's the one," she told me, after meeting him, and she seemed pretty convinced of her selection.

Next, we took all three candidates to an outside area provided by the shelter, to observe them beyond the confinement of the cages. This is another step I strongly recommend for all shelter adoptions, because a dog's behavior can change 180 degrees from inside a cage to outside a cage. When we took the dogs outside, we discovered that all three of them were males, which goes to show you that energy has nothing to do with gender. But Sylvia was in for a surprise. Letting the three dogs explore each other in a fenced-in space, it became clear that her favorite Chihuahua mix was a dominating little fellow, at least when it came to relating to the other dogs. He and one of the other candidates began to engage in a not-so-subtle competition for territory almost immediately upon meeting each other. Meanwhile, candidate number three, whom we christened "the Environmental Guy," did what I always want to see a balanced dog do before he starts focusing on the other dogs around him—he started respectfully exploring his environment. It's a dog's nature to ask these questions in this order when she enters a new place: (1) Where am I? and then (2) Who else is here? From inside the cage to without, this third dog maintained his calm-submissive state of mind, all while showing a healthy level of energy and curiosity. I tested him for food drive (a strong food drive can be extremely helpful if you want to employ positive training methods in the future) and found him to be enthusiastic but polite when it came to taking food from my hand. This guy had all the hallmarks of a ready-made canine companion, and Sylvia changed her mind right there. She decided to take the Environmental Guy home with her, and from the reports she continues to give my team, it seems that a year later, she is still ecstatically happy with her decision.

SHELTER CHECKLIST

1. Prepare yourself emotionally before entering. Work through all your feelings of pity and sympathy in advance. Remain as calm-assertive and as unemotional as possible.

2. Always apply my no-touch, no-talk, no-eye-contact rule, and approach the cages sideways while letting the dog inside approach you. This allows dogs to show you more of their true selves.

3. Look for signs of calm submission. These include a healthy but respectful curiosity, consideration of your personal space, and physical signs such as the tail in the middle, head low, and ears slightly back. Observe the dog's level of excitement, fearfulness, aggression, or anxiety.

4. If you can, observe the dog outside the cage area. See how she interacts with humans and other dogs. Test to see if she is motivated by food.

5. If possible, see if the shelter workers will let you take the dog for a short walk on leash. Make a close observation of the animal's energy level.

6. If you have another dog at home, bring him along and introduce the two to each other. Make sure their energies are compatible.

7. Ask the shelter workers about the dog's behavior and habits since they have known her. Has she been returned from a previous adoption? What was the reason given? Does she have any health issues that they know of?

8. If you aren't certain, ask if you can return the next day. This will give you a chance to weigh your decision less emotionally and also to see the dog again, perhaps in a different state of mind.

9. Once you decide to bring home a shelter dog, make sure he or she is spayed or neutered, and take the dog to a vet as soon as possible after adoption to be checked for illness or infection and to get any necessary vaccinations that the shelter or previous owner might not have provided.

10. Make sure you go for a long walk with your dog after you leave the shelter.

Adopting from a Rescue Organization

As I do shelters, I greatly admire rescue organizations for their dedication to finding good homes for abandoned animals. Many are committed to having "no kill" policies, meaning they are committed to keeping most or all of the animals they rescue, even if they can't find homes for them. Often, they are run on a shoestring budget by a handful of unpaid volunteers. My wife, Ilusion, and I have started a nonprofit foundation, the Cesar and Ilusion Millan Foundation, to help these organizations with their endless obligations and expenses. But not all organizations that claim to be rescue organizations are reputable. Some puppy mills and Internet scams can masquerade as rescues. Before going to any rescue organization for your pet, I recommend you check to make sure the organization has a nonprofit status. Petfinder.com and Pets911.com are two good sources if you are seeking a reputable rescue organization in your area. You can also call the Humane Society of the United States (HSUS) at 202-452-1100 (ask for the Companion Animals section), and they will help you find out if there is a breed-rescue group near you.

Unlike shelters, many rescue organizations don't take just any

SHELTER SUCCESS STORY

Allyson Tretheway—an Unlikely Adoption

Allyson Tretheway's dogs

In the fall of 2006, I started watching the *Dog Whisperer*. I have a pretty well behaved male five-year-old border collie/Brittany spaniel mix. I used to think about getting a second dog as a playmate for him, but I feared two dogs would be too hard to handle. My mother reminded me of some of the negative two-dog situations they'd had over the years—fights, territorialism, overexcitement—and warned me that when you get two dogs, they bring out the bad behavior in each other. But watching *Dog Whisperer* had given me the confidence that I could control two dogs.

So in March of 2007, I went to the pound to pick out a second dog. Like Cesar recommends, I brought along my other dog, Corey, to make sure he'd get along with whatever dog I chose. I also took my own energy into consideration. I am high energy; I like to run, hike, and be outdoors. I wasn't too concerned with adopting a high-energy-level dog because I enjoy being active.

I had always believed all the media hype about pit bulls being aggressive, child-mauling monsters! We didn't set out to get a pit bull, but sadly that's what the shelters are full of. Cesar's show had given me the belief that (a) pit bulls should be judged as individuals, and (b) with good leadership, they could be great canine citizens. That day, I adopted Dixie, a one-year-old female pit bull. Before Cesar, I would have passed her right up just because of her breed.

Right off the bat when I took her home from the shelter, I started applying Cesar's tips. My boyfriend, Randy; our dog, Cory; Dixie; and I took a walk before we went into our house. Dixie had just been spayed so it couldn't be a long walk. But we established that we were all a pack right from the start. I always made sure she was calm and submissive before giving her food. I would give her a bone and take it away from her, repeating it a few times just so she would know that I control the food and treats. One of the very first things I did was to get her a dog backpack. I enrolled her in an obedience class that was an outdoor hiking class. Also she's taking agility and fly ball classes, too. She's not real great at either one yet, but we'll keep working on it.

I've taken her to the retirement home to visit my gram, and Dixie basically charmed everyone there. Not a single elderly person who saw her could resist petting her. And Dixie loved every minute of it. She is just the most loving dog. She never tires of getting love from people! If I hadn't watched Cesar, I probably would not have had the confidence to adopt a pit bull. I'm so glad I did because she's turned out to be such a sweetheart!

dog. That's because they have an individual commitment to each dog they take in, and therefore they can't afford to have the high rate of return that many shelters have. Some rescue organizations will put you through an interview process and even a home visit before they'll allow you to go home with the dog of your choice. A Southern California greyhound rescue that I know of actually will bring a "test dog" into your home, to make sure that it is "dog friendly." Some will require landlord or even employer references. All of these rules vary, and it's best to confer with someone from the organization ahead of time, to make sure you are willing to comply with their requirements.

You want to avoid the well-known story of comedian and talk-show host Ellen DeGeneres, who, with her partner Portia de Rossi, adopted a puppy named Iggy from a local animal rescue organization in October 2007. When Iggy didn't get along with Ellen's cats, the celebrity gave the dog to her hairdresser and her young daughters. About three weeks later a representative from the shelter came to the hairdresser's home and seized custody of Iggy. The rescue group claimed Ellen had signed a contract stating that if she could no longer keep Iggy he would be returned to the rescue organization, and it reiterated its policy of not placing dogs in homes with children younger than fourteen. The hairdresser's girls were eleven and twelve years old. The girls were devastated and asking that Iggy be brought back. But since the rescue group owned the microchip Iggy was wearing, legally he was still theirs.

The story has a happy ending for Iggy at least—he was placed with a new family and apparently is doing very well—but the trauma suffered by Ellen and the family to whom she transferred Iggy, and the damage to the rescue group's reputation, cannot be undone.

Another advantage to rescue groups is they often employ volunteer "foster families" to house the dogs in their care. Usually, experienced dog owners take on this job for the love of it, and they can provide you, the potential owner, with a wealth of information about the breed of dog you want to adopt. Often, the group or the foster family will preevaluate the dogs in their care, to see if those dogs are kid-friendly, cat-friendly, dog-friendly, and so on. If you have some experience with dogs, fostering is also a good way to find out if a certain breed or dog is for you. If this is something you're interested in, ask your local shelters or rescue groups if they have a fostering program available.

For the video *Your New Dog: First Day and Beyond,* I helped a young couple, Angelo and Diana Barbera, adopt a basset hound to add to their already balanced pack consisting of a cat, a Siberian husky, and a mastiff/Great Dane mix. I took the couple and their dogs to a fantastic local rescue organization, "Daphneyland," in Acton, California. Daphneyland is a model of breed-specific rescue. At any one time, this rescue can have up to a hundred hounds at its spacious indoor-outdoor ranch, most of which come to them through other rescue groups without the resources to care for many animals. Dawn Smith, Daphneyland founder, has hands-on experience with over a thousand basset hounds and shares my "power of the pack" philosophy. Because they have been bred to hunt in packs, basset hounds tend to be "ultra-pack-oriented" dogs, and Dawn uses group socialization as a way to create "balance" among all the dogs in her care.

The first thing I wanted Diana and Angelo to do when we arrived was to observe the individual energy levels of the various pack members. Though basset hounds as a breed have the stereotype of being lethargic and low energy, the truth is, some basset hounds are every bit as high energy as high-energy terriers; some Jack Russells have lower energy than basset hounds. Remember, it's not breed that determines a dog's character, it's the energy the animal was born with.

When adding a dog to a pack that you already have at home—whether that pack be human, canine, feline, or all three—it's vital to choose a dog with an energy level the same or lower than the existing pack. Diana and Angelo's current pack were both medium to high energy levels, so we were seeking a basset hound with a medium to low energy level. As soon as we entered the facility, a curious but respectful female hound began following the couple around, sniffing them daintily. Diana liked the energy of this girl, so we tested her behavior when Dawn Smith offered the rest of the pack treats. The female in question hovered around the edges of the pack, not fighting her way in, but not shying away from the other dogs, either. This suggested that she was neither dominant nor fearful, two characteristics that would bode well for her likelihood of fitting in with the Barberas' other dogs. Our next step was to do a "test introduction" with the Siberian husky and mastiff/Great Dane. Both dogs approved of her energy, though she was a little bit shy around them at first. I explained that this was normal, because the new girl obviously still felt that she was a part of the Daphneyland pack, not the Barbera pack. After spending a little time near the Barbera dogs, the basset began to come out of her shell, and the three dogs checked one another out thoroughly. When the new girl made a friendly face-to-face overture toward the Barbera's Siberian husky, we all knew that she had the right energy for the family. But how would she fare with the cat? Since bassets are hunting dogs at heart, cats can sometimes stimulate their prey drive. How could the Barberas know they wouldn't have a cat conflict once they took their new pack member home?

Fortunately, Dawn Smith keeps a cat on her property for that very reason. She makes a valiant attempt to socialize all the bassets around the cat, and to identify right away which dogs might have problems with it. When we tested the Barberas' bassett with the facility cat, she treated the cat like a superior pack member. Now that we had covered all possible contingencies, the Barberas were ready to commit to the dog by filling out the appropriate paperwork and paying a fee to help cover medical costs and to ensure the continuation of Daphneyland's efforts. After a refreshing bath to wash off the grime and scent of her time at Daphneyland, the dog the Barberas named Daisy was ready to begin her new life. Just as I always recommend with a shelter adoption, I had the Barberas walk with Daisy and their other dogs as a pack before putting her in the car for the drive back to Los Angeles. That way, Daisy's trip to her new abode would begin as a member of the pack, not as an outsider.

RESCUE ORGANIZATION CHECKLIST

1. As with any adoption, consider the situation of your "pack" at home.
2. Find an organization with a good reputation by checking its nonprofit status, calling the HSUS, or contacting Petfinder.com or Pets911.com.
3. Call the organization to find out what the requirements are for adoption. If you're not willing to agree to the home visit, interview, application process, or fee that the organization requires, seek another source to adopt from before you get your heart set on a specific dog.
4. Bone up on any breed-specific knowledge you might need to have.
5. Don't feel sorry! Once again, cultivate your calm-assertive demeanor before you meet the dog or dogs available for adoption.
6. If you have other dogs, ask if you can bring them along for a face-to-face meeting.
7. Observe the energy of the dog you wish to adopt. Does he or she have an energy level the same or less than your family and/or the other animals in your pack?

8. Make sure the dog is spayed or neutered and has all his or her shots before you bring the animal home.
9. Walk with the dog as soon as you leave the facility.

Adopting a Dog from a Breeder

If you are set on adopting a dog of a certain breed and don't want to risk going the rescue organization route, please don't just go rushing out to your nearest pet store, and don't buy any dog sight unseen over the Internet! Chances are, the dogs you'll find there are "puppy mill" dogs. Puppy mills, which the HSUS has been fighting to regulate since the 1980s, are breeding facilities that literally churn out litters of puppies in bulk to be sold in pet stores or on Internet websites. The conditions in many puppy mills are deplorable, especially for the female dogs used as breeders, who sometimes spend their whole lives in cages, often with no exercise, companionship, or veterinary care. These dogs will continue to bear litter after litter, until they are too old or sick to reproduce anymore, when they might be abandoned or even killed now that their "usefulness" to the puppy mill is over. Inbreeding is so common among puppy mill dogs that many of the offspring suffer from serious genetically transmitted conditions and diseases. But these shady operations continue to thrive because there's still big money to be made from the uneducated dog lover who falls in love with an irresistible little puppy in the pet store window.

If your child does pine over that "doggy in the window," you can use this opportunity to explain to children how wrong it is that puppy mill dogs live in cages, that they don't have normal lives, that they don't walk or get physical exercise, that they don't get groomed or bathed. And just as I counsel my clients not to nurture unstable behavior in their dogs, you should not reward a human being who makes money from puppy mills.

The Internet poses similar problems for potential dog owners. The Internet gives you access to a picture, and you feel the rush of instant love. It has been a great tool for many shelters and rescue groups, which use websites to show what dogs they have available, so people can know what to expect before they go there. But when you're dealing with a breeder, it's like playing poker, especially if you "order" your dog from far away. Even if the breeder is legitimate, there is no substitute for meeting him or her in person, checking out the facility, and observing your potential new dog's parents. In the vast Internet, the odds are higher that you will encounter people who, like puppy mill owners, are only about making money. There's no guarantee. You can get lucky, but I'm an old-fashioned guy and I like to meet the parents.

In a world where humans can so wantonly abuse animals just to make a buck, how do you go about finding a breeder who's reputable? You can get referrals from your veterinarian, local breed clubs, or AKC or other certified dog shows and competitions. Don't just go pick up a cute puppy from a local owner whose dog has "papers" (certification of lineage); if someone is willing to take your cash for a dog and let you walk away no questions asked, then they aren't a knowledgeable or responsible breeder. If the breeder is a good one, she will be able to answer any questions you might have about each dog and the dog's lineage (including the temperament of the parents and grandparents) and will be able to provide references for others who have adopted from her in the past. I always like to meet a puppy's parents, to get a sense of their health and temperament. The HSUS provides an excellent downloadable checklist for determining if a breeder is the real deal or not. If, after using its checklist, you have any doubts at all, put a lid on your emotions and have the courage to walk away. If you don't, you could be risking spending a lot of money and making a lifetime commitment to a dog with genetic abnormalities or lack of normal socialization abilities—both conditions that could end up costing you and your family in cash and heartache for years to come.

An advantage of getting a dog from a good breeder is that the breeder is going to know everything about the DNA background of the dog you are selecting. Since you are looking for a dog with the correct energy level for your family, you will be able to ask the breeder what kind of dogs she is selecting for. A breeder who mostly provides dogs for police departments or search and rescue work might be selecting for much higher-energy dogs than a breeder whose clients are primarily show dog owners or families. This way, you have a better chance at finding a dog with the energy level you are seeking.

Once you have found the right breeder and decided to take the plunge, make sure you don't just grab the cutest pup or adolescent dog that catches your eye. I suggest you compare at least three dogs, so you can sense the differences in their energy levels from the start. Remember, even dogs in the same litter can have wildly varying energy levels. If you don't want a high-energy dog at home, then the puppy that is bouncing on its hind legs trying to jump up on your chest won't be the best choice for you. Similarly, the shy guy in the corner may tug on your heartstrings, but you might have a family with too many boisterous kids to risk having to rehabilitate a low-self-esteem dog (many times, the smallest in the litter comes with a few ready-made insecurities). If the dogs you are looking at are old enough, follow the procedures I outline in the shelter and rescue organization sections and take the dog to a place where you can observe her away from her littermates. How does she relate to her environment? Is she open and accepting of mild corrections to her behavior? Are you able to walk her and feel the beginnings of a bond?

Responsible breeders won't allow you to take a puppy before he or she is at least two months of age. This is because those first two months are vital in the development of your dog's identity as a dog.

BREEDER CHECKLIST

1. Find a breeder with an excellent reputation. The HSUS website, www.HSUS.org, provides a checklist for identifying a reputable breeder.
2. Research the breed you are interested in. The more purebred the dog, the more likely her breed will influence her behavior.
3. Try to compare as many dogs as possible to find the right energy "fit" for your family.
4. Make sure to take the dog for a walk before leaving the breeder's, or after the dog has arrived at your home but *before* you invite her inside the house.

Wherever you find your dog, the joyous day will come when you will be bringing your new companion home. Believe it or not, how you handle that simple situation is almost as important as how you choose your dog!

The Homecoming

Welcoming Your New Dog
into the Family

The Barberas with their dog

So now you've done it. You've completed your research on dog behavior and dog breeds and most important, you've held at least one soul-searching family meeting with everybody involved. You've put it all on the line and been brutally honest about what your family's energy level is, what your real needs are as opposed to your fantasies, and you've ensured that every member of your family unit is onboard with the concepts of commitment and consistency when it comes to owning a dog. Armed with this new encyclopedia of knowledge and information, you went to the shelter, rescue organization, or breeder of your choice, and selected the dog you are certain will soon become the next, much-loved member of your family.

If all of the above is true, then great work so far! When it comes to predicting what kind of life you will have with your new dog, I cannot stress enough the importance of making the correct choice at the beginning. But as important as the selection process is, the hard work of owning a dog doesn't stop here. I've helped clients make the most informed, most wise choices in the world for themselves, then been called back weeks later because they didn't follow through after the choosing was done. Even the most happy-go-lucky, mellow, easygoing dog in the world can develop issues if his owners don't follow through from the moment they walk the dog out of the shelter.

The most important rule to remember here—and you will find me repeating it again and again in the chapters to follow—is that when it comes to relating to a dog, everything you do *counts*. A wise parent I know once said about children, "They're like little cameras that never shut off," and the same thing can definitely be said of dogs. Like a child, a dog is going to be observing your energy and behavior at all times, and processing that information in order to decide what his behavior is supposed to be. The difference is, of course, a dog isn't learning to be *human* from you, the way a child is. A dog is learning what his role and function in the pack will be. And everything you do, from the first moment you meet him, will play a part in what he takes home from this lesson. Here we'll focus on adopting an adult dog, covering puppies beginning on page 71.

The first thing you need to do when you remove the dog from his previous place of residence (shelter, pound, or rescue organization) is to take him for a walk, even before you get into the car to drive back home. This accomplishes two important things. First, unless you're adopting the dog from a huge ranch where he had ample room to romp, he's probably been in a confined space for a while and has built up large amounts of negative, pent-up energy. An energetic, ten- to thirty-minute walk will help begin to drain that energy and will begin the process of uncovering the real dog beneath the tension. Second, and more important, is the process of bonding that will begin with that very first walk. The walk is the single best tool you have available to every member of your family to create the ideal relationship with your dog, from day one and beyond.

BASICS REFRESHER

Mastering the Walk

1. Always begin the walk with calm-assertive energy. You don't need to "psych your dog up" for walking by telling her in an excited voice what you guys are about to experience. The walk is about bonding and creating a primal pack experience, not going to Disneyland.

2. Don't chase after the dog with the tool you are using, be it a simple 35-cent leash like the ones I use, a harness, or a haltie. To your dog, the tool you are using is an extension of your own energy, so it should have a pleasant (but not overstimulating!) connotation. Let your dog come to the tool, not the other way around. Many dogs seem to grasp the concept of the leash right away. Others will need your patience. Create a pleasant experience around the leash, associating it with food and mild affection. Remember, even your approval is affection to a dog!

3. For your very first walk with your dog, wait at the threshold of wherever you are leaving from—be it a shelter, your car, or your home. Make sure your dog is in calm-submissive

(continued)

waiting mode beside you, and then step out the door first. Ask your dog to follow. Whoever leaves the dwelling first, in the dog's mind, is leading the excursion. You want that leader to be you!

4. Hold the leash in a loose, relaxed manner like you are carrying a purse or a briefcase. Hold your head high, put your shoulders back. Your dog should be walking beside or behind you, not pulling you from in front. If your dog doesn't get that concept right away, use an object, like a walking stick or an umbrella, to create an obstacle until he gets the picture. Gently put the object out in front of the dog's path in order to create a boundary that will soon become an invisible one. The dog should not be fearful of the object, just respectful of it. Your energy will determine which of these it will be.

5. When encountering obstacles or distractions on the walk, never become reactive to the dog's behavior. Remember, you are setting the tone for everything you do together. If a dog gets excited when he sees a commotion or another dog across the street, this is not a signal for you to get excited, too! Keep your focus and, most important, your calm-assertive energy, and continue walking. A slight side-pull correction on the leash will communicate, "Don't get distracted, keep on walking!" Your dog will pick up that "This is okay, it has nothing to do with us, we're just moving forward." If your dog is especially hard to convince, calmly give eye contact, ask your dog to stop and sit beside you, and wait until he is calm and submissive before you proceed. If necessary, turn your dog's back to the commotion that is causing the distraction. By doing this (and again, waiting until he is calm-submissive before

continuing on), you are communicating the message that "We ignore dogs that are causing trouble across the street."

6. When you and your dog have had a successful fifteen- or twenty-minute walk, then allow your dog the freedom to wander a bit on the end of the leash, to smell the ground or pee and poop. This is a reward! After about five minutes, return to your structured walk.

7. When arriving at your destination or returning home, repeat the procedure outlined in step 3. Step over the threshold first, then invite your dog in after you. Remember, in your dog's mind, whoever goes through the door first owns that space! Make sure he is calm and submissive as you remove the leash.

Ideally, as many family members as possible have joined you on the first adoption excursion, but not so many as to create unneeded chaos. If you fear that once you get to that shelter or that breeder, some family members will still be focusing on their emotional response to the dogs, then you may need to leave some of your pack at home. If you are worried about bringing your excited young children or bored teenagers along to the shelter when you make this first, vital impression on your new dog, then your instincts are probably correct. It's okay—as long as you follow the correct procedures I'll lay out later, when introducing the dog to *every* member of his new pack.

In the meantime, bring your new dog into the car using the same calm-assertive energy and "pack leader first" technique you employed on the walk. If you are using a kennel, do not force the dog inside. Instead, invite the dog into the kennel by using food or something else he is attracted to. Wait with the kennel door open until the dog is resting in calm-submissive mode—closing the door while a dog is still anxious will make him feel trapped. Then put the kennel in the back of the car, turning it to face you, so he can smell and see you on this first auto trip. This helps to increase the feeling that he is not alone and that you two are together on this great adventure. Make sure he is settled in a safe place and is calm-submissive before you start the engine. You may have to wait patiently, but this is an important time. Once you start an activity with an anxious dog, you run the risk of his forever associating that activity with anxiety. Remember, the more perfectly you accomplish each of these rituals the first time around, the less likely you'll have to "fix" an issue later on.

When you arrive home, once again remind yourself that calm-assertive energy must be the order of the day. This goes for everyone else in the family who've been impatiently waiting to greet the new arrival! You need to explain to even your smallest children that your new dog is a living being needful of respect, and that in order to acclimate him to his new home, they will need to refrain from showering him with all the affection and excitement they surely must be feeling, at least in the very beginning. Everyone in your home, from the youngest child to the oldest grandparent, needs to be educated in and committed to the no-touch, no-talk, no-eye-contact rule. I'd advise you to take a page from my dog behavior tips and tire out your most excitable kids before the dog arrives.

I always advise owners to take their dog for a second walk before entering the house or yard itself. This will be to try to re-create the process of "migration" from one place to another. If possible, park a few blocks away and walk around your dog's new neighborhood for as long as possible—an hour or more if you can. Remember, even though you may be "rescuing" your dog from a cramped kennel or cage and taking him into the spacious, tastefully decorated home you worked so hard to earn, in your dog's mind, you are simply moving him from one kennel to another. Walls aren't natural to dogs, no matter how beautiful those walls might be.

A five-acre backyard surrounded by woods and trees is definitely an improvement over a kennel, but if you don't structure space so your dog gets the best possible use out of it, you might as well be in a studio apartment. In fact, some of my apartment-dwelling New York City clients do better than my suburban Los Angeles clients in terms of providing balance for their dogs, simply because they *have* to take their dogs out and walk! For a New Yorker, an hour walk across Central Park and back isn't a big deal, while for a family in Calabasas, California, even a trip to the local grocery store involves a ride in the car. Suburbanites can always go to the gym to get their primal exercise, but what are their dogs going to do?

For any dog, wandering around aimlessly in a big backyard—no matter how expensive the landscaping—is no substitute for a walk with his trusted and respected pack leader. This fact is all the more

The Dilbeck family walks Lacey

important when your dog first arrives home with you. Please, resist the temptation to simply let him out in the yard to wander. Take another walk; help him get used to the scents, sights, and sounds of his new neighborhood. And more important, help him get used to thinking of you as his pack leader.

When humans go into a church, a mosque, a synagogue, or any other kind of temple, we know that we must be very respectful from the moment we walk in. We speak in hushed tones and bow our heads. Upon entering, we obey the rituals and regulations of that particular religion—we might take off our shoes, cover our heads, anoint ourselves with water, or kneel down in prayer. The point is, we recognize that this particular environment is a place we must honor by obeying the rules, boundaries, and limitations that have been established there. Think of this temple metaphor every time you bring your dog into the house. If your dog springs across the threshold and darts in any given direction every time you open the door, then your dog is not honoring the temple of your home.

When faced with bringing a dog home for the first time, most owners do the polar opposite of what I advise. They open the door to the house, and watch with joy and fascination as the dog wanders about on his own, exploring, sniffing, knocking things over—doing all the things that a normal, curious dog is supposed to do in a new environment. What's wrong with this picture? It's not just any new environment. It's *your* environment. It's your home, and you—and the rest of the humans in your family—own it. Your home is your temple . . . and you need to communicate this to your dog right off the bat.

For the first introduction into your home, open the door and enter in front of your dog, then invite him to come in after you. Since you have just walked your hearts out, lead the dog directly into the kitchen, or wherever his feeding area may be, and give him food and water. Ask him to sit quietly while you prepare the meal, and don't let him wander around too much on his own. I advise keeping the leash on your new dog for most of his introduction into his new home.

After having exercised and eaten, your new dog should be in a much more relaxed state than he was when you first brought him out of the kennel. Now, one by one introduce him to the rest of the family. Keep excitement to a minimum. The less sound you use, the better. Let the dog meet each family member one by one, so he can become familiar with each distinct scent. Once your family members have practiced no-touch, no-talk, no–eye contact, if the dog gravitates to any of them, *then* they can show affection—but only if the dog initiates it. Remember this important adage: The pack leader doesn't chase after anyone; followers always come to the pack leader!

Now is a good time for a walk-through of your house. Imagine your dog as a new guest who has come to visit for the weekend, or pretend you are a real estate agent giving a potential buyer (your dog!) a tour of a house. Keep the leash on the dog and quietly take him to each room or area of the house into which he will be allowed. Stop at the threshold, make him wait, and then invite him in. Let the dog explore the room in a controlled manner, then bring him out and go to the next room. This is your way of communicating to your new dog, "This is *my* bedroom. This is *my* den. This is *my* couch." Though your dog doesn't understand that you paid $700 for that couch at Pottery Barn, he does understand the primal concept of "ownership." In dog packs, a dominant dog expresses ownership by standing over the object in question, and "claiming" it with his energy. This says to the more submissive dogs in the pack, "Stay away from my stuff."

If you do decide that a certain couch or room is off-limits, your dog won't take that personally. Your dog doesn't need an explanation of *why* you allow him on one couch and not another. In that sense, it's easier to give a dog rules than it is an inquisitive child. But you have to be sure to communicate those rules *clearly and consistently* to your dog. Dogs live in a black-and-white world when it comes to codes of behavior, so if there's any gray area at all, you message simply won't get through. Walking your dog from room to room as soon as you bring him into the house will help open those lines of communication right from the start.

Finally, you should show your dog to the place where he will sleep or what will be his "den." Though you may allow your dog to sleep with you in your bed later in your relationship, I don't recommend you allow it on the first night, or even the first week. This is because of the three proxemic zones—the public space, the social space, and the intimate space. Although most humans will never let another person into his or her intimate zone without some preexisting level of trust, Americans tend to take dogs into their intimate zones instantly, before either human or dog really knows anything about the other. This can feel strange and unnatural, even for animals as affectionate and companionable as dogs. Sleeping with an animal or a human is the most intimate act you can share, even more intimate than sex. That's because for two animals to sleep together, both must have total trust. Once you are asleep and your eyes are closed, you are in the most vulnerable state of your life. It takes complete trust and submission to be able to do that and still feel perfectly safe and secure. When we adopt an adult dog, we shouldn't share that kind of intimacy right away. First, we want to establish our position as pack leader; second, we want to have total trust with each other. I am a big believer in sleeping with dogs (we'll address sleeping arrangements for puppies on page 74), but I also believe sharing your intimate zone is something that should be earned through following rules, boundaries, and limitations. That way, it will have an even deeper meaning for both you and your dog.

Instead of bringing your dog into your bed right away, set up a kennel or a dog bed in a designated area, and make that be the one area where he is allowed to sleep for the first one or two weeks. If your dog has been properly exercised and is tired and fed, he shouldn't have too much trouble adjusting to his new place to sleep. Invite the dog into the kennel, or garage, or guest room, or laundry room—and make sure he goes there on his own. Never force; tempt with treats if necessary. You must make it a calming, pleasant experience. Make sure the dog is totally relaxed, in resting mode, before you close the door or the gate to the sleeping area. If the dog starts to whine, give him eye contact and ask him to relax, then wait until he shows total submission—as long as it takes. He is learning that the only way to get your approval is by relaxing, and that the "den" you have arranged is the place where he must practice calm submission.

It may take you forty minutes the first night, then thirty the second, then twenty the third, but eventually, your pet will feel natural in the new space. If your dog whines and cries during the first night or two, don't comfort him, even if your best instincts urge you to do so. That's good human psychology, but dogs' minds don't work like ours in that way. With a dog, when we give affection to an unstable mind, we only reinforce and encourage that state of mind. After a night or two of becoming accustomed to this ritual, your new dog will calm down and sleep more comfortably. And so will you.

BASIC CHECKLIST FOR THE FIRST HOMECOMING

1. "Migrate" with your dog to his new house.
2. Step over the threshold first.
3. Introduce your dog to other pack members.
4. Give your dog a walk-through of his new home.

5. Introduce your dog to the rules, boundaries, and limitations of your home.
6. Introduce your dog to where he will sleep, making sure to give it the most positive associations possible.

Dealing with New Dog Anxiety

Your new dog is entering an unknown environment, so if he has any anxiety issues at all, they might be exacerbated by the newness of your home and family. If you have thoroughly exercised the dog and remained calm-assertive during the introduction process, that should help to relieve the stress of the new situation. In extreme cases of anxiety, however, your dog might become startled and dart under your furniture. If he does this, don't go crawling in after him, yell at him, or pet him. Instead, move a comfortable distance away, and use gestures to try to draw him out. Dogs instinctually understand our gestures; in fact, they are the only species on the planet besides primates that understand if we point, they need to look or go in that direction. You can also use food to draw your dog out. Be sure to wait until he is in the clear and showing a calm-submissive posture before you give it to him.

Another way to minimize the anxious stress that a new dog might have is to introduce him to something loud or startling right away, communicating with your energy that it is nothing to get upset about. Doorbells are a good example. Don't wait until company comes over to discover whether your dog will jump six feet in the air at the sound of the buzzer! Instead, have a family member use the buzzer to go in and out calmly, ignoring the dog. Condition him to associate the sound of the buzzer with something other than the excitement of a new arrival. By gently introducing these potential stressors into a dog's life early, you will be much less likely to have difficulty with them later.

Adding a New Dog to the Pack

If you already have dogs and have followed my suggestions so far, your new dog is a dog with an equal or lower energy level than the dogs you already have. You have also made sure that your current pack is balanced, has few if any issues among one another, and every dog in that pack looks to you as leader.

The first step in this process is to introduce the dogs to one another in as natural and unthreatening a way as possible. In an ideal world, you already set up a first meeting before you made the final decision to adopt the new dog, just as Virginia and Jack did in Chapter 1, by introducing both their new dog candidates to their current pack member, Spike. This vital first meeting convinced Jack that the dog he was so emotionally attached to was not a compatible choice energy-wise for Spike. Likewise, the Barberas brought both their dogs with them to Daphneyland to make sure they were compatible with the basset hound they wanted to bring home. By adopting a dog with an equal or lower energy than the dogs in your existing pack, you are defusing the possibility of dominance struggles arising. If the new dog is the right energy, he is more likely to adapt and blend in with the current pack structure.

Whether before or after the adoption, you should be sure to arrange the first meeting on neutral ground, away from your home, to avoid a territory dispute. Never allow new dogs to meet head-on. In the dog world, face-to-face meetings and unsolicited eye contact often imply that a confrontation is about to explode. Instead, use your own body to mediate the interaction, allowing your dogs to explore each other around you. In the dog world, a new dog stands still, allowing the rest of the pack to sniff its rear. This is the equivalent of a human handshake, or more accurately, a handshake and a business card, since the dogs doing the sniffing will be getting a passel of new information about who the dog is and where he has been. It will be up to you as a pack leader to set the boundaries, making sure none of the dogs cross the line into unacceptable behavior. However, taking your dogs all together in a "pack walk" is the very best way to begin to integrate them into one cooperative unit.

Before the pack walk, it is a good idea to take the new dog and your current pack on separate walks to drain any pent-up tension or physical energy that might be lingering. Once every dog has had his or her preliminary exercise, it's time to bring them all together. When you first begin to walk, keep your existing pack to one side and your new addition to the other in order for them to get comfortable with each other and become accustomed to walking together as a unit. You can allow one dog to move ahead of the other; this will give the other dog a chance to become familiar with the smell of his new companion. Then switch it up; let the other one have a chance to be behind and experience the scent of his new mate. The new dog will not only be looking to you for direction, but also to the other dogs as role models. If they follow you, your new dog will pick up on that. Your current dogs will teach the new arrival the appropriate way to behave within the structure of the pack you've created.

INTRODUCING YOUNG CHILDREN TO THE NEW DOG

When it comes to children and dogs, my three top rules are: supervision, supervision, and supervision. Children are attracted to animals like magnets to steel. But wanting to be close to animals and Mother Nature doesn't mean that kids always understand rules, boundaries, and limitations. Teaching children these things is the job of a parent or guardian. Until you are absolutely sure that both your dog and your child each understand the rules of being together, you always need to be aware of how they are interacting together.

Repeat the mantras of "no touch, no talk, no eye contact" to your child long before he meets the new dog. Chances are, your child will have a friend or know someone who does not practice this way of being around the dog and will predictably ask you why Amy is allowed to pull her dog's tail, or play tug-of-war, or do some of the things that you will instruct your own child never to do. This is the time for the "why" questions, and it's good to get them out of the way before the dog's arrival. It is also something to bring up in your family meeting, to discuss how *your* family does things as opposed to things you have seen your friends, relatives, and neighbors do. It might be helpful to bring up something unpleasant about Amy's dog—for instance, it jumps on you every time you come to the door. Explain that this behavior doesn't mean that the dog is "happy"—it means the dog is too excited and hasn't learned manners. Don't try and make the neighbors wrong; just explain that you have been exposed to good information that has convinced you that this is the way our family should do it. Young children will almost always want to get onboard with the family plan, but they need to understand it clearly, and rightly so.

When your child has his first meeting with a new dog, it's important that he be in an instinctual/psychological, not a physical state, which means the child has already exercised and is relaxed and on his best behavior. If the child is overexcited, it can either overstimulate an anxious or hyperactive dog or a dog with aggressive or dominant tendencies, or it can intimidate a fearful, shy dog. Have your child stand still (but not stiff) and let the dog come to him, to check out his scent. If the dog is overly assertive, you need to claim the space around the child and communicate to the dog, "This is my kid's space, you have to be invited in!" When you do this, you will not only be establishing a circle of respect around your child, but you'll be teaching him to claim his space on his own in the near future. If the dog shows hesitancy or fear, make sure the child doesn't follow a natural impulse to reach out to the dog to give comfort. By now, I hope you've communicated to everyone in the home the concept that giving dogs affection or sympathy when they are under stress doesn't help them, it hurts them.

BASICS REFRESHER

Claiming Your Space

1. Claiming space means using your body, your mind, and your energy to "own" what you would like to control. You create an invisible circle of space around a person, place, or thing that belongs to you, a space that the dog cannot enter without your permission.

2. When you want to claim space, commit 100 percent into projecting an invisible line around the space or object you do not want your dog to go near. Say to yourself, "This is my sofa," or "This is my ball." You are having a verbal conversation with yourself, but a psychological/energetic conversation with your dog.

3. Never pull an object away from a dog, or pull a dog away from a place, person, or object. When you pull things away from a dog, you're either inviting her to compete for it or you're inviting her to play. This only increases the dog's prey drive. Instead, step calmly and assertively forward toward the dog, making firm eye contact, until the dog backs up or relaxes.

4. To get your dog to drop an object, you must first claim it with your mind and your energy. You cannot be hesitant

and you must be totally clear about your intention. Don't negotiate or plead with your dog, either mentally or verbally. Your dog will not take it personally. He shouldn't have a problem giving you what he now knows belongs to you.

I always recommend that people refrain from giving a dog too much affection for the first days or weeks after they bring the dog home. I also realize that most people won't take my advice. The logic behind this request is what's best for the dog. When a dog is in a new environment and a new pack, the first things he's concerned about are "Who's running this place?" and "Is it safe?" By providing leadership and boundaries before affection, you are answering those questions for him—*you* are in charge, and *you* are going to keep him (and the rest of the pack) safe. It's only after knowing the answers to these questions that a dog can truly relax and bond and become a full-fledged, trusting, respectful family member. Young children are naturally affectionate and may not understand why they can't pet the dog as much as they want right away. You can help them control their impulses by explaining how they should interact with the dog before he arrives, and by always supervising the interaction. By the time the dog is living with you, the children should all understand that what is best for the human isn't always what's best for the dog.

Another great way to help your child bond with the new dog, while also providing rules, boundaries, and limitations, is to start the child and the dog exercising together right away. If your child is still in a stroller, illustrate how you leave the house with the dog, and how the dog follows behind. After the walk, let the child pet the dog and give it a treat, when the dog is calm and relaxed. If your child is older, it's never too soon to start teaching him how to master the walk. Make it a family walk until you are 100 percent certain the child can handle the dog by herself; by watching you, she will be absorbing the right calm-assertive way of being around the dog. Kids and dogs make great walking companions, and they are attracted to each other because each lives totally in the moment. By teaching both dog and child rules, boundaries, and limitations and mutual respect from day one, you are creating an incredible kid/dog team. By nurturing this relationship, you will be introducing another wonderful pack leader to a world that needs as many calm-assertive pack leaders as it can get!

INTRODUCING YOUR NEW DOG TO YOUR CAT

Since I am a "dog person," I often forget that "cat people" consider their cats to be members of their families as well. Making that first meeting between dog and cat go smoothly begins with the work you do before bringing your new dog home. The Barberas' experience at Daphneyland is a great example, They were able to make sure the dog they adopted was already socialized with cats since that was a service that the Daphneyland rescue group already provided. Many rescue groups prescreen dogs to see how they react to cats, children, and other dogs. Some dogs with a very high prey drive aren't the best candidates for homes with small creatures running around underfoot.

The next thing to remember is that all-important concept—energy. A human is energy, a dog is energy, and a cat is energy, so you must consider your cat's inborn energy when selecting the dog you will bring home, just as much as you must consider the energy of any dogs you already have. Energies attract and energies repel, so ideally, you will want to select an energy that is compatible with the energy of the pet you have at home. If you have a dominant, high-energy cat, the cat will take care of itself in almost every situation. On more occasions than I can count, I have been called in to help humans with an "uncontrollable" dog—only to find that the family cat has had no problem at all giving the dog rules, boundaries, and limitations.

However, if you have a cat that is skittish around humans, or is shy, elderly, weak, or ill, then you must make sure you bring home a very submissive, low-energy dog in order to keep the balance in the household. If you have any doubts, introduce the cat to the dog as part of your own space. If you present yourself as the pack leader to the cat—in other words, you *own* the cat—then the dog will give the cat some space in deference to you. Don't keep dog and cat apart; your objective is to create one family pack, not several. In one *Dog Whisperer* case, I actually advised a couple to walk their dog and their cat (in a stroller!) together, in order to strengthen the pack bond. As odd as my suggestion may seem, the couple tell me it worked, and their cat and dog, formerly mortal enemies, are now playful pals.

HOUSEBREAKING AN ADULT DOG

On some occasions, a dog may be available for adoption that hasn't been properly housebroken in its previous placements, or hasn't been housebroken at all. For instance, dogs rescued from puppy mills, from laboratories, or from racetracks may have gone through their whole lives without learning a housebreaking routine. The good news is, a dog naturally does not want to eliminate in his "den." You can help him in this by providing a consistent routine, which you will have to be extremely disciplined about for the first two months.

TIPS FOR ADULT DOG HOUSEBREAKING

- Take your dog out first thing in the morning, then every four hours if possible. Gradually decrease to three times a day.
- If you work during the day, keep your dog in a small area or kennel while you are gone and thoroughly clean and disinfect any area in which there have been accidents.
- Take your dog to the same place every time.
- Do not allow a large area for the dog to roam at first.
- Reward with affection—praise, a treat, or just your energy—after your dog has used the bathroom outside.
- Feed your dog on a very regular schedule and control the amount of water you give, at least until a routine has been established.

Some dominant dogs will want to pee to mark their territory, as opposed to just relieving themselves. It's important that you break this habit right away, by making sure your dog is always in a calm-submissive state whenever he goes to pee. If you have a dog that is urinating from a dominant point of view, every time you see him going toward a tree with that energy, you have to stop him and wait until he's in a submissive state in order to release him. What you are teaching him is that it's not excitement that makes him pee, it's you who allows him to do it. This is basically reprogramming his organs through his mind, controlling his physiology through his psychology. In an adult dog, this can take a lot of patience and commitment on your part, but don't forget that you are taking a few short months to establish a lifetime pattern of good behavior.

Puppy's First Day Home

Bringing a puppy home from the breeder, shelter, or rescue organization is a very different process from welcoming an adult dog into your life. A grown dog can actually hurt somebody, so you have to make sure he respects the environment by immediately welcoming him into the pack in the way I've outlined. While, for the most part, respect is the first thing you want to earn from an adult dog, *trust* is the first thing you must establish with a new puppy. The puppy needs to learn to trust the new environment you've brought him to. He can't hurt anybody else, but he can hurt himself.

Your role with the puppy is to take over the role of pack leader from the mother, while still allowing the puppy to explore and process things on his own. This means you want to pick up the puppy by the scruff, the way the mother does, and when you put him down, always let two of his feet touch first, so he can experience finding the place you are putting him with his own body. These can be the back two feet, if you are holding the puppy upright, or the front two feet, if you are putting the puppy onto or into a foreign object like a car. Put two feet down with a puppy and eventually the other two will follow. Most people carry puppies around like babies, so they never get a sense of how they get to where they're going.

When you put the puppy into the car on your way home, don't just place the puppy in the box and carry the box to the car. Take the puppy to the car, put the front two feet down, and the brain will automatically want to put four feet wherever the other two landed. If you wait for that moment, the puppy will be able to figure out how to be on a human lap, in an automobile, or in a new environment. By introducing the puppy to new places the way the mother would, the puppy instinctually understands, "Okay, this makes me feel the way I used to feel at home. Now it's very important that I follow this

human who is familiar to me from the moment he picked me up."
You become the puppy's last link to his mom, or his first pack. The
puppy will want to explore first with his body and then with his
nose, so if you want to transport the puppy in a box or a kennel, you
can use food to lure him there so he goes in on his own.

If you have removed the puppy correctly from the mother and introduced him to the car the way I've just described, it will be natural
for him to follow you because you are already the closest thing to his
family. Now it's time to bring the puppy inside your house. It's important for a puppy to have a sense of the environment he's going to
live in; to get a taste of the smells, sounds, and sights of your yard,
home, and neighborhood.

Let's say you have the classic yard with the white picket fence in
front. You must communicate to the puppy that this fence marks the
beginning of your territory. Put the leash high up on the puppy's
neck, so you can have a comfortable amount of control. Then place
the puppy on the ground, back feet first, then walk toward your
home, letting him follow you inside the front door. If you live in an
apartment, place the puppy just outside the apartment door and
wait for him to follow you inside. Patience is key here, because he
may be a bit disoriented and a little reticent in the beginning. Hesitancy is normal in puppies, because everything is new to them, but
don't force the puppy inside if he is "putting the brakes on." Wait
until the puppy's nose gets into the act. Then he will show natural
curiosity and willingness to come in after you, and at that time you
can help him come inside. Remember, the energy you share with
your puppy will become his energy. If you are tense and impatient
with him, he will reflect that tension right back at you. The good
news is that all puppies are programmed to follow at this age, so give
him time—he'll go inside the house eventually.

Once you are safe inside your domain, watch and see how the
puppy adapts himself to the new environment. Some puppies will

look around and begin whining, which is how they tell you, "I'm not familiar with this place." Some might cautiously explore in a small space; but don't forget, any time you enter a new area, you must be the one to cross the threshold first. If the puppy begins to wander ahead of you, use your leg as an obstacle to block, to silently say, "This is the line you don't cross." Some puppies might come in and immediately shut down out of fear and confusion. It's important that you do not feel sorry at this time. Remember, the mother dog will never feel sorry for her pups! Stand nearby, remain calm and assertive, and let the puppy go through the transition period on his own—this is how he builds self-confidence. If you pick him up right away to pet and comfort him, you are actually thwarting him from developing the necessary self-esteem he'll need to be able handle new situations in the future.

The best thing for you to do for your puppy at this time is to use scent to unlock the brain when it shuts down. Puppies at this age are driven by two main needs—food and companionship—so you can lead the puppy to where you want him to go both by your presence, and by waving food in front of the nose. Once the puppy moves forward toward the scent, you give him the food, and quickly he will realize that if he follows that scent, he gets fed. You are also making the association between moving forward and a safe, positive, pleasant experience.

At this point, a more confident puppy will be looking to you for direction, as if asking, "What do we do now?" If that's the case, then let the puppy follow you around your environment until he gets tired. Once he shows signs of slowing down, let him follow you where his resting place is going to be. But if he's already worn out or already in a shut-down state, then you want to grab that opportunity to introduce him to his pen, bed, or kennel, indicating, "This is where we practice quiet behavior." Once again, don't just pick him up and plop him down on the mat—not only do you disorient the pup by doing this, you also run the risk of associating the resting place with a negative experience. You may have created the most beautiful, comfortable sleeping paradise in the world, but if you introduce it in a negative way, it will always be ugly to your new puppy. Instead, try to lead the puppy with food, or place the puppy down a foot or so away from the place you want him to rest. By going there on his own steam—especially if led by a treat—he will associate his new "den" area with pleasant relaxation.

Sleeping arrangements are also a different matter between a puppy and an older dog. Puppies always sleep with the mother and siblings in their natural world. Since I always have a pack of dogs, all my puppies have slept with their new packs from day one; in Chapter 4, I'll talk about how my pit bull Daddy became a parent figure to my new puppy, Junior. If you don't have another balanced dog that is ready and willing to take on the role of "nanny" to your puppy, then it is up to you to reduce any trauma the pup might have on his first night away from his birth family. This means keeping a strong pack leader presence in close physical proximity to the pup for the first two or three nights to minimize any feeling of abandonment the puppy might have. Be sure to bring a towel or blanket or toy that has the scent of the puppy's first family on it. Smelling his mother and siblings will help soothe him as he tries to adjust to a life without them.

Next, set up the puppy's crate, box, or kennel near or next to the bed of an adult member of the family. The crate keeps the puppy safe, helps to start house training (since pups don't like to soil their sleeping areas), initiates crate training, and allows the new human "parents" to get some sleep while knowing the pup is safe and secure. The crate should be lined with newspaper or a towel with a raised bed in the back. Crate training should never include the puppies sleeping in their own waste, and there will be accidents. The crate should also have a soft mat or cloth in it that contains both the scents of the puppy's birth family, and the scents of his new human family as well. Add a stuffed toy or two with familiar scents on them to provide physical warmth and comfort. Many pet stores sell "beating heart" plush toys that remind the youngster of the sound of the mother's heartbeat. Remember, never close the door to a crate if the puppy isn't totally relaxed.

If you don't plan to have your puppy remain in your bedroom, then three days should be long enough to acclimate him to his new environment. He may whine through the night when you move his sleeping place, but if you tire him out and make sure he is relaxed before you put him down for the night, it won't take long for him to adjust to the place you want him to stay. Don't forget that your own energy and attitude toward your puppy's sleeping arrangements will have a powerful impact on how he himself views them. If you feel terrible about putting your puppy's crate in the laundry room and are wracked with worry that he'll feel lonely out there, then your puppy will probably pick up on and come to share your negative emotions. Deciding on a sleeping arrangement that makes *you* feel that you are providing the best for your puppy is the best way to guarantee that he will become comfortable sleeping there.

Your puppy's first nights home are only the beginning of his exciting new life with his human family. In raising a puppy, you have a wonderful opportunity to "create" the dog of your dreams.

4

RAISING THE PERFECT PUP

Puppies 101

My pit bull Daddy is now fourteen years old, and he has had a remarkable life so far. He's been all over the United States; he's been on the Red Carpet at the Emmy Awards; and he's even been to the White House. Daddy originally belonged to a rapper named Redman. In the rap culture, it's still considered a status symbol to have a big tough dog like a pit bull or a rottweiler. Daddy certainly looked the part. But once Redman had brought Daddy home, he looked around and saw friends and colleagues of his with badly behaved pit bulls who were biting people—people who would, in turn, slap their owners with lawsuits. Redman traveled a lot, was in the studio or touring constantly, and couldn't afford to be watching his dog like a hawk all the time. He also couldn't afford to be going to court again and again to explain that his dog was unfriendly to humans. So Redman made a responsible decision and sought out a professional to help him. Blessedly, that professional turned out to be me.

Daddy was only three months old at the time, and I had the opportunity to provide him with everything he could possibly need to be fulfilled, balanced, and challenged. I, my family, and a pack of rottweilers that I was rehabilitating at the time raised Daddy. Of course, we all know that Daddy has grown up to become the ultimate ambassador of his badly maligned breed. Though Daddy spent most of his years with me, he officially belonged to Redman until a few years ago, when he legally became mine. Though I never like to admit favoring one dog over another, Daddy and I have a bond that supersedes anything nature or science can explain. We've reached that wonderful level of companionship where we read each other's thoughts and communicate without words almost instantly.

The truth is, however, the train of life on this earth only goes in one direction, and Daddy is now a senior citizen. That's just a fact. One day, he won't be able to be here with me on this planet. Because of the way pit bulls are vilified in our society, I believe it's important to always have a pit by my side that will disprove all those terrible stereotypes against the breed. Among my pack, there are many wonderful pits that have helped with rehabilitating dogs, both at the Dog Psychology Center and beyond. But none of them have Daddy's unique brand of medium-level energy, calmness, experience, and wisdom. I can take Daddy anywhere, and I know that every human and animal who meets him falls in love with him, too.

For a long time, I could not admit to myself or out loud that Daddy was getting older. He survived cancer and chemo with flying colors, and he manages well with arthritis. Though I monitor him closely, making sure he's not too hot or tired or has gone too long without a bathroom break, I try to live in the moment and never think about the time when he won't be my sidekick. A close friend of mine, an excellent vet tech who also happens to be from Sina Loa in Mexico, wasn't quite so subtle. "He's not going to be around forever, you know," he said to me. This friend told me that he had a female pit who had been wonderful with his own kids for years, and who just had a litter of puppies. He said, "Come on over to my house, maybe you'll find the next Daddy."

Introducing Junior

My friend had been pretty blunt about some things I wasn't ready to face, but I took him up on his invitation. I wanted to see his female pit bull around his own small children, so I went to his house. She was absolutely wonderful—the perfect family dog, very submissive to the kids. My friend showed me a photo of the father, who was also a well-bred, healthy pit bull—a show dog, in fact. When I went in to see the puppies, one immediately caught my eye. He was all gray with a little white on his chest, and he had powder-blue eyes. But what attracted me most to him was his energy. Though he didn't resemble Daddy physically, his energy made me feel as if I were going back in time and seeing Daddy again when he was a puppy. In my heart, I heard myself saying, "That's him. That's the one."

As attracted I was to this particular pup, I wasn't going to commit to bring him into the pack until he met Daddy, the guy I wanted to be his "surrogate father." As always, a dog can tell you much more about another animal—dog, cat, or human!—than any person can. First, I decided to see how Daddy reacted around some of the other puppies in the litter. I had noticed one of the puppies acting a little dominant around the children in the family, so I tried introducing him to Daddy. Daddy immediately growled at him and turned away. Another pup I picked out didn't interest Daddy at all; he totally ignored him. Older dogs often ignore puppies that annoy them—they just don't have the energy or patience to deal with puppy antics. But how would Daddy react to the gray pup I had been so attracted to? I had my fingers crossed, but I know Daddy—and I just had a feeling he and I would be drawn to the same dog.

I lifted the little gray guy up by his scruff the way the mother would carry him and presented his rear to Daddy. Daddy checked him out and signaled for me to put him down. When I put the puppy down, he automatically lowered his head in a very polite, submissive way to Daddy. Daddy continued to smell the little guy, and it was obvious there was an interest and attraction there. But the most wonderful thing happened next! When Daddy finished checking the puppy out and began to walk away, the puppy started to follow him.

Daddy and his protégé Junior

My heart leaped up inside me, and I knew that this little gray bundle of fur was going to be Daddy's spiritual "son."

THE CRUCIAL MONTHS OF PUPPYHOOD

One of the most important things to remember about puppyhood is that it is the shortest stage of a dog's life. A dog is a puppy from birth to eight months, then an adolescent from eight months to three years. With good nutrition and veterinary care, a modern dog's life span can last from ten to twelve to sixteen years or more.[1] So when the children in a family come back from watching *101 Dalmatians* and beg parents, "I want a puppy, I want a puppy!," both parents and kids need to remember that in the blink of an eye, this puppy will physically resemble a grown-up dog. A puppy is not a stuffed animal that will stay small and cuddly forever. If someone in your household seems enamored only with the charming antics, size, and shape of a pup, then I advise you not to give in to a whim and bring one home for the novelty of it. Sadly, this is something that occurs far too often. Human beings are naturally attracted to "neotenized" animals, that is, animals with big eyes and heads and tiny bodies that resemble helpless babies. They appeal to the caring, nurturing needs in all of us, from children to grandparents. That could explain why puppies and small dogs are generally snapped up from rescues and shelters first, leaving older and larger dogs to wait for owners who will never come. Often, these dogs are the first to be put to death. A person who adopts a puppy on an impulse, or who receives a puppy as an unsolicited gift, may ultimately end up bringing the grown dog to a shelter or rescue group once it has outgrown its endearing "cute factor." Puppies require commitment, focus, energy, and above all, patience. If you are not prepared to care for a dog for the rest of her life, then please don't fall for an adorable face and bring a puppy home on a whim.

If you are certain you want to commit to a puppy for life, however, despite some hard work, you have a wonderful opportunity in front of you. This is truly your chance to create the dog of your family's dreams. Pups are like lovable little clean slates, programmed in their DNA to absorb the rules, boundaries, and limitations of the societies they live in. If you clearly communicate your family's rules to the puppy from day one, you can mold a companion that will respect, trust, and bond with you on a level that you never imagined possible. But like children, puppies are constantly observing, exploring, and working to figure out how they fit into the world around them. If you consistently send them the wrong signals during this phase, it will be a lot more difficult to rehabilitate them once those bad habits are ingrained.

Mother Nature is all about balance, and it is to nature that I turn whenever I want to explain about the correct way to bring up puppies. From the moment they are born, the canine mother gently but firmly lets her new offspring know that they must follow her rules if they want to survive. Mother dogs do not "coddle" their young. In fact, if one of the pups in her pack has trouble finding a place to feed, she will only help her up to a point. If the puppy can't get with the program, the mother may even let her die. This may sound harsh, but it's up to every dog to learn to survive in the pack, and even the weakest member of the litter has to learn to adjust on her own.

When the pups are about six to seven weeks of age, the mother begins to be a little less possessive of them and begins to let other members of the pack participate in their socialization. Among packs of wild canines, rearing the young is truly a family affair. In canid species such as wolves, jackals, and wild dogs, many of the adults in addition to the mother share the job of feeding the maturing pups, returning from hunts and regurgitating food for them. The whole pack also shares in the education of the pups, including disciplining them.[2] If another adult member of the pack feels the pups are getting a little too boisterous in their play, he may use physical touch—a nudge, or even a firm but nonaggressive bite—to communicate the limits. The mother doesn't come running, crying, "How dare you touch my puppy—I'm the mother here!" This is because the mother's rules are the same basic rules that are enforced consistently throughout the pack. In this way, all the pups learn right off the bat that they have to take direction from all the adults, and although they will test their limits like all maturing mammals do, they fall into line pretty quickly. This should be the model your human family emulates when working together to bring up your new puppy.

Mother Knows Best

When a puppy is first born, she experiences her mother as first energy, then touch. When a mother dog gives birth, she does so in private and the whole experience is very calm and quiet. It's a mother's instinct to be very protective about the birth experience, and newborns in general. In the wild, she will often issue threats to other dogs that come near her during this time. Even if the mother dog has a lower-energy, more submissive temperament by nature, having puppies will always bring out the calm-assertive side of her. The first energy that any dog experiences upon coming into the world is the mother's calm-assertive energy, and that will remain the energy that attracts them the rest of their life. Calm-assertive energy will always make them feel safe, stable, and secure.

Puppies' noses first open right after they are born, and thus, after touch, scent becomes the strongest of all their senses. Not until about fifteen days after birth will they open their eyes, and not until twenty days after birth will they have full use of their ears.[3] This is why I counsel all dog lovers to remember to approach all dogs with this order in mind: start to function.

1. Nose
2. Eyes
3. Ears

When we are around puppies, we humans tend to resort to sound—usually, excited sound. "Oh, my God, they're so cute!" would probably be the most common response from a person presented with a litter of squirming, squealing newborn dogs. But puppies are not little humans, they are little dogs, and they experience the world in a completely different way than we do. Relating to puppies via nose-eyes-ears not only gives them the respect that they deserve; it gives us better access to influence them in a natural way. For the first few months after I brought him home, the little gray pit bull pup that I adopted to be Daddy's spiritual "heir" had no name. I rarely used sound to communicate with him, making a point of using only scent, energy, and touch to get my messages across. After I knew that he and I were speaking fluently without words, I decided to name him "Junior," in honor of his role as "Daddy Junior" in the pack.

Unless you are a breeder, you should not be taking a puppy from her or his mother until after eight weeks of age. Those first two months of development are crucial to the pup's identity as a dog, and pups removed from the natural canine family before that period will often have behavioral issues right out of the box. If your puppy was fortunate enough to have a confident, dedicated mother, then you will have a head start on raising a happy, balanced dog. Dogs make terrific parents, and the dog pack is the best classroom in the world for learning how to adapt and survive.

Human researchers call puppies' first three months their *developmental period* and divide it into three distinct stages:[4]

PUPPY DEVELOPMENT CHART

Neonatal Period

Birth to two weeks	• Sleeps 90 percent of the time • Only senses are touch and scent • Nurses, crawls, seeks warmth of littermates and mother • Needs stimulation to urinate and defecate • Can usually right herself if turned over • Nervous system is rapidly developing

Transitional Period

Two to three weeks	• Eyes open • First formation of teeth • Stands on all fours and takes first steps • Begins to lap with tongue • No longer needs stimulation to eliminate

Socialization Period

Stage 1: Becoming Aware	3–4 weeks	• Can hear and see • Sense of smell much more acute • Begins to eat food • Begins to bark, wag tail, and bite siblings
	4–5 weeks	• Walks and runs well but tires quickly • Chases and plays prey-killing games • Bares teeth and growls • Begins pawing

(continued)

Stage 2: Curiosity Period	5–7 weeks	• Weaning begins • Very curious • Plays dominance games with littermates	
Stage 3: Behavioral Refinement	7–9 weeks	7 weeks	• All senses function • Will investigate anything
		8 Weeks	• Becomes fearful and startles easily • Is cautious about anything new in environment

A Natural Upbringing

For a true understanding of the way dogs learn rules, boundaries, and limitations from birth, there is no substitute for watching how a good bitch raises her own litter among a pack of dogs. Fortunately, we recently had such a blessed event occur at the Dog Psychology Center when we rescued Amy, a pregnant pit bull, from the local pound. When Amy came to the Center, she immediately started searching for a place to make her nest. A pregnant bitch becomes very private and protective of her space, and she can send other dogs away from her with just a look. I wanted my sons to witness the miracle of birth because it was something they had not been exposed to before. Because I spent so much time at my grandfather's farm as a kid, by the time I was their age, I had seen dozens of animals born, and I believe it has helped me appreciate the wonders of the natural world. Amy was an amazing mother. She patiently delivered each puppy, removing each sac, eating the placenta, and chewing off the umbilical cord. Every time a mother dog licks her pups, she strengthens the bonding between them in both directions. She begins to recognize the pups by their smell and taste, and the pups learn the smell of her saliva and come to recognize that "this is my mother." The saliva trail also helps lead the pups to nipples where they will soon be nursing.[5] For the first two weeks (the neonatal period), the pups do little more than eat, sleep, defecate, and seek the warm comfort of their mother's body. Amy was a fastidious mother, licking her pups to stimulate their elimination, and then cleaning up the nest by consuming the rest of their waste. Although I checked on Amy frequently and handled the pups myself every day, I didn't allow any other humans to interrupt this special bonding time between mother and pups. Research shows that sensitive early handling by humans actually makes for smarter pups with better coping mechanisms, but too much stimulation is bad for them.[6] That's why it's best that only very knowledgeable humans handle newborn pups.

By the end of the second week, Amy's pups were entering what's called the transitional period. Their eyes were open now and their hearing was beginning to develop, but their primary interest was still in their mother and littermates. By four weeks, the pups were just beginning to become curious about things outside their immediate environment, including the humans who visited their den.

As Amy's experience indicates, during the first two months of a dog's life, the pups don't really care about meeting the other dogs of the pack. They're extremely happy with just one another and with their mom, and they really don't explore more than four to six feet away from where they normally sleep. The mother teaches them

Amy's puppies

social boundaries, and they also learn limitations by playing games with their littermates.

After two months of age, however, puppies begin to show signs of wanting to see the world beyond the den. By this time, the mother is no longer nursing them, so she starts distancing herself from them a little bit, as if to say, "Okay, now you guys are strong enough and healthy enough; it's time for you to meet the pack." We kept Amy's pups in an enclosed area on one side of a fence, and as they moved into their more curious stages, I would come out to see them sitting next to the fence, just watching the other dogs, waiting until they were invited to come to the other side.

Once the pups begin to venture out and explore the rest of the pack, they hold their bodies low because the other dogs are taller, and they begin to investigate the adult members of the pack by cautiously smelling their feet, toenails, and the lower parts of their bodies. Thanks to both the mother's consistent discipline and the social instincts they are born with, the puppies are very respectful of the environment and the other dogs in it. Some of the dogs will growl right away, and the puppies get their first lesson in corrections. Then they will try to visit with another dog and experience a different way of being—they might be invited to play, or simply to relax and lie down. Some of the adult dogs will move away and avoid them, but some dogs will stay there and patiently let the puppies investigate them. Others will investigate the pups, and the puppies will sit or stand very still, trying to figure out how they should feel about submitting and letting a stranger smell them. When challenged, the pups roll over on the ground right away and learn very quickly to let the adults smell them completely before moving away. This is an important cue we need to take from the dog world—the pack expects good social behavior from the puppies from day one, and it always gets it.

In the beginning, Amy's puppies would get their social "fix" from hanging out with the pack between fifteen and thirty minutes, and then they'd return to the den. They'd stay in the den for up to five hours, just resting and watching. Then the urge to explore would kick in again and they'd venture back into the pack territory. They naturally wanted to learn from the other dogs. Each time they would stay with the pack a little bit longer.

Although a pack of unrelated domestic dogs don't all pitch in to raise the puppies as wolves would in the wild, many of the litters we've had at the Dog Psychology Center over the years have found "nannies" in some special pack members with particularly strong nurturing instincts. I've written before about Rosemary, a rescued fighting pit bull who had been set on fire by her handlers after she lost an illegal dogfight. After I rehabilitated Rosemary and integrated her into the pack, she proved to be Nanny 911 to all the pups that came through the Center. Often this job appeals to females like

Rosemary who've never had puppies, but still retain their mothering instincts. As a nanny, Mary Poppins had nothing on Rosemary. She was absolutely the best. She would watch out for the puppies in the pack, groom them, comfort them, correct them gently when necessary, but also protect them from other dogs that weren't quite as patient.

Respect Your Elders

By six months of age, the pups in the pack are approaching adolescence, are in a much more exploratory phase of their lives, and are hanging around with the pack all the time. When they approach six months, they start wanting to go on longer walks with the pack, and they begin exploring a broader range around their home territory. At the Center, I make sure to challenge them constantly with the obstacle course, the pool, scent and sight games, and other behavioral enrichment tools—this is a crucial time in their learning development. This is also the age when they begin eating with the pack, and learning just how powerful the older pack members are. Watching a pup learn to negotiate mealtime with the rest of the pack is a great way to understand how dogs use dominance—not aggression!—to keep order and peace among one another. The pups are drawn to the food by the smell, but when they sense the intensity of their elders around the food, they spontaneously stop as far as ten feet away. When they get closer, they roll over and show their bellies without even being challenged. They show the ultimate respect to the older dogs when they're eating, practically melting right in front of them. They'll come close to the food but they won't touch it or even look at it, even though it's right next to them. They are saying to their elders, "I'm avoiding the food, submitting to you. I am no threat to your possession of the food."

If a pup does make the mistake of venturing forward to take food, or if he gets too close to the food without permission, an adult dog will turn and growl or snap at him. The reaction among all the pups will be like a tsunami—one growl from the older dog and all the pups will scurry back four or five feet. From there, they'll stay and wait patiently, and once the bigger dog moves, they will come and lick the plate, even though there is no food in there. They've just learned that the only time they can come to the food is when the grown dogs have walked away. They're learning how to communicate in the social language of canines, which is very specific about the right time and the wrong time to take initiative in the pack. And the pups learn their lessons quickly.

If they do persist in a mistake, one of the older dogs will correct them instantly. She will give them a warning growl, and if that doesn't work, she will immediately correct them by biting. She will bite the puppy in the muscle, but there is a tremendous amount of control in the correction. She never draws blood when correcting, even though sometimes she'll grab the puppy's whole face and hold it in her mouth. The bite and the timing are amazingly precise. The pup may squeal, as if to say, "I mean no harm! I mean no harm!," but the older dog won't let him go until he settles and stops moving. But there are no hard feelings in the dog world.

Nobody feels bad, not the one who corrected or the one who received. Dogs don't harbor resentments when they are reminded not to break the rules, and in fact, the corrector and the corrected can be grooming each other in friendship moments later. That's the beautiful thing about dogs. Humans need to understand that feeling bad about giving a puppy a deserved correction actually goes *against* the master plan of Mother Nature.

ADOLESCENT CHALLENGES

For puppies, this respectful, polite, submissive stage continues until around eight months, when they hit their adolescent period. When rams or buffalo get to the age of sexual maturity, you'll see a lot of head butting. In the dog world, you will see the formerly acquiescent pups challenge one another and even their elders by tentative displays of dominance—they'll put their heads on the shoulder of another dog, try to take food away from another dog, and compete with one another in a much more intense way. If the dogs are not spayed or neutered, the mating urge just increases this teenage rebellion. This is when the adolescents will unconsciously challenge their elders; because the mating urge is so strong, it will override good manners. Unfortunately, the mating urge also lessens the tolerance level of the adult dogs, and they'll have little of the patience they displayed when teaching the pups how to act around food. If an adolescent dog challenges an older or higher-rank dog for a mate, then this time, the pup will walk away bleeding. The upshot is that the mating urge only lasts fifteen days maximum, so if they can make it through this phase, adolescent dogs can make it to adulthood in one piece.

Another behavior that comes along with adolescence is urine marking, especially among males. When we take dogs into our homes and don't plan to breed them, then spaying and neutering at six months will ease this physical and psychological frustration for dogs of both genders. It has also been shown to greatly reduce the risk of cancer.

The rest of their short puppyhood (the adolescent phase lasts from eight months to up to three years) is spent learning to become fully engaged in the social dynamic of the pack. They'll learn their rank in the pack, where to walk, how to hunt, how to track. Dogs take great joy in being accepted as full members of the pack and helping the pack survive, but it's important to remember that in their natural habitat, not everybody makes it. Although African wild dogs can have as many as twenty members in a pack, for most canines—wolves, coyotes, jackals, hyenas, foxes, and feral dogs—packs are very small, with a maximum of eight to ten members. One of the reasons there is such an enormous overpopulation of *Canis familiaris* is because, living in civilization, dogs don't face the dangers and hardships that naturally select only the strong for survival.

PUPPIES AND ENERGY

Finding a dog with the right energy level for you is the most important first step you can take in creating a fulfilling lifetime with your pet. When you are evaluating an adult dog at a shelter, you may find it hard to separate a dog's true energy from the issues she carries with her from previous life experiences or placements, but with puppies, there are no issues to get in the way of your selection. Puppies are born with a certain energy level, and, overall, that energy will be with them for the rest of their lives.

Breeders often employ a process called "puppy temperament testing," a test administered by a professional at around seven weeks of age that attempts to predict what the grown-up dog will probably be like.[7] Based on the puppy's responses to several basic challenges, the test attempts to quantify responses in such areas as social attraction; following; restraint; forgiveness; acceptance of human dominance; willingness to please; touch, sound, and sight sensitivity; and energy levels. Breeders use the results of these tests to help categorize their dogs from cautious to aggressive, and to assess how likely they are to be suited to certain specific jobs, such as therapy dog, search and rescue dog, police dog, and so on. If you are getting a puppy from a breeder, you might want to ask her if she has the results of these tests for the dog that you are interested in. They may aid you in assessing whether the puppy's personality is right for your lifestyle.

However, even those breeders who use these tests religiously will tell you that their results don't always tell the whole story. When evaluating energy, other factors can make a big difference, such as the dog's bloodline, her birth order, or more important, her day-to-day interactions with other dogs. Since dogs speak in energy 24/7, a dog can tell you more about another dog than any human system of measurement. When I first took Daddy to meet the pit bull puppy that would carry his legacy of calm-submissive energy to the next generation, I allowed him to show me the energy levels of the puppies I was considering. Remember how Daddy growled at the puppy I noticed was displaying dominance toward my friends' children? Daddy knew right away that the puppy's behavior was not his cute "friendliness" or "spirit," but the kind of dominant energy that can cause problems within a pack. Take your cue from Daddy and don't let your emotions get in the way of evaluating a puppy's inborn energy.

YOUR PUPPY AT HOME

Most puppies are adopted by humans at around two to three months of age. Once we become their teachers, they enter a new phase—the phase of learning to live not only as a dog, but also as a dog in the human world. During this time, we must show them that humans are in charge in this new social structure they're entering. Nature didn't program them to know about cars, glass doors, or electric wires. Because they're going to live in our complicated world, it's very important that we become their pack leaders to guide them through it.

SURVIVING PUPPYHOOD

When I brought Junior home from my friend's house, he was just two months old—the optimum age to adopt a puppy—and he had already had his first round of vaccines. From seven weeks to twelve weeks is the best time for a dog to cement her socialization with humans, and it's the best time in her life to learn to bond with you as her pack leader. If you bring home a puppy from a breeder, by two months it's likely that she will already have had two sets of vaccines, though many veterinarians recommend four.

A newborn pup is antibody-free, meaning it has no natural immunity to any viruses or diseases. Of course, Mother Nature has provided puppies with a built-in protection for the first few months of their lives. This comes in the form of the colostrum, special milk the mother secretes shortly after she gives birth. The colostrum contains all the mother's own antibodies and provides a temporary shield to protect her offspring. Not all puppies get the same amount of colostrum; in true survivor-of-the-fittest form, the firstborn and the most assertive nursers will end up with more antibody protection than the last in the litter or the weakest nursers. But colostrum is only a temporary buffer. Every nine days, the pups' antibody levels drop by half until, at around four months of age, the level is too low to protect them anymore, and they are potential targets for any virus in their environment. This is why a vaccination regimen is usually started at around six weeks of age and continued until sixteen weeks (four months). However, there is a week or so period during which puppies no longer have much leftover immunity from their mothers and the new vaccines haven't taken effect. This time can be an open window through which even the best cared for puppies can get sick.

RECOMMENDATIONS FOR PUPPY VACCINATIONS

Before twelve weeks, the mother's immunity protects against parvo, so unless the mother is unprotected, parvo is not recommended until six weeks. A typical recommended vaccine schedule is as follows:

3 weeks	worming
6 weeks	worming for the common parasites passed through the mother's placenta and milk, fecal exam for coccidia, and combination DHPP (for distemper, infectious hepatitis, parainfluenza, and parvovirus)
9 weeks	worming, DHPP
12 weeks	possible worming, DHPP, possible rabies. Leptospirosis and Lyme if in endemic area (The last two will need to be boosted in three weeks if given.) Possible bord (bordetella) if puppy is going to be boarded or groomed frequently
16 weeks	Possible DHPP, final fecal exam, and rabies if not done previously[8]

The biggest worry during this time is the parvovirus. Parvo is an extremely contagious organism that finds a happy home in the intestinal lining of puppies. If caught early enough, parvo isn't always fatal, but the treatment involves quarantine and is extremely expensive. Parvo is spread through the feces of infected dogs, and some adult dogs can carry the virus without showing symptoms. It's very hardy and can't be killed with simple soap; you can disinfect parvo-contaminated areas with a solution of one part chlorine bleach to ten parts water. It's tricky to vaccinate a puppy for parvo because if there are any parvo antibodies left over from the mother's colostrum in the puppy's body, they will attack the vaccine as if it were the disease. This is why many vets recommend that puppies be kept away from public outdoor areas—the dog park, the playground, dog training classes, a doggy day care center—until after their vaccination series is completed at sixteen weeks. They should also be kept away from any dogs you don't know.

In my personal opinion, fear of parvo obsesses some people to the extent that they totally deprive their puppies of the outside world, which can be detrimental to both their physical and psychological health. Overly protective owners sometimes keep their dogs in an indoor environment until the adolescent stage, at which time the dog is becoming very powerful, doesn't need your guidance as much, and is more difficult to teach. What these well-meaning owners forget is that from birth to four months, puppies have a preinstalled program to "follow," making it an ideal time to start teaching rules, boundaries, and limitations. The grass in your own backyard—as long as it's not a highly traveled area for strange dogs or a shortcut to the dog park—or a back patio or driveway are great places to start to condition them to walking on a leash, which they can easily learn to do while keeping their heads up and without sniffing the ground. When puppies are under four months of age, they naturally don't want to venture too far from their home base. The leash can be your friend here, and this is the perfect time to introduce it. If you are still worried, spraying a solution of bleach on the sidewalks around your property can offer added protection. As far as socialization goes, an older dog that has had his or her vaccines is highly unlikely to be carrying parvovirus and is probably a safe playmate.

There is some debate over which vaccinations are necessary and how often vaccines should be given. Some veterinarians think that we are overvaccinating our dogs and causing as many problems as we are preventing. I believe that we must find a balance between Mother Nature and science. Vaccines can help protect your dog from many life-threatening illnesses, but the body also has its own natural defense systems. It is equally important that you keep your dog physically fit and psychologically healthy in order to give her the strength she needs to fight off potential diseases.

Because of my belief that a balanced, healthy lifestyle is better for a dog than an extra vaccine, I did not give Junior any parvo vaccine after his first round. From the age of two months, I took him everywhere with me, and I started him helping out in dog rehabilitations right away. I leash trained Junior from the start to keep his head up and away from the ground, and I obviously kept him in the company of only healthy dogs. In my opinion, a lot of vigorous exercise, plus exposure to the outside world and all the adventures and challenges it offers, was, for Junior, a kind of vaccination all its own. I'm happy to report that Junior is in outstanding health and has never had an illness in his six months. I'm not recommending this course for everybody, and I would never advise you to go against your vet's advice, but this is what worked for me.

Vaccines can play an important part in helping your dog live a long, healthy life, but you should feel confident that your dog is not receiving unnecessary shots. I recommend that you discuss your options with your veterinarian, do your own research, and discuss vaccinations with other dog professionals or owners whom you trust and respect. Make an informed decision about which vaccinations your dog receives and how often. See Chapter 7 for more information on vaccines.

HOUSEBREAKING

From two to four months, most pups pick up on the concept of housebreaking quite easily, since it is, in a way, part of their natural programming. When the puppies are born, they eat and they relieve themselves in the den, but the mother always cleans them. The mother stimulates their bodily functions, and her environment is always clean. There is never the scent of urine or feces where they sleep or where they live. It's not natural for a puppy to live in its own mess, so the DNA of the puppy is working for you.

Another built-in plus when it comes to housebreaking is the puppy's digestive system, which works very rapidly. Five to thirty minutes after a puppy eats, she'll want to defecate. From the time you get your puppy until about eight months, you should be feeding her three times a day. I recommend you keep to a very consistent feeding schedule, and that you take your puppy outside immediately after eating, and also right after naps or long play sessions. Every time she eats, you must be ready to take her outside, which becomes the pattern. Puppies are looking for direction and quickly pick up on routines and patterns. A routine makes a puppy feel safe and secure. You want to be sure to take the dog to an outside area where there's dirt, grass, sand, rocks—the natural things that stimulate the puppy's brain to look for a place to relieve herself. You also want that area to be one that is already familiar to her, so she feels relaxed there. If a dog is panicked, nervous, unsure, or insecure, she will shut down and not be able to eliminate. If you are feeling impatient or trying to rush a puppy, that, too, can stress her out. Share only calm-assertive energy, and your puppy will be able to tune in to her natural instincts and learn the lessons of housebreaking smoothly.

FEEDING

AGE	STAGE	FEEDING SCHEDULE
0–8 months	Puppy	3 times a day
8 months–3 years	Adolescence	2 times a day
3–approx. 8 years	Adult	Once a day
Approx. 8 years and up	Senior	2 times a day

THE WHYS, WHENS, AND WHERES OF WEE-WEE PADS

Many puppy owners—particularly puppy owners who live in the city—don't want to go through the chore of taking a puppy outdoors five or six times a day, so they decide to housebreak the dog using wee-wee pads. Though wee-wee pads are a wonderful invention and my dogs use them all the time when we travel, it's very important that puppies don't learn housebreaking inside a house. To dogs, a floor, walls, and a ceiling mean a den, or home base. It's not natural for them to eliminate in their own dens. Often when people start by conditioning puppies to use wee-wee pads alone, they are shocked when the dog won't eliminate outdoors. Learning to eliminate only inside the house also increases the likelihood of accidents and messes, because the natural inclination not to go inside the house has been removed.

The best way to incorporate wee-wee pads into your housebreaking routine is to set them out at times when you won't be able to supervise. Set out four pads at first, in order to zero in on exactly the part of the pad where the puppy will relieve herself. As the puppy begins to use them correctly, and begins to refine and mature her behavior, you can remove the pads until there is only one left, at exactly the spot where she will go every time. To attract the puppy to the pad, find a piece of grass or dirt with the scent of urine or feces from another dog on it. This may sound distasteful to you, but the presence of another dog's excrement will stimulate your puppy's brain to go and pee right over it. Eventually you won't need to do this, once the puppy gets conditioned to the pads.

In the area of my house or hotel room where I keep the wee-wee pads, I always use an air filter to make sure the scent doesn't travel, and I make sure to give the dogs a place to sleep that is far away from the pads, since, like humans, dogs like their bedroom and their bathroom to be distinct locations. As soon as I get up, I will roll up the used pads and mop up the floor beneath the pads so there is no more scent. This is a *must* for using wee-wee pads, newspapers, or anything you put on the floor for the puppy to relieve herself on: *always* replace the used pad immediately and clean up the floor underneath, because a dog doesn't want to pee on a place she herself has already peed. In addition to helping train your puppy to use that spot again, you will be keeping your own environment clean and sanitary.

Wee-wee pads are a great convenience and can be an asset to both you and your dog—but only if you make sure to use them in combination with a regular outdoor elimination schedule. Remember, when you break it down, wee-wee pads are for the humans, not the dogs!

LEARNING BY EXAMPLE

One of the best ways to teach a puppy about proper bathroom etiquette is to let an older dog lead by example. Although Daddy is Junior's role model in most things, being an older dog, Daddy doesn't need to go outside as much. Daddy defecates twice a day, in the morning and nighttime like clockwork, and he only goes out to pee about once every four hours. However, Junior also lives with our other small dogs—Coco the Chihuahua, Molly the dachshund, Sid the French bulldog, and Minnie, our new diminutive Chihuahua-terrier mix. The small dogs are on a more regular schedule, and Junior automatically imitated them. They are also already housebroken on the wee-wee pads, so Junior picked that up right away as well. Puppies are programmed to look to other dogs as role models, and in our family, there is never a shortage of dogs willing to share their knowledge with a new member of the pack!

Of course, accidents are a part of the housebreaking experience. Never "blame" a puppy for an accident; don't get angry at her for a bodily function she can't control, and please, don't buy in to the old wives' tale that you should push a puppy's nose into her excrement or hit her if she happens to go in the house. Instead, remain calm and assertive, and immediately take the puppy outside to where she is supposed to relieve herself (or to the pad). If you catch a puppy in the act, use a touch or a simple sound to snap her out of it, then immediately remove her to her spot outside and wait until she relaxes and finishes her business. Then thoroughly clean and disinfect the area of the accident, so there is no lingering odor. Don't get upset or make a big deal over an accident and never berate your puppy with a long speech, because the dog can learn that if she poops in a certain place, she gets your attention. She can also wrongly interpret your reaction as a cue to never eliminate in your presence. Stay consistent, and keep your energy neutral. Your dog's digestion is a normal part of her biology; you just want to teach her some control over the whens and wheres of it.

DOS AND DON'TS OF PUPPY HOUSEBREAKING

1. DO take the puppy outside first thing in the morning, immediately after each meal, after she awakens from a nap, and after long play sessions.

2. DO take the puppy to the same general area outdoors each time.

3. DO supervise your puppy closely! You are investing a lot of time in these first months to establish a lifetime of good behaviors. Keep your puppy with you as much as possible. If you can't be with her, put her in a safe, enclosed area or in her crate. If you think you might forget about your puppy's needs, set a timer for forty-five-minute intervals to remind yourself.

4. DO remain consistent! Daily consistency is the key to good habits. Feed and walk your puppy at around the same time every day. Remember, dogs don't understand the concept of weekends or holidays. If you want to sleep late on a Sunday, take your puppy out first, then go back to bed.

5. DON'T punish a puppy for an accident, or do anything to create a negative association with her bodily functions! Stay calm and assertive and quietly remove the puppy to the place where you want her to go.

6. DON'T potty train a puppy on wee-wee pads alone. It's not natural for a dog to relieve herself inside her "den." Make sure you alternate between outdoor and indoor bathroom habits.

Leash Training a Puppy

I believe it is never too early to begin conditioning a puppy to the leash, or to any obedience work you would like her to master as an adult dog. For pups or small dogs, I often use a lightweight 35-cent leash that I loop around the dog's head. Puppies are very easy to "steer" and direct, and they do best with less—a soft nylon collar or a thin leather collar. Never use a choke chain or a heavy training collar on a puppy; check to make sure whatever tool you buy is safe for young or small dogs. The collar should fit tightly enough so it won't slip off, but leave enough open room so that you can fit two fingers between the collar and the dog's neck. Remember, at this age, your puppy's desire is to follow you. Whenever using a tool with a dog—be it a puppy, an adolescent, or a senior-aged canine—never force the tool on the dog. Never, ever allow a dog to associate a training or conditioning tool with something negative! Instead, let the dog's natural curiosity lead it to the tool. If necessary, use positive reinforcement—food, a toy, or whatever particular item or action attracts your dog to something new. I am a big believer in positive reinforcement, but I always remind my clients that they shouldn't think of positive reinforcement as being just treats or toys. Remember, in their natural environment, the mothers and adult dogs never need to bribe the pups with food or toys to get them to behave! To me, positive reinforcement is making sure you provide a healthy stimulus that triggers a good, natural response. It can be praise, it can be petting, it can simply be your silent joy at what the dog has achieved. If you are happy with your puppy, you can tell her without words. Your energy, body language, and eye contact will telegraph to her loud and clear what you are feeling.

When you use the leash to correct a puppy or to snap her out of an unwanted behavior, please remember that puppies are small,

lightweight, and very sensitive. They are also preprogrammed to follow their pack leader's instructions. A very gentle but firm touch or
pop on your leash should be all you ever need to communicate to
your puppy. It's important to remember that if you remain consistent, firm, and loving during your puppy's most tender years, you are
investing in an insurance policy that will prevent you from having to
deal with the sort of extreme behavior problems I'm often called in
to help correct. By conditioning a puppy to the leash early, you are
also conditioning *yourself* to pass your calm-assertive energy through
the leash, greatly reducing the odds you'll ever need more forceful
methods in the future.

TEETHING

Between four and six months, most puppies will pass through a
teething phase. This process is uncomfortable, and the increased
chewing binges you'll see in the puppy's behavior at this stage are her
attempts to relieve this discomfort—usually, on your most expensive pair of shoes, since they are at her eye level and because they
carry your scent. It's very important to understand that teething is
not rebellion or a personal attack at you. It's not really play, either.
During this stage, all the puppy is focused on is "How can I relieve
this irritation that I have in my mouth?" A big no-no at this time is to
wear gloves and let the dog chew on them, or to play games where
you allow the dog to bite you anywhere on your body. It may seem
harmless now, but you will be conditioning your dog to see your
hands or your body as a source for relieving her frustration.

Teething behavior is not the same thing as obsessive chewing in
an adult dog and should not be corrected but instead redirected.
There are thousands of teething toys in pet stores just for this purpose. Place the shoe in front of you and then each time the puppy

touches the shoe, get her attention with a treat, and redirect her toward the teething toy. Then you claim *your* space around the shoe. This becomes a psychological challenge; the puppy is learning the sophisticated concept of "Just because it's there doesn't mean it's mine." They are also learning what is appropriate for them to chew on. Pulling the shoe away from the puppy isn't a wise thing to do. It doesn't send a clear message to the dog; it inadvertently involves you in a dominance game, which you might actually win the first few times if the puppy is small enough, but it is one you won't keep winning forever. Once the puppy wins, or figures out how to hold on to the shoe by running away with it, you will find yourself in a situation where you've taught your own dog how to use her strength and speed as weapons to defeat you.

Teething discomfort can also be minimized through exercise. I've used swimming in the past, and not necessarily in a large pool. A bathtub or wading pool for a small to medium-size dog will get her legs moving in the water, give her something healthy to focus on, and distract her from what's going on inside her mouth. I managed to distract Minnie, my tiny Chihuahua-terrier mix, by letting her move her legs in a large bucket! After the exercise, give the dog an object of your choice to chew on, and be relieved that the teething stage for puppies goes by quickly—a month or two at the most.

When puppies approach adolescence—from six to ten months of age—they will go through a second chewing phase. Their permanent teeth are coming in now and the urge to chew is powerful. Remember to make the appropriate toys available to your "teenager" at this stage, and provide as much healthy exercise as possible. Often, dogs that don't teethe at this stage may have dental problems later in life, so make sure you are seeing your vet regularly and reporting on your pup's teething behavior.

Kids and Puppies

I believe all children should be exposed to the life cycle of animals. As parents, it gives us opportunity to teach them to respect and honor Mother Nature, and help them understand the rhythm of life in a deeper, more profound way. However, children—especially small children—need to be supervised around puppies. It's important to condition young puppies (less than seven weeks of age) to human touch, but if they are handled too frequently or in the wrong way, the pups can actually develop a fear of humans. If you have puppies in your home younger than two months old, make sure you never allow children to touch, lift, or play with them without adult supervision.

Once you bring a new puppy home—assuming the dog is older than seven weeks—you should take the time to teach your children the correct way of meeting a dog. Remember, puppies around eight to ten weeks of age can be very shy and skittish about new experiences, so explain to your children about no-touch, no-talk, no–eye contact until the puppy has signaled that she is comfortable with the new human in her presence. Just as you challenge your puppy by playing "waiting" and "patience" games, this is a way to help foster good patience in your children as they learn to wait and watch for the puppy to show that she accepts them. Explain to your children about the public, social, and intimate zones of space that exist among all animals, including humans. This is also a good way to help teach your children about their rights when an adult or another child invades their own space in a threatening manner. Then, take the time to watch your child play with the puppy, standing back until you're needed, but supervising any behavior that is veering into the danger zone.

When children are too young to understand the concepts of personal space or no-touch, no-talk, no–eye contact, they are still able to learn these skills from simple correction and redirection. If a baby is crawling toward a dog that is giving off the wrong kind of energy, you have to simply block and redirect. I used to physically block my boys from encroaching on a dog's territory when the dog had not invited them, often by just putting my arm in front of them. If the boys' energy was too energetic, aggressive, or otherwise unstable for a dog, I would do the same thing. I explained to my boys from the time they were toddlers that dogs are not toys, and that they are never allowed to pull a dog's tail or ears, or tease a dog. Likewise, I would block a puppy from becoming too playful with my boys if I felt the puppy was not giving them the proper respect or honoring my sons' personal space.

Remember, you are dealing with two species of animals, both young, and both learning for the first time how to approach the other one. By the time your child is walking, however, you can begin the ritual of the pack walk with dog and child together. Teaching a child to properly walk a dog or puppy is a wonderful way to build the child's self-esteem, and to create the kind of human-dog bond that will enrich your child throughout her life.

My wife, Ilusion, and I get immense satisfaction when we have the chance to speak at schools and other children's groups about animal safety issues. I always explain to the children what a dog's body language can mean, with a special emphasis on the myth of the wagging tail. Children's books the world over stress that a wagging tail always means a happy dog, and that is true most of the time—but if you watch my show regularly, you'll see dogs wagging their tails right before an attack. Any one gesture in a dog's repertoire of body language can mean several things, just like one word in the English language can have several meanings depending on its context in a sentence. In a dog's case, the context includes both the situation the dog is facing, and more important, the energy the dog is projecting.

It takes practice for a human of any age to be able to read a dog's energy accurately, so the first, most important thing to teach children about dogs or puppies is that they should never, ever approach a dog they don't know without adult approval. Ilusion and I have observed time and again that once children understand the concept of how to show respect to animals, they are more than willing to comply.

Play Behavior

Dogs are playful animals by nature, but for puppies, play is their career. In nature, all young animals use play as a way to practice the survival skills needed to survive as adult animals. It's innate for puppies to play games mimicking the things their wild ancestors would have to do to survive in the wild—games involving hunting, domination, and submission. Most purebred dogs will start exhibiting signs of their breed in their play activities—wanting to chase, to track, to retrieve, and to dig. As your puppy's pack leader, it's up to you to observe your puppy's playful activities early and help channel them in productive ways.

Puppies are natural explorers, so giving them safe, recreational areas to explore is a wonderful way to challenge them and build their confidence. I have created many obstacle courses at the Dog Psychology Center and have built softer, safer miniversions for the pups to play in. A small puppy can also begin to learn to fetch for coordination, and hide-and-seek games with food and scents are wonderful methods that can sharpen the senses. It's important to have soft and chewy toys available for teething.

One way that I like to challenge young pups involves asking them to wait patiently for food. I hold the food dish high over their heads until they sit, wait patiently, and make eye contact with me. Teaching patience is an important skill that requires psychological concentra-

COMMON PUPPY MISBEHAVIORS AND CAUSES

BEHAVIOR	POSSIBLE CAUSES	SOLUTIONS
Chewing and Mouthing ("Inhibited biting")	Exploring the environment, relieving frustrating, easing the pain of teething, testing dominance	Provide proper chew toys, monitor teething, but don't allow overly intense biting as dominance or to relieve anxiety—it can become a habit. Instead, provide distractions in structured exercise and games.
Nipping	Communicating that something is unpleasant; an extension of mouthing that has not been discouraged early on	Nipping should never be allowed. Remember, in nature, the older dogs would step in and correct a pup the first time she steps out of line. A firm touch should be enough to manage a young pup's nipping; don't let her learn that this is a way to control the humans and dogs around him.
Marking	Can indicate sexual maturity (may begin to mark around five to six months of age); in nature, it is to prevent intrusion from romantic rivals; can also signify dominance	Spay or neuter your dog by six months of age, and consistently reinforce rules, boundaries, and limitations as they apply to house-training.

BEHAVIOR	POSSIBLE CAUSES	SOLUTIONS
Submissive or Excited Urination	Can be a sign of complete submission or respect, a skittish temperament, or can be a sign that the pup has not learned to completely control her bladder muscles	Check with your vet to make sure there is nothing physically wrong. Stay calm and assertive when enforcing house-training rules, and employ the no-touch, no-talk, no-eye-contact rule with a pup that seems to react nervously on first meetings.
Digging	An inborn behavior used to expend energy or frustration, or to find a cool place in warm weather; for some breeds (like terriers), an inbred activity created for finding game	Never punish a dog for digging. Instead, provide a safe, "allowed" place for digging. If your dog is frustrated, provide additional structured outlets and exercise.
Crying or Barking	Used by puppies to call their mothers and siblings if they are lost; when living with humans, they sometimes cry during times of separation, hunger, or if they need to relieve themselves	Make sure to tire your puppy out before bed, and make sure she's on a regular feeding and bathroom schedule.

tion—something that is essential for a healthy dog to develop. Sometimes, I make an obstacle course out of the same food game by moving the food dish behind a chair or box or table. I ask the dog to wait, and then she has to go find the dish where I've hidden it.

You can think of unlimited challenges for your new puppy, and her rapidly developing brain will gratefully devour all of them. The important thing in initiating any games with a pup, however, is to make sure you, the pack leader, are the one to start the game, set the rules, and stop the game. When clients of mine complain about a dog that is "obsessed" with a tennis ball or a certain chew toy, it almost always turns out that these clients skipped the important process of setting rules, boundaries, and time limits on the game when it first began.

I'm often asked how owners can differentiate between healthy puppy play and potential budding behavior problems. I've found that inexperienced dog owners sometimes worry too much that a typical puppy trait—such as hesitancy at entering a new environment—means their dog will end up fearful and skittish, when in reality, it's perfectly normal for a puppy under three months of age to go through a period where they want to go slowly and cautiously into every new experience. Other owners go too far in the opposite direction, by explaining away bad behavior, such as the fact that their puppy jumps on and bites guests to the home, as "just a basic phase." The best answer I can give here is that normal puppy play has a light, clumsy, innocent quality about it. The puppy is testing her limits and learning what skills she is going to need as an adult dog. Therefore, you may see a normal, healthy puppy exhibit dominance, aggression, fear, anxiety, or insecurity at any given time.

What you as an owner need to be watching out for is the frequency of the behavior and, more important, the intensity of it. Puppies' behavior that involves playing with you, touching you with their mouth, or exploring you with their mouth is perfectly normal.

But as the pups get caught up in the excitement of that play, if they don't get feedback from us that "that's enough!" they can intensify the behavior until it becomes an obsession. Remember our role models, the natural dog pack. An older dog might let a puppy mouth or chew on its paw or ear, but the second the pup gets too rough, the adult will whirl around, growl, or even pin the puppy with its teeth. The pup will instantly get the message. Because we don't communicate with dogs in their innate language, we tend to say "Ow! Ow! Bad dog!" and move back if a puppy chews too aggressively. We forget that when we move back, we trigger the prey drive in our puppy's brain and this makes them move forward and want to hold on to us with more intensity.

Likewise, it's a puppy's nature to want to explore, examine, and understand the environment. Let's say your puppy makes a tear in your carpet while you are not watching her. This may be due to a natural curiosity about the environment—she smelled something interesting under the carpet and wanted to find out what it was. But if you note your puppy digging away at the carpet with such a single-mindedness and ferocity that you can't distract her away with a treat or something else that she usually enjoys, then you can be sure she is learning that digging at the carpet is a way to release frustration. When a dog begins to intensely focus on something as a way to release frustration or anxiety, you have the beginnings of a behavior issue that could escalate into an obsession or a phobia. The key here is to immediately redirect the dog, and make sure you are providing her with healthy things upon which to work out her energy—more exercise in the form of structured walks, more time on the treadmill, more fetch games, or other challenging activities.

The longer you live with your puppy and the more time you spend with her, the more you will be aware and alert to her individual changes of mood, energy, and focus. If you can monitor your pup's intensity in all her activities and, as if you were a grown-up dog in her pack, put the brakes on her before any of her playfulness crosses the line into obsession, you will be raising a dog that is still joyful but also has the proper respect for limits and boundaries.

HUMAN MISTAKES

Although adopting a puppy is the best chance you have for raising an issue-free dog, it doesn't come with an unconditional guarantee. It's just as easy to "ruin" a puppy, as it is an adult dog you picked up from the shelter, if you don't abide by the basic rules of dog psychology. The most common mistakes people make with puppies are, to me, the same kinds of mistakes humans make when raising their own children—they are either overprotective, too lax with discipline, or both. Many times these mistakes begin when the puppy is very small, when the human insists on carrying the puppy everywhere, as if she were a primate. Carrying a puppy in your arms like a baby or in a pouch like a kangaroo's joey may look cute and make you feel like a warm and protective parent, but it is totally unnatural for the dog. A pup's mother only carries her around to move her from one place to another; from inside the den to outside the den, for instance. As soon as the puppies can get around on their own, she lets them figure the world out for themselves. This is a vital part of a puppy's learning experience in life. Without being able to walk from place to place, puppies don't have a sense of geography or environment. They find it harder to make associations between things. And most important, they can't develop the vital self-confidence that comes from exploration and trial and error. This also goes from always bringing food to the puppy, not conditioning the puppy to come to the food, to carrying a puppy up the stairs instead of allowing her to learn how to climb. In nature, unless the puppy learns life's lessons on her own, she is no good to the pack. In our world, such a puppy will feel useless. For a puppy to get everything in life without earning it isn't natural, and it is a setup for a grown-up dog with behavioral issues later on.

Junior's Progress Report

As for Junior, he is now six months old and has just been neutered, so he will never have the unpleasant experience of sexual frustration. Junior is growing every day, but even though he is energetic and playful like any normal puppy, he already shows a disposition that is respectful, easygoing, and very much like Daddy's. Junior has an ideal life, because he is being conditioned and nurtured and fulfilled by his adoptive "father"—a dog that has fourteen years of experience and wisdom. He's also being nurtured and conditioned by a human who has raised a lot of dogs and has the confidence to earn his trust, respect, and love. Junior gets hours of exercise with the pack, and my sons and I play with him and challenge him regularly at home. Since Junior was three months old, I have been bringing him out on *Dog Whisperer* cases. His first case was in Santa Barbara, around very excited dogs. Although he obviously doesn't have the life experience to help in the way that Daddy can, he can assess the situation and copy the way Daddy responds to it. Daddy is essentially teaching him, "We don't react to overexcited dogs like these; we ignore." Junior is an amazingly fast learner. And in a way, I think he may surpass Daddy's ability to rehabilitate dogs someday, not only because he has access to Daddy's lifetime of wisdom, but also because, over time, I have become a better handler than I was fourteen years ago when Daddy first came into my life. Much of that is thanks to Daddy himself. Daddy has been the greatest guru I've ever had.

Is it really possible to "raise the perfect puppy"? I believe Mother Nature is perfect. Balance is perfect. And I maintain that we can truly create the perfect relationships with our dogs when we raise them with exercise, discipline, and affection; give them rules, boundaries, and limitations; and offer them both consistency and new challenges every day. Perfection to me is peace and joy; it's connection, and understanding. It is knowing how to fulfill another being, and becoming happier yourself because you have succeeded in that challenge. That's perfection to me, and that's my goal for the future life my family and I will share with Junior.

RULES OF THE HOUSE

Providing Rules, Boundaries,
and Limitations

Cesar with the Valesquez family

From the moment your new dog arrives home, it's your responsibility to start making clear the rules of the house. Remember, in a dog pack, every dog is responsible for upholding and reinforcing the pack's rules, so your first job is to hold another family meeting and determine what the rules of the house will be. Everyone, from small children to elderly grandparents, must be clear and consistent on what those rules are going to be. Many of my clients write down their rules (and hints on enforcing them) and leave them in prominent places around the house. For instance, "Sparky is not allowed on the velvet couch. Command: Off!" Or "Sparky must be sitting quietly before you feed him." Because your home is your castle, you have the right to make any rules that make sense for your family's lifestyle. However, I suggest all family dogs should respect a few general limits. These are all rules that are compatible with the limits a dominant dog or pack leader would set for the dogs that rank below him in the pack:

CESAR'S RECOMMENDED HOUSE RULES

No nipping or biting (unless invited in play)
No leading or pulling humans on the walk
No jumping on guests or family members
No herding guests or family members
No playing alarm clock (you—not your dog—decide when to wake up)
No stealing human food off counters or tables
No whining or begging for food during human dinnertime
No stealing or destroying things that belong to humans
No dominating a human's bed

In my opinion another "must" for a dog's psychological well-being is for his human pack to make sure he works for food and water every day of his life. In nature, dogs don't go to the grocery store and pick up kibble. They don't go out to restaurants when they get hungry. From the time they are old enough to hunt with the pack, they learn that their purpose in life is to work for food and water. They migrate together, sometimes walking for many miles until they find the nourishment they seek. After they eat, they celebrate together, and then they rest. This is the program that nature has ingrained in them. It is the kind of routine that makes them feel good about themselves, reassuring them that they have something important to do and to contribute to the survival of the pack. When we roll out of bed and give our dogs food before they have had a chance to work for it, we are robbing them of a very important ingredient to their self-esteem. This is why I recommend that you take your dog for a minimum thirty-minute walk every morning, before feeding time.

Most important, all discipline must start with consistency! If rules aren't put into effect with consistency on the part of *all* human pack leaders, it's not reasonable to expect the dogs to follow them consistently, either. The first step in setting rules, boundaries, and limitations for your dog is to create a structured life for him in which all those rules make sense.

CREATING THE FAMILY SCHEDULE

When you've got everyone sitting around the kitchen table to talk about your dog's routine, get out a pencil and paper (or boot up the Excel program on the family computer or laptop!). Next, go over everybody's schedule, and see whose lifestyle meshes best with each dog-related task. Who gets up earliest in the morning? Who has the most time for the longest walks of the day? (Remember, your dog must have at least two walks of a minimum thirty-minute duration each day, no matter how big your backyard is, or whether or not your kids play Frisbee with your dog every day!) Who is the last to go to bed? If anyone in the family balks at taking responsibility, remind him or her that since the entire family decided together to bring the dog home, all family members must participate as best they can in fulfilling the dog and making sure he fits smoothly into the family pack.

Here's an example of an imaginary family who have worked out a successful schedule for caring for their adult dog: a five-year-old high-energy terrier named Sparky. Let's say that fifteen-year-old Caitlin gets up at 5:15 A.M. every morning but must be at track practice at the high school by 6:00. No one else in the household gets up until 6:30 A.M. Caitlin agrees to wake up fifteen minutes earlier, to walk Sparky for about ten minutes, just to the end of the block and back so he can relieve himself. These early morning visits allow the busy teenager some quiet bonding time with Sparky, reminding him that even though she's not around much, she's still one of his pack leaders. Before she rushes out the door, Caitlin provides Sparky with water and makes sure he's resting calmly on his dog bed.

The next person to wake is Eddie, "Dad," at 6:30. He's in a rush to get breakfast for Tom and John, the ten-year-old twin boys, and to get them and him out the door by 7:30. Because Sparky has already relieved himself and had water, their only responsibility at this time is to make sure Sparky stays calmly and submissively in the background—despite all the chaos—and to reward him with affection when he complies. By 8:00 A.M., Betty, "Mom," comes downstairs. She works the nightshift, from 7:30 P.M. to 11:30 P.M. every weeknight. Betty makes herself a quick cup of coffee and takes Sparky for a brisk forty-five-minute pack walk. When they return, she feeds him, making sure he is in a calm-submissive state before giving food. Betty spends the rest of the morning running errands and takes a computer class in the early afternoon, so she makes sure Sparky is resting comfortably before she leaves.

By 2:30 in the afternoon, Mom arrives home in time to meet

Tom and John as they get off their school bus. Now it's the twins' turn. They get on their bikes with Sparky running alongside of them. Their destination is the local dog park (about twenty minutes away), where they supervise him as he socializes with his friends for another half hour. Then it's another twenty-minute ride home, water for Sparky, and time for the boys to retire to do their homework.

Caitlin has after-school activities, so she and Eddie arrive home around the same time, near 6:00 P.M. Caitlin goes upstairs to start her homework, while Dad unwinds by playing Frisbee with Sparky in the backyard for ten minutes or so. The family sits down to dinner together. Sparky is tired from the afternoon activities, so after water and a couple healthy treats, he curls up on his bed while the family eats. Then Mom's got to rush off to work. Caitlin goes to sleep early, while Dad and the twins watch television downstairs until it's time for them to go to bed at 9:30 P.M. Sparky is calm and submissive, so the twins let him cuddle with them on the couch. At 10:00 P.M. Dad takes Sparky on another ten- to fifteen-minute walk to the end of the block, so the dog can relieve himself before Dad goes upstairs to read in bed. When Mom comes home at 11:30, since she's the last person downstairs, she takes Sparky outside one last time if he needs it, and she makes sure he has water and is settled into his bed before she retires, too.

A chart of this imaginary family's weekly routine follows on the next page.

This is an imaginary example, of course, but I use it to illustrate how even the busiest of families can work together to make sure a dog lives a happy, fulfilled life. In this scenario, Sparky gets plenty of exercise, is in a resting state when alone, and has a chance to bond with every member of his pack on a regular basis. He has exercise, discipline, and affection, all in the correct proportions.

FAMILY RESPONSIBILITIES FOR SPARKY

MONDAY THROUGH FRIDAY SCHEDULE

Time	5:00 A.M.	8:30 A.M.	9:30 A.M.	2:30 P.M.	6:00 P.M.	8:00 P.M.	10:00 P.M.	11:30 P.M.
Caitlin	10-min. walk; pee. Water.							
Twins				40-min. round-trip bike ride; 20 min. at dog park (or other similar exercise and activities). Provide water.		Give affection and cuddle during TV time only if dog is calm and submissive.		
Mom		45-min. walk.	Mealtime ritual and water. Make sure dog is resting before leaving house.					Take out to relieve if necessary, water, put to bed.
Dad					Play Frisbee in yard. Water.		15-to-20-min. walk; water; leave resting before retiring.	

WEEKENDS, HOLIDAYS, AND SPECIAL OCCASIONS

In the dog world, there are no such things as weekends or holidays. Dogs don't understand the concept of "taking the day off"; they work for food and water and expect to follow rules, boundaries, and limitations every day of their lives. Therefore, just because it's the weekend doesn't mean your family members can shirk their dog-related responsibilities. However, a dog is one of nature's most adaptable animals. Though he thrives on consistency, he doesn't have to do—or even want to do!—the exact same thing at the same time, every single day of his life. Dogs love new adventures and challenges! The basic structure of their lives should stay the same, but every day shouldn't be a cookie-cutter replica of the day before.

In the case of our imaginary family, perhaps on some weekdays, the twins split up responsibility for Sparky in the afternoons, when one of them has Little League practice or wants to go over to a friend's house. This allows them to think of different, creative ways to exercise Sparky and condition him to enjoy new activities. Sparky also doesn't have to get up at 5:00 A.M. every morning. He can come to understand that on the mornings that Caitlin doesn't come down by 5:00 he has to wait quietly until, say, 7:30 A.M. Perhaps on Saturdays, Caitlin comes downstairs at 7:30 so she can go for an hour-long jog by herself. She can take Sparky with her on these mornings, further cementing the bond between two family members who don't get the chance to spend a lot of time together. On these mornings, perhaps it's the twins who want the privilege of feeding Sparky before they head out for their weekend activities. On Sunday mornings at 8:00, the whole family goes to church together, and of course they can't bring Sparky. So Dad volunteers to get up a half hour early and take Sparky for a thirty-minute walk before everybody leaves. These kinds of variations make the dog's life more interesting, and they also give everyone in the family a chance to experience all the different dimensions of being a pack leader in Sparky's life. The key is to keep the basics of the routine similar, making sure Sparky gets a minimum amount of primal exercise and works for food and water around the same time every day.

Weekends are also a great time to add breed-specific challenges to your dog's routine.[1] Perhaps on Sunday afternoons after church, Mom and the boys take Sparky to an agility class. Or after taking Sparky on a long walk, the whole family brings him along in the car to visit Grandma, who lives in the next town. Grandma has an older dog that Sparky loves to play with, but since the older dog is lower energy than the terrier, the family makes sure Sparky gets an extralong walk or run before they bring the two dogs together. The more challenges and fresh adventures you add to your dog's life, the more fulfilled and adaptable he will become. But the key is an overall consistency in which the basic rules of the house stay the same.

UNITING THE PACK

When it comes to family life, I believe dogs should be uniters, not dividers. Too many times, I'm called in to help a family where a dog's uncontrollable behavior seems to have everybody at one another's throats. This saddens me, because I believe dogs are given to us to help us reconnect with our animal nature, our intuition, and our pack instincts. They should be a tool to help a family communicate and to teach every member to work together, not an obstacle to get over. When dogs divide a family, it not only creates a dysfunctional family, it creates a dysfunctional dog, too.

A HOUSE DIVIDED

Shelley Gottlieb is an interior decorator sharing a large, elegant house in the San Fernando Valley with her sister and brother-in-law, her two nephews, her mother, three dogs, and one cat. They're doing what close-knit families are supposed to do—supporting one another during transitional times. Both Shelley and her sister and brother-in-law, Deborah and Mike Jacobson, are saving money, and the house is big enough for all of them. For six human beings living on top of one another, everybody gets along pretty well—except when it comes to one resident, Shelley's ten-year-old female Chihuahua, Peanut. It's not enough that the anxious, unfriendly dog barks ceaselessly whenever the doorbell rings, and snarls and snaps at any visitor who happens to cross the threshold, Peanut also turns her bad temper on everyone sharing the house with her. Shelley received her little dog as a gift from her family ten years ago. By the time I met the extended Gottlieb-Jacobson clan, however, this same little dog was tearing everybody apart.

Shelley's brother-in-law, Mike, is the ultimate target of Peanut's territorial dominance. When Mike walks into any room, Peanut will start barking and growling and won't stop until Mike leaves the room. It has become nearly impossible for Mike and Shelley to be in the same room together, and totally impossible for them to sit close to each other, say, on the same sofa. Needless to say, this has caused a lot of stress among everyone. And there's another problem. Mike's calm-submissive yellow Lab, Scout, follows him everywhere. When Peanut starts barking at Mike, Scout stands in the middle and starts barking at Peanut. The noise level in the house is deafening, and stress levels are at the breaking point.

"I worry about her stress levels," Shelley says of Peanut, choking back tears. "She's older now and I don't think this can be good for her." I agreed. An animal that is not being fulfilled and that is always on constant alert is not a happy one. And stress hormones are just as bad for dogs as they are for humans.

When I met the Gottlieb-Jacobson clan, I immediately felt the energy of a chaotic household. Though all the residents of the house loved one another, they were basically coming and going and doing their own thing, with no real cohesive family rules. We often forget that the energy of the humans in any household will be transferred to the animals that share it with us, and they will learn to adapt accordingly. Peanut seemed especially sensitive to this chaotic energy. She picked up on everybody's stress and tension and was mirroring it right back to them all in her dominant territorial temper tantrums.

The problem, however, originated with Shelley. Shelley was looking at Peanut as *her* dog, and hers alone. Shelley also projected a very soft, tentative energy toward Peanut, as if she didn't want to upset her. This created two major problems. First, Shelley was not behaving as part of the pack. No matter how independent the members of a household, when we bring a dog into a group living situation, that dog has to belong to everyone in the household, and everyone has to play the part of pack leader. Dogs have no problem understanding this concept if this is what we communicate to them. "The dog doesn't know she was a gift," I told Shelley. "The dog just knows she came into an environment. And everybody in the environment has different energies and is practicing different activities. She's thinking, 'I'm confused! I'm supposed to live with a balanced pack!' " In Peanut's case, she had grown up believing that she and Shelley were a separate pack from everyone else in the house. She felt it was her duty to be protective and dominant over Shelley, and that everyone else in the house was a threat or a rival. No wonder Peanut was not winning any popularity contests at home! Shelley had created in Peanut an animal that divided the household, because Peanut believed that was her job.

When I sat down to talk with Shelley and Mike—Peanut's number one target—he didn't hesitate to tell me how he felt about the dog. "I hate this dog right now," he said. Of course, dogs give us back what we give them, and Mike was exacerbating the situation by teasing Peanut whenever she tried to nip at him, escalating her level of frustration and stress. I told Mike that when he walked into the room with Scout and Scout tried to get between him and Peanut, only one of the three—Peanut, Mike, and Scout—was doing the right thing. Of course, that one was Scout. Scout was the mediator, a role often played by dogs in the middle of a pack hierarchy. Just like a middle child in the family, Scout was wondering why everyone else couldn't just get along. While Mike and Peanut were acting as if they were part of separate packs, Scout was trying to get everyone to work together. Scout had a lot more wisdom than any of the humans in the house, and I was there to give him a helping hand.

CREATING THE FAMILY PACK

Scenarios like the one playing itself out in the Gottlieb-Jacobson home are incredibly common in dog-owning families where one member "claims" the dog as his or her own. I often find myself trying to unite several different "packs" living under one roof. If we want our dogs to behave in a calm, balanced manner, we can't draw them into situations where they have to align with one faction of a family against another faction. This makes the other members of the family into rivals or targets and causes the dog to be on constant alert in his own home—the place he should always be able to relax and remain calm-submissive. Even if it makes us feel good as humans to have a dog that "loves us best," it's not good for the dog, or the general state of affairs in the pack.

HOW TO CREATE A PACK
IN A DIVIDED FAMILY

Enforce consistent rules for every member of the family.

Make sure everyone plays a role in the dog's care and fulfillment.

Give everyone a chance to "migrate" with the dog at least
once a week.

Switch off dog-care responsibilities from time to time.

Don't allow the dog to "disrespect" any family member.

Teach every family member how to achieve calm-assertive
energy.

A dog is always going to give you back what you give him. If you
give chaos, you will get chaos back, many times over. In Peanut's
case, I taught both Mike and Shelley how to work together to project
the same calm-assertive energy toward Peanut. Shelley had to become more assertive, and Mike had to learn how to become calmer.
It was time for them all to be more honest about their feelings and
energies. Mike felt angry and resentful; Shelley felt frustrated and de-
feated. Each of those states of mind is, to a dog, an unbalanced energy he needs to dominate or attack. Shelley needed to start seeing
herself as a source of harmonious rather than chaotic energy, and
Mike had to stop seeing himself as the target.

Next, I counseled all the family members on how to correct
Peanut when her neurotic behavior began to escalate. Even though
Peanut is ten years old, she is like all dogs—always willing and ready
to return to a balanced state. Shelley and Mike turned out to be excellent students. When the *Dog Whisperer* crew and I went out for our

lunch break, they continued to work with Peanut and saw for themselves that they could control Peanut on their own, without the Dog Whisperer around! Two months after my visit, the Gottlieb-Jacobson clan reported a changed dog, and a much more peaceful household.

ENFORCING THE RULES

In my previous books, *Cesar's Way* and *Be the Pack Leader*, I write in depth about how to communicate your boundaries to a dog and how to deal with any canine behavioral issues that might arise. These are the basic skills everyone in the family needs to master in order to manage a dog's behavior:

1. Have a picture in your mind of the behavior you desire.
2. Clearly and consistently communicate that desired behavior. In this communication, energy, intention, and body language are more important (and more easily comprehended by your dog) than verbal commands.
3. Ignore very mild misbehaviors using the no-touch, no-talk, no-eye-contact rule (they usually correct themselves when they aren't reinforced).
4. Immediately and consistently give corrections to more obvious misbehaviors.
5. Always apply corrections with calm-assertive energy—never take your dog's misbehavior personally!
6. Always give a dog an alternative acceptable behavior every time you correct an unwanted one.
7. Reward good behaviors—with affection, treats, praise—or simply your silent joy and approval, which your dog immediately senses and understands.

Jumping Up

An example of a behavior that I suggest you always forbid is letting your dog get into the habit of jumping on you, your kids, or your guests. In the dog world, jumping on a new arrival to the pack or a returning pack leader would be considered to be the epitome of rudeness and disrespect, yet my clients always insist their dogs are just "happy to see them!" when they practically knock their owners over as they step across the threshold every night. If your dog always jumps on the next person to pass through your front door, he is telling you that he is overexcited—perhaps he has too much pent-up energy and isn't getting enough exercise. Too often, humans inadvertently add to this hyperactive state of mind by giving the dog affection when he jumps on them, or by shouting, "Hey, buddy, we're home!" as they open the door. When a dog jumps on you and your guests, he is also telling you that he doesn't have enough rules, boundaries, and limitations to create true peace and balance in his life. He may also be making sure that every new arrival to your home understands that he is the one in charge.

Here are some suggestions for putting the brakes on this particular unwanted behavior:

• **Make sure your dog is receiving adequate exercise.** Jumping can be a sign of hyperactivity, which is caused by pent-up energy. Exercise provides a positive outlet for this energy.

• **Practice no-touch, no-talk, no–eye contact.** Don't shower your dog with affection when you walk through the door. Jumping is often simply an attention-seeking behavior; by providing attention, you are reinforcing the behavior. Ignoring the dog until he calms down is often an effective strategy.

• **Correct bad behavior.** If jumping is excessive, simply ignoring the behavior may not be enough. Remember, corrections should be immediate—don't withhold tomorrow's trip to the dog park, or tell the dog he isn't getting a treat later that day. Never hit or otherwise harm your dog—instead use sound, energy, and eye contact, or a firm, physical "touch" correction.

MEALTIME MANNERS

Mealtime is a ritual with great significance in the dog world, and when dogs live with us, we can use this time as a wonderful opportunity to connect with our pets as well as to help to shape their good behavior. In a dog pack, animals of lower rank always respect the food that belongs to those above them, and nobody ever bothers a pack leader while he is eating! By creating firm rules, boundaries, and limitations around the feeding ritual, you are not only providing your dog with nutrition, you are also helping him lead a more balanced and happy life.

MOST COMMON MEALTIME MISTAKES

- **Not letting a dog work for food.** In nature, all animals work for food and water. For canines this means migrating in search of a meal. You can re-create this experience for your dog by taking a long walk. By properly challenging your dog before mealtime, you are allowing your dog to stay in tune with Mother Nature.
- **Associating food with excitement.** Many humans talk and gesture in an excited way when providing food for

their dog. They create and encourage the dog's excited state, which can lead to problems or exacerbate existing ones. You need to be calm, and you should ask your dog to maintain *calm* energy before feeding time.

- **Rewarding negative behaviors.** Excitement is just one of the states that should not be rewarded with food. Dogs will often become anxious, territorial, or aggressive at the prospect of being fed. If you feed your dog when he displays negative behaviors, you are reinforcing the behavior, and it will almost certainly reoccur.

- **Not establishing a routine.** While you fill the bowl, ask your dog to sit. If he sits quietly and projects calm-submissive energy with no negative behaviors, place the bowl of food in front of him. Some of my clients think this routine sounds too rigid, but from your dog's perspective, it is instinctual. Focusing the mind and body brings the dog back into a more natural, balanced state.

SOCIAL GRACES

Often, the dogs I bring to my Dog Psychology Center for heavy-duty rehab are dogs completely lacking in the social graces; that is, they haven't been taught the basic rules and etiquette that allow them to get along with and enjoy the company of other dogs (and sometimes, humans). "My dog just doesn't 'like' other dogs," a typical client will tell me. "But other than that, he's perfect." I have to break it to them that a dog that doesn't "like" other dogs is about as far from perfect as a dog can get. Nature designed dogs to be social animals. Being curious about one another; sniffing one another to get a sense of the other dog's energy, lifestyle, and history; and playing with one another is simply what healthy, balanced dogs are supposed to do.

Often, owners inadvertently reinforce antisocial behavior in their dogs by comforting them if they growl at or cower from other dogs, scooping them up and taking them away from situations with other dogs, or avoiding contact with other dogs altogether. An antisocial dog is always an unhappy dog, a dog on edge, a dog that doesn't get to experience the joy of being a dog by being able to share dog activities with others of his kind. If you are fortunate enough to be raising a puppy, you have the opportunity to begin socializing him with balanced, friendly dogs, a variety of humans, and even other animals from an early age. But some dogs that have been adopted from a shelter or rescue organization come with antisocial tendencies already built in. Returning these dogs to a normal social state can take patience on your part, but it is rarely impossible. Here are some of the activities I suggest:

1. Make sure your dog gets plenty of primal exercise before you introduce him to any other dogs. If necessary, add a backpack on the walk, or add biking and Rollerblading with your dog to his routine to help him expend any pent-up frustrated energy.

2. Seek out dogs with the same or slightly lower energy than your own dog as companions. Make sure any dog you invite to meet your dog has calm-submissive, balanced energy.

3. Before introducing any two dogs to play together, walk them as a pack. Begin with one dog on either side of you, then once you are all "in the zone" of the walk, move the leashes to the same side so the two dogs are walking next to each other. A pack walk is the single best way to create bonds—both human-dog and dog-dog.

4. If your dog has a tendency to shrink away or engage in hostile eye contact right off the bat, help him return to communicating the natural way, using "nose-eyes-ears." Staying in calm control of the situation, gently maneuver the two dogs so that each can sniff the other's rear. This ritual is an equivalent of the human practices of shaking hands or bowing to each other. In the dog world, each animal takes turns at standing still and symbolically "submitting" to the other, allowing the other dog to investigate him.

5. Keep your dog leashed—at least in the beginning. This will ensure that you maintain control while still allowing for normal dog behavior.

6. Monitor your own energy. If you are anxious and "holding your breath" to see what happens, you will be communicating to your dog to remain tense as well. Accept the fact that you may not succeed the first few times, but that nothing will stop you from repeating the process until your dog regains his nature-given right to calmly befriend other dogs.

7. When your dog can play easily with one dog, then gradually add more dogs to the "playgroup." Once your dog accepts new members into the circle without fear or challenge, you can consider bringing him to a neighborhood dog park—but only after you have scoped it out to make sure there are no out-of-control dogs or owners dominating the activities there!

8. Make sure your dog socializes with dogs that play at his level of intensity. Dogs play at four levels of intensity: low, medium, high, and very high. Dogs that play at a high or very high level can easily escalate into an aggressive state that could result in a fight. If possible, condition your dog to play at a low or medium level of intensity and find other dogs that also play at this level of intensity.

To help your shy or suspicious dog become more comfortable socializing with strange humans, you have an advantage in that you can instruct friends to help you, teaching them the correct way to act. The most important thing to teach them, of course, is how to project calm-assertive energy and how to honor the no-touch, no-talk, no-eye-contact rule. Ask them to ignore the dog until the dog's natural curiosity draws him forward to investigate. You can provide your friends with treats as "lures," but they should only provide them once the dog takes the initiative to approach. Once your dog is comfortable around a group of friends, invite them over for a party—once again, instructing them to ignore your dog. Eventually, his natural instincts should prompt him to want to become part of the group.

Home Alone

In the wild, members of dog packs are rarely separated from one another. Sometimes one or two "aunts" or "uncles" will stay behind to tend to the pups while the mother and the rest of the adults in the pack go out hunting, but this is one of the rare situations in which wild canids split up. Now that they live in our modern, urban world, dogs often face being left at home while the rest of the human pack goes out to earn a living. Because being home alone feels so unnatural for a dog, many of them suffer from separation anxiety. This condition can arise in even the most balanced dogs with no other behavioral issues at all. Most of the time, my clients make their dogs' separation anxiety worse—and sometimes, even create it—by making a fuss over the dog before they leave the house. Trust me, all the explaining in the world about how you must work to pay for dog food and that you will be back in only a few hours will do nothing to curb your dog's anxiety; in fact, it will probably intensify it.

You must remember that any interaction you have with your dog begins and ends with energy. If you want to do away with the whimpering, howling, chewing, and the other symptoms of separation anxiety, you must take control of your dog's energy.

FRANTIC FELLA

In *Dog Whisperer*'s second season, I was called in to help a recently divorced mother, Cindy Steiner, and her ten-year-old daughter, Sidney, who were facing eviction from their Los Angeles apartment complex because of their recently rescued beagle mix, Fella. From the first time Cindy left Fella alone in the apartment when she left for work, neighbors complained that he barked all day, every day. After several months, the apartment manager laid down the law. Though she liked Cindy and Sidney personally, unless something was done about the dog, she would have to evict them. Of course, Cindy and Sidney couldn't lose their home—but they also realized that to return Fella to the shelter might ultimately result in his death.

Sometimes, separation anxiety is only one symptom of a larger problem. After talking with Cindy and Sidney, I learned that Fella also became territorial in the car, showed aggression toward other dogs, and worst of all, got only fifteen minutes or so of exercise a day. Fella had a very boring life. Fella needed to wake up every day with a challenge. The problem related directly to Cindy and Sidney's failure to give him what he needed, and also to take strong leadership positions in the home. I felt we could not even begin to address the separation anxiety issue until the women had brought Fella's overall level of stress under control through exercise, and after they had demonstrated to me that they understood the concept of calm-assertive leadership.

I gave Cindy and Sidney a homework assignment—ride their

bikes with Fella for at least a half hour, twice a day. After two weeks of keeping to a strict exercise routine, I returned to a changed Fella. Even Cindy was floored. "Everyone is remarking about how calm he is, how he listens to me." Now we were ready to tackle Fella's separation anxiety. After Fella's morning workout, I taught the mother and daughter how to make the moment of departure less traumatic by constant repetitions of putting the dog into a calm-submissive state, then leaving for a little while, first for just a few minutes, then staying away longer each time. Like many of my clients with dogs that suffer from this issue, Fella had owners who were compensating for their guilty feelings by making a big production of leaving every morning, trying to soothe his anxiety "It's okay, Fella, we'll be back soon," they would coo. Instead of soothing Fella's nerves, they were only increasing his anxiety and excitement by this behavior.

Eventually, we conditioned Fella to go into his kennel every morning after exercise and breakfast. All on her own, ten-year-old Sidney came up with the plan to put her own shirt in the kennel with him, so he would have the comfort of her smell. Three months after my visit, Fella was no longer the scourge of the apartment complex. He understood that for several hours after exercise and mealtime, he was supposed to enjoy resting time in his kennel. Even the neighbors agreed. "I would ask them, 'Did you hear the dog?'" Cindy told me. "And they're, like, 'No, we haven't heard him in months.'"

DOS AND DON'TS FOR PREVENTING SEPARATION ANXIETY

1. DO take your dog out for a thorough exercise session before you leave him alone. This could be a nice long walk or a vigorous run. Either way, make sure your dog gets a good workout and is tired.

2. DO provide water and food to your dog after exercise. Some dogs will need to rest a while before eating to prevent bloat, but you can hydrate them immediately. Different dogs require different periods of rest after exercise, and with time, you will get to know your dog's preferred routine. The combination of exercise and food will naturally put your dog in a calm-submissive state. Let your dog out to relieve himself after about fifteen to twenty minutes, or at least one more time before you go for the day.

3. DO practice no touch, no talk, no eye contact. This is the best way to leave your dog, and the best way to return home to him. By simply speaking to your dog when he is in an excited state, you only exacerbate his mania. Wait until your dog is in a calm-submissive state, then you can initiate contact.

4. DON'T make a big deal about leaving! Allow your dog to remain in his post-workout/feeding calm-submissive state.

5. DON'T blame your dog if he acts destructively while you are away. It isn't personal—he's just frustrated. Instead, rethink your strategy for leaving him alone. Consider conditioning him to stay in a smaller space or a kennel.

Remember, dogs respond best to my three-part formula—exercise, discipline, and affection, in that order. By setting and keeping consistent rules of the house, you are actually helping to make sure your dog is happy, fulfilled, and challenged.

6

AWAY FROM IT ALL

Traveling with and Without Your Dog

Traveling by car

Sometimes, our careers and the other obligations of our human lives force us to travel far from our homes. Sometimes, we simply need to take a vacation. The advantage of having dogs as pets (as opposed to cats) is that dogs thrive on going new places and attempting new adventures. Today more than ever, American society is adapting to make it easier for us to bring our animal companions with us on our sojourns away from it all. Airlines, trains, and ships all have well-established policies for transporting pets as well as people. The key to making traveling with your dog a positive, happy experience is to plan ahead—and to set rules, boundaries, and limitations—not just for your dog, but for you and every other human on the trip!

Before You Travel

Before any trip, have your veterinarian examine your dog to ensure that she is in good health. It's also a good idea to have copies of your pet's medical records close at hand. If you and your dog will be traveling across state lines, you must obtain a recent health certificate from your vet and a certificate of rabies vaccination. With the exception of Hawaii, which requires a 120-day quarantine period, dogs can travel anywhere in the United States with just a rabies vaccination certificate. However, other countries have varying policies and quarantine requirements that you should research long before you pack your bags.

Although life can be hectic before a business trip, vacation, or long-distance move, remember that your stress is also being transmitted to your dog. Don't forget to stay consistent in your routine of exercise, discipline, and affection before you leave, and try not to project your own anxiety about the sojourn to your dog. Dogs can learn to enjoy anything as long they associate it with a positive—but if you are dreading the annual trip to see your mother-in-law or driving across state to your high school reunion, don't be surprised if your dog "mysteriously" acts up before the trip.

Traveling by Car

Many dogs genuinely enjoy traveling by car. They relish the opportunity to stick their heads out the window and experience the psychedelic circus of scents that bombard them as they whiz by. As much as your dog may delight in this experience, however, in my opinion it's a real safety hazard for the dog. If you can crack the window just a little, she can get a taste of the world outside without the risk of being injured by flying particles of debris or becoming ill from having cold air forced into her lungs. For safety's sake, it's not a good idea to travel with your dog in the passenger seat, where she could be injured by an exploding airbag. I suggest the rear-bed area of a station wagon, hatchback, or SUV, or the backseat. Never travel with a dog outside in the bed of an open pickup! It will soon become law in many states, including California, that all dogs not traveling in a kennel or case must be restrained while a vehicle is in motion. Most pet supply shops carry a wide range of doggie travel harnesses that buckle into most standard seat belts to secure your dog safely and securely.

Of course, there are also a number of dogs that become carsick during long drives, or just don't seem to appreciate the great invention of the automobile as much as you do. If your dog has issues with the car, spend the time to acclimate her to auto travel long before you have to take her on a trip of more than an hour. Make sure she is well exercised before the ride, so she can curl up and nap in her kennel or travel case. Provide plenty of water in the car, some cookies to help settle her stomach, and a chew toy to relieve anxiety. Dramamine or a stronger motion sickness medication prescribed by your vet can help with severe motion sickness, but personally, I would choose a more homeopathic approach and use some of the flower remedies recommended by holistic veterinarian Dr. Marty Goldstein, such as Rescue Remedy, herb ginger root, peppermint—either a few drops of the herbal tincture or even making the dog some tea to drink or just a little raw honey before the trip. Some specific homeopathic products available in natural pet stores and organic food markets include PetAlive EasyTravel

Solution, Dr. Goodpet's Calm Stress, and Professional Complementary Health Formulas: Travel Sickness.

Remember, *never* leave your dog alone in a parked car. On warm days, the interior temperature can rise to 120 degrees in a matter of minutes, even with the windows opened slightly.

If you really have a good relationship with your dog, the best time to travel with her is at nighttime, when she'll be more inclined to rest and relax. If you choose to travel in the daytime, remember that although your kids understand that this is vacation and we are doing things differently today, your dog doesn't rationalize like that. Dogs may love adventures, but they also depend on routine. On a long car trip, I suggest you ask yourself, "What would my dog normally do at 7:00 A.M.? What would she normally do at 10:00 A.M.? What would she normally do at lunchtime?" Then try to provide some similar activity around the same time.

For me, the rule is that at least once every four hours, I'm going to stop my car and let my dog have at least fifteen to twenty minutes to stretch, relieve himself, and maybe take a miniwalk. If a dog is a playful dog, I will throw the ball, play a game, burn some energy, and give water. Speaking of water, before you take a long car trip, know your dog's signals and the way she communicates "I gotta go!" to you. I have seen dogs that actually live with truck drivers, and they know when they are going to stop. They can smell, "Oh, we're getting into Camarillo; I know we're going to stop in a few minutes." But it took time for those dogs to adjust to that style of life.

I love driving across the country or across the state with my wife, my kids, and my dogs; to me, it's a fun bonding experience for all of us. I try to remember, however, to think of every family member's individual needs when it comes to rest stops, food, stretch time, and exercise. Those family members include the dogs!

Traveling by Air

Many airlines (not all—be sure to check ahead) are set up for pet travel, but they aren't about to give your dog a free ride. The Animal and Plant Health Inspection Service (APHIS) of the U.S. Department of Agriculture (USDA) sets and enforces regulations for the transportation of live animals and you must comply with the applicable laws, which require your pet to be at least eight weeks old and fully weaned before traveling by air. Some airlines will allow you to travel with a small pet in the cabin of the plane if your pet will fit in a carry-on kennel or approved carrier under a passenger seat, but prepare to pay between a $50 and a $100 service charge each way for the privilege. Some airlines also consider your pet a part of your carry-on allowance—in most cases, only one carry-on bag and one personal item—so you need to consider this before you pack.[1]

The good news is, little dogs often do very well when traveling by air in the cabin with the family. They often have previous experience being transported in cars or small carriers, the cabin environment has a regulated temperature, and the energy of the people around them is normally relaxed, as the people around them are in a calm-submissive mode—watching the in-flight movie, reading a book, or napping. It's not a completely unnatural experience. For the sake of your dog as well as your fellow passengers, however, please don't make an airline flight your dog's first experience spending a long period of time in a carrier! You don't want a whining, barking traveling companion. Take her on a few car trips first, until she learns that the carrier means relaxation. And of course, take her on a long walk beforehand, so resting for a while feels natural.

PRECIOUS CARGO

On many airlines, you have two other options. The first is to fly your pet as "accompanied baggage," in the cargo hold alongside your checked luggage. This option is only available if you are traveling on the same flight as your pet. The second choice is to transport your pet as a "live animal" cargo shipment. In the cargo system, the animal may travel unaccompanied, either through the regular cargo channels or through a specially expedited delivery service that many airlines have developed. Animals in the cargo systems are transported in the same pressurized holds as those in the checked baggage system. If you do either of these things, by all means consult with your trusted veterinarian to be sure that your dog is fit to travel. Senior dogs (over seven and a half years old) may need a more extensive health examination (that is, liver and kidney screens). Some breeds—for example, flat-nosed dogs (for example, English bull dogs and pugs)—simply do not fly well because they may have difficulty breathing even under normal conditions. You will need a health certificate in order to comply with the rules of most airlines as well as state and federal rules. To be valid for your trip on most airlines, the certificate should be issued no more than seven to ten days prior to departure.

Personally, I do not recommend flying dogs as cargo unless you have absolutely no other choice. Whenever I take Daddy or any of the other pack members to *Dog Whisperer* shoots in different parts of America, the dogs typically drive in the mobile home with our crew member Rojo, or we have a production assistant drive them in a car. Everybody loves traveling with Daddy. In the mornings, he always welcomes the day by bringing the person he is with a toy as an offering of friendship and simply to celebrate the start of a new adventure! Of course, driving across country involves more logistics and

Try to keep your emotions in check when visiting dogs in a shelter or kennel.

It's hard not to feel sorry for a row of winsome puppies, but emotions may cause you to make a bad choice.

Cesar demonstrates the correct way to meet a dog in a kennel or shelter: stay calm and always approach from the side.

Cesar helps Sissy out of her kennel.

Cesar remains calm and assertive while applying medication.

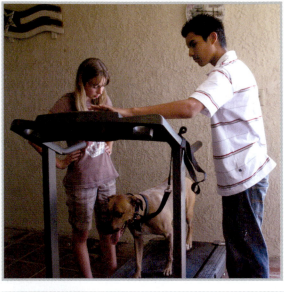

Exercise is essential for a happy, healthy dog, and no matter which activities you decide to do together, every family member should be involved. Here, Chipper's young owner helps prepare him for a run on the tread-mill.

True obedience from a dog—such as having him come to you on command—is something that will require patience, leadership, and respect.

Agility classes that incorporate ramps, hurdles, and other obstacles are excellent outlets for high-energy dogs and will help build a stronger connection between you and your dog.

Swimming, especially fetching items in the water, is an excellent activity for sporting dogs. Here, Gavin the ATF dog retrieves a Frisbee during a therapeutic swim at the center.

Cesar demonstrates how swimming can help calm Gizmo, a high-energy beagle.

A bike ride with Cesar helps Abbey, a fearful beagle, overcome her reticence on walks.

Dogs in the herding group thrive when presented with a challenge, such as corralling a pasture of sheep.

Working breeds like Swiss mountain dogs flourish when given a job to do. Cesar shows Joy how pulling a cart can help Barclay expend excess energy and help him feel useful.

planning ahead than flying, but I don't trust the unpredictable temperature conditions of cargo holds, not to mention the fact that there are no humans around to supervise.

I realize many people don't have an option when traveling and must sometimes make the decision to fly their dogs as accompanied baggage or as cargo. If this is the case, I recommend you take the time to prepare your dog physically and psychologically for the trip. When humans become astronauts, NASA doesn't just hire them off the street, put them in a capsule, and send them up into outer space! They prepare new astronauts years in advance, by easing them into the kind of new experiences the human body will undergo in a zero gravity environment. If I am going to put my dog on a long airline flight, I will prepare him as if I want him to become a kind of astronaut. I will start by easing him into longer periods spent in his crate. I will buy a crate with wheels and let him experience being pulled around in a crate on wheels, until I know that he is relaxed and comfortable in that situation. I will take him to the airport in his crate so that he can get used to the sound of airplanes taking off and landing. I will take him into the swimming pool and hold him in the water so he can have access to that kind of gravity-challenging sensation. The goal of all this is to condition the brain to have experiences of different sensations, so when he's in the cargo hold, he can put it all together—"Okay, I've been in a crate before and everything was fine. Okay, I've felt this floating feeling before and everything was fine."

In order to do this preflight training right, I'm going to start conditioning my dog at least a month before the trip. Of course, future trips won't need this kind of intensive preparation, but my goal is to create as low-stress an experience as possible the first time around, so the travel doesn't become a negative experience.

Before the flight itself, give your dog the ultimate exercise session—a long Rollerblade outing or a run next to your bike, for example—to thoroughly tire her out. If your veterinarian is familiar with acupuncture or homeopathic remedies, you might ask about a preflight treatment or any natural remedies that can help create calmness. In my opinion, this is far preferable to medical tranquilizers or "doggie downers," which I would never give my dogs before a flight. Most veterinarians advise against sedating, since the effects of tranquilizers on animals at higher altitudes are unpredictable. Choose a flight that is direct or nonstop, and avoid the stresses of holiday or weekend travel. Avoid traveling through any kind of temperature extremes; morning or evening flights are preferable during the summer. In the cargo system, it is possible to reserve space on a specific flight by paying for either priority or special expedited delivery service. Airlines have the right to prevent your dog from flying in very severe weather conditions.

The USDA requires that you offer your pet food and water within four hours before check-in with the airline. Do not overfeed or overwater your dog before travel. When you check in with the airline, you must sign a certification of the time when you last offered food and water to your pet. Never leave food or water in the dish in the kennel.

Traveling by Train or Boat

With the exception of assistance dogs, only a few cruise lines accept pets—and usually on ocean crossings only. Some lines permit pets in private cabins, but mostly they are confined to kennels. Contact cruise lines in advance to find out about their policies and which of their ships have kennel facilities. If you must use the ship's kennel, make sure it is protected from the elements. I have had to travel by ferry with dogs a couple of times, and the rules there were that dogs had to stay in the car. It was my choice to stay in the car area with the dogs for the duration of the trip. If you are traveling with the whole family, I suggest you create a schedule and switch off dog-sitting responsibilities until you arrive at your destination.

As for trains, in America, Amtrak currently does not accept pets unless they are assistance dogs. (There may be smaller U.S. railroad companies that permit animals onboard.) In Europe, many train systems allow pets. If you're going to travel with your dogs on a train, I suggest you go through the preparation ritual for this specific means of travel, bringing your dog near a station in a casual way, to get her used to the sounds and smells of train travel.

STAYING IN HOTELS

According to Tracey Thompson, who runs the website Pet Friendly Travel.com, more and more hotels are accommodating travelers with pets. "In the past it was only low-end motels that would let you have a dog in your room," Tracey tells me. "Four-star and up hotels have just recently jumped on the pet bandwagon. In the last five years the trend has really become . . . well, it's not just a trend anymore; it's a way of life." But Tracey reminds us that each hotel is different with its restrictions. Always do your homework before you hit the road. "The good thing and bad thing about the Internet is there is a lot of information out there, but it could be inaccurate. Don't trust a website or chat page just because it says you can take a dog to such and such hotel. Always call and get the details."

I check into hotels with my dogs all the time, and this is what I've learned: it's up to you as an owner to teach your dog how to enjoy and respect this new environment. You will not have a good stay if your dog is not socialized well to be in unfamiliar surroundings, with unfamiliar people, and possibly other dogs. First of all, it's important for your dog to understand where she is. Walk her around the neighborhood, introduce her to the doormen, the desk clerks, and the housekeepers using the no-touch, no-talk, no-eye-contact rule. If you do your job right, she will adapt quickly. Wee-wee pads are great inventions to bring with you to a hotel or vacation house. If your dog is conditioned to use a wee-wee pad, you can avoid any potential property-damaging accidents that might occur. But the most crucial thing, in my opinion, is to immediately get your dog used to whatever new schedule she will have to abide by during your time away from home. Once she understands the routine, she can adapt to it—but if she feels confused, she is going to be wondering how to channel her energy, and she might just express it in negative ways unless you give her the guidance she needs.

Rules for Relaxation

Often, people complain to me that their dogs are "out of control" on vacations. Once again, to me this comes down to the fact that we forget that our dogs don't see vacations in the way that we do. Humans often want to use vacations to relax, do nothing, and have no schedule at all. Or they want to experience new and different activities and forget all about the dog. I'm here to tell you that you may be able to punch out on your job during vacations—you can even punch out on your own diet and exercise regimens—but you simply cannot punch out on your responsibilities as pack leader to your dog! Even if your schedule is different from the schedule you keep at home, you need to create a compatible routine for your dog and make sure she is comfortable with it from the very beginning.

My own life with my family recently offered me a new metaphor for understanding how to help dogs adapt to a new environment and new rules. On my kids' last spring break, Ilusion and I took both boys to Club Med in Punta Cana in the Dominican Republic. When we arrived, we were a little disoriented. It seemed to us that everybody else knew what was going on except us. Then the Club Med organizers showed up and gave us our schedule. It was completely different from the schedule we were used to at home, so it took us a day or two to acclimate to the rules—what time do they serve breakfast? How do you find the various activities? How do you get your towels at the pool? Once those things became clear to us, we were able to become part of the group and enjoy their new routine. We ended up having a fantastic time and plan to go back as a family soon.

When you travel with your dog, think of yourself as the activities guide from Club Med. First, you have to introduce your dog to the new environment: give her a tour of the neighborhood and show her where she is going to eat and sleep. Next, set up a daily schedule that is as consistent with her schedule at home as possible. Then, add in any new activities. Today we're going to swim. Today we're going to do kayaking. Today we're going to explore. If you are going to take the family out for activities that don't include the dog, you must make sure she's tired, knows where she's going to rest, and is not in an excited mode when you close the door to leave her behind. You are basically reminding her of the things that she already knows how to do at home, but doesn't necessarily know how to do in this new place, with the different smells, and different energy. Our job is just to teach her, "Look, the way we normally behave over there, we have to do here, too."

Vacations may represent a break from discipline for humans, but if we let them represent a lack of rules, boundaries, and limitations for our dogs, we are in for big trouble. Some of my clients like to sleep late on vacations, but I have to break it to them—they can't vary their wake-up time too much if they're going to bring the dogs along. Your dogs need consistency, especially when it comes to the morning walk. If people usually wake up at six but sleep until ten on vacation, it will take them several days to get the dogs used to the

10:00 A.M. wake-up call. By that time, it's time to go home, and it will take you several days to get them back on the 6:00 A.M. schedule. Why would you want to go through that trouble to break a habit that's already so healthy for your dog? Personally, I'd rather get up at the regular time on vacations, walk the dogs and feed them, then go back to sleep—or take a nap on the beach later. It's much better for everyone involved if I just "take one for the pack."

Staying at Home

If you can't travel with your dog, you still have options. You may have trusted friends or family with whom your dog is comfortable and who have good experience and instincts about caring for animals, so leaving your dog with them is one choice to consider. If this is a possibility for you, I suggest you allow your dog to get to know these new people and the new environment with a trial visit. Provide those people with a list of your dog's rules and her daily schedule (and make sure they're willing and able to follow it!). Then let the dog have a "sleepover" there for a night or two. Every time you take the time to adapt your dog to a new situation, it's going to be a plus for everyone.

Other options are professional doggie day-care businesses, pet boarding kennels, and pet sitters.

Doggie Day Care and Boarding Kennels

First, find out whether your state requires boarding kennel inspections. If it does, make sure the kennel you are considering displays a license or certificate showing that the kennel meets mandated standards. Also ask whether the prospective kennel belongs to the American Boarding Kennels Association, a trade association founded by kennel operators to promote professional standards of pet care.

Never take your dog to any facility that you haven't checked out thoroughly yourself for cleanliness, ventilation, and the attitude and energy of the staff. Make sure the kennel provides adequate exercise for all animals. Don't just do a walk-through of the facility; ask if you can observe for a few hours to see how the place runs on an average day. Be aware that some facilities will require a vaccination for bordetella, or "kennel cough." If you are leaving your dog at a doggie day care for a few days, make sure your dog is socialized and calm-submissive enough to fit into the center's environment. Just as with the boarding kennel, spend a day at the facility to observe the routine. If the owners won't let you watch as a quiet, respectful observer, then it's not the place for you.

The good news is, there are many outstanding boarding facilities out there. Some are designed to seem like houses, with carpets, furniture, television sets—everything that would remind a dog of home. Some even have webcams available so you can see your pet from afar. You'll have to do your research, of course—and often, having your dog stay in such posh quarters can be expensive.

PET SITTERS

One other option for leaving your dog home when you travel is to find a trusted pet sitter. Great pet sitters don't just stop by their clients' houses to feed the dogs and take them out to pee and poop; they'll also spend quality time with dogs, exercise them, and keep an eye on their medical conditions. Many pet sitters also offer house-sitting services, such as bringing in mail and newspapers or watering plants. Some will actually live in your house with your pet for the duration of your trip.

The National Association of Professional Pet Sitters and Pet Sitters International are organizations that offer pet-sitter accreditation to those who demonstrate professional experience, complete pet-care-related home study courses, attend professional conferences, and abide by a code of ethics set by the organizations.

Once you find a pet sitter you like, make sure he or she comes to meet with your dog at your home, and observe how they get along. If something seems wrong (beyond the dog being slightly unsure around a new person at first meeting), trust your dog's instincts. Some pet sitters will keep dogs with them at their own homes. If this is the case, make sure that any other dogs that will be "rooming" with your own don't have aggression issues that could put your own dog in danger. And ask for guarantees that all the dogs at the pet sitter's home have their basic immunity protection against parvo, distemper, and rabies.

Of course, even the most trustworthy, experienced pet sitter will have trouble if you haven't also kept your end of the bargain. Here are your responsibilities:

- Make reservations with your pet sitter early, especially during holidays.
- Ensure your dog is well socialized and allows strangers to handle her.
- Affix current identification tags to your dog's collar.
- Have an identification microchip implanted in your dog.
- Maintain current vaccinations.
- Leave clear instructions detailing specific pet-care responsibilities and emergency contact information, including how to reach you and your veterinarian.
- Leave food and supplies in one place.
- Buy extra supplies in case you're away longer than planned.[2]

I'm very close to my mom, back in Mexico. So close, in fact, that if I'm not feeling well or having a hard time with work, she'll call me to tell me she's sensed something's wrong. It's also been my experience that when I travel, my dogs can sense when I'm not comfortable with the arrangements I've made for them, and it only heightens their bad experience. This is why it's so important not to leave travel decisions about your dog to the last minute. Long before you even know you have to go on a trip, begin to work through solutions to the different travel issues you might have, be they vaccinations and travel kennels, or finding a pet sitter whom you totally trust. A great advance plan is the key to happy traveling with or without your dog, and peace of mind whether you're together or apart.

AN OUNCE OF PREVENTION

The Basics of Health Care for Your Dog

Barnes jumping in a pool for the ball

When you bring a dog into your life, you are responsible from that day forward for his nutrition, his safety, and his health care. In my pack of forty to fifty dogs at the Dog Psychology Center, I've overseen the physical well-being of dogs that were never sick a day in their lives, senior dogs with the usual old-age complaints, and dogs with genetic and neurological disorders that could never totally be cured. Caring for these diverse "patients" over the years has schooled me in some of the basics of health care for canines, but like any other dog owner, I rely on trusted veterinary professionals as the mainstays of my pack's health and well-being. Through nearly twenty years of working with dogs in the United States, I've been fortunate to have made the acquaintance of and consulted with many amazing, dedicated animal health-care professionals.

But finding stellar vets doesn't just happen by accident. I suggest to all my clients that they meet with and interview prospective vets long *before* they bring a new dog or puppy home, and not wait until an emergency to see if they can find someone they trust with their dog's life. One of the first things you may have to do, whether you have a grown dog or a puppy, is take the dog in for his shots or checkup, and if you the human are even a little unsure about that strange man or woman in the white coat, then you can bet your new dog will pick right up on it, too—on top of any anxiety or fear she may already be feeling. So take some of the stress off both your family and your dog by interviewing and meeting with veterinarians several weeks in advance.

I believe selecting the right veterinarian for your dog should be much like selecting the right pediatrician for your kids. Sure, someone can have a wall full of diplomas, but that just means he did well in medical school, not that he necessarily has the right energy to care for your loved ones. When I first came to Los Angeles, I needed to find a vet immediately when one of my rottweilers, Gracie, had a seizure. Without any recommendations to go on, I checked out several clinics in my area. I was seeking a person I sensed to be honest and who made me feel at home, but at first many of the doctors I encountered seemed to convey an air of superiority. In other words, "I am the doctor; I am very important—you are the Mexican immigrant and if you're very, very lucky, your dog may get to be my patient." This is not the kind of healing energy I want around my family or my dogs; to me, a real healer is someone who addresses his patients directly, as one human to another, or one human to one dog. Perhaps that person can save your dog, but can he give you real hope and support? Giving hope is, to me, one of the most important gifts any kind of doctor can offer us. And there is another thing, another kind of diploma that only a dog can give you. When a dog is able to trust, respect, and relax around a person, when a person can ease the anxiety of a nervous dog or earn the trust or deference of a dominant, territorial, or aggressive dog— that is the kind of degree that no piece of paper can give you.

Fortunately, a friend of mine who was a vet tech learned of my frustrating search for the perfect veterinarian and referred me to Dr. Brij Rawat of the Hollypark Pet Clinic in Gardena, California. I went to Hollypark Clinic and asked to meet with Dr. Rawat. He was from India and I am from Mexico, and we had both come to America because of our love for animals. That fact alone immediately gave us something in common. Back then, I was a "nobody"—but Dr. Rawat didn't treat me that way. He welcomed me and talked to me at length about his philosophy of dogs, which meshed perfectly with mine. It was clear to me that Dr. Rawat did what he did not because he wanted to get rich, but because he considered it his mission in life. Like me, he was passionate about animals and making their lives better. I was living hand to mouth back then, but Dr. Rawat was more than fair with me when it came to financial arrangements. He allowed me to pay him in installments when I had emergencies that I hadn't been able to save properly for. To me, that kind of honesty and integrity always deserves loyalty, so I'm forever grateful to him, and I take all my dogs to Hollypark to get spayed and neutered.

Dr. Rawat will never do a procedure or a test that he feels is unnecessary, even if it will make him more money. When there are situations or procedures that are not in his area of expertise, I always consult with him first and listen to his suggestions for specialists. Dr. Rawat is involved in the community around him, and he likes to meet dogs and owners in times of health, not just sickness. He is concerned with the overall wellness and balance of the dogs and people around him. To me, that is first and foremost the most important consideration for a great, dedicated veterinarian.

TEN TIPS FOR CHOOSING THE RIGHT VET

1. Get the family together for another conference. Share your thoughts about what qualities in a health-care professional are important to all of you. Make a list of questions and concerns to ask every vet you interview.

2. Get references from breeders, shelter and rescue organizations, or other dog owners.

3. Investigate the veterinarian's education and experience. Does the clinic or hospital have American Animal Hospital Association (AAHA) approval? Although many excellent clinics are not AAHA members, such a membership does ensure a certain level of medical care.

4. Check out the veterinarian's involvement in the neighborhood and community. Does he invite dogs and owners to visit the clinic and staff socially, during times of wellness as well as need?

5. Ask the vet about her goals and philosophies. Do they mesh with yours? How does the vet respond to your own questions and concerns? Does this seem like someone with whom you'll be able to communicate? Someone open to relating equally in a give-and-take conversation?

6. Address the issue of access. What are the hours of operation? Will a doctor or a technician return your calls and answer your medical questions promptly? If your pet is hospitalized, can you call as often as you want for updates?

7. Inquire about any areas of health care that are specific to your pet. Does the doctor/clinic offer those special services?

8. Observe how the vet interacts with the animals in his clinic. Does he project calm-assertive energy? If possible, introduce the veterinarian to your dog in a casual, friendly manner—long before you go in for a checkup. What does your dog tell you about this person who may become very intimately involved in your family's life?

9. What about the vet techs, assistants, and other helpers in the clinic? Do they seem knowledgeable about and sensitive to animals? Ask about the longevity of the medical and nursing staff. Staff members who feel empowered to do good medicine and nursing care tend to stay with a practice longer.

10. Request a tour of the hospital, clinic, or facility. Does it have a welcoming atmosphere? Is it clean, cared for, and not overcrowded? A good hospital should have access to x-ray, ultrasound, dentistry, in-house lab tests, IV pumps, blood pressure and eye pressure monitoring as well as the ability to send out to labs and refer to specialists.

THE ANNUAL VISIT

A degree in veterinary medicine costs more than $100,000 and takes at least four years and an enormous amount of hard work and dedication to earn.[1] It's a profession that attracts many fine minds devoted to the well-being of animals, so I can guarantee you that the right vet for you is out there. Once you have selected a medical professional with whom you are happy, you need to make and keep routine wellness visits, usually once a year—more for an older dog or dogs with specific health issues. Every vet has slightly different recommendations, but the common components of the "annual" may include blood work and other lab tests; weigh-ins; eye, ear, and oral exams; preventive medications; checking fecal samples for parasites; and any vaccinations for which the dog may be due. As a consumer you can choose which parts of the exam you can afford to do financially, but medically they all have value.

The single most important part of the annual is the physical exam. Especially as your dogs get older, there are many conditions that a physical can detect so that you can provide early intervention. The lab tests are the second most important part of an adult dog's annual evaluation. Most local labs now provide yearly profiles at a very reasonable price. A blood profile will help to detect certain hidden conditions early enough to prevent serious disease and establish "normals" for future comparison. Heartworm prevention is very important in the areas where this condition is widespread. On average, treating a dog for heartworms costs the same as a lifetime of prevention, so even though it seems expensive, in the long run it has good value. When the Dog Psychology Center rehabilitated three Katrina dogs in 2005, all of them had been infected with heartworms during their ordeal in the murky floodwaters of New Orleans. A fecal evaluation is also very important because it can reveal parasites that can be dangerous to your children as well as your dog.

Maintaining oral health should also be a big part of your dog's annual health-care routine, especially in smaller-breed dogs. A clean and healthy set of teeth does much more than free your pet from his persistent "doggie breath"; dental plaque can actually lead to systemwide infection that may cause cardiac or renal disease. Making sure dogs have abrasive items to chew on, and tooth brushing, if possible, can delay the development of oral problems.

AVOIDING FINANCIAL SURPRISES

When measured against the skyrocketing costs of human health care in America, the cost of "just the basics" in veterinary care for your pets has remained comparatively steady.[2] However, as we continue to view dogs as not simply "pets" but equally valued members of our families, more and more of my clients are willing to consider expensive treatments and procedures to save or prolong their animals' lives. I always advise families to honestly consider their financial situation long before they make the decision to bring a dog home. Make sure you add a line item to your family budget that allows for your dog's yearly vet expenses, food, and preventive care. Saving money isn't easy these days, but try your best to set aside a reasonable amount for any canine medical emergencies that might arise.

It's also important to be up front with your vet from the beginning about your financial constraints. Ask the vet to prioritize the recommended tests at your dog's yearly exam. Be sure to go in for regular checkups to find problems early. If there is an emergency, taking your dog to the vet before he becomes too ill often avoids costly overnight stays. Waiting until the end of a day when the problem has been going on since morning or the day before is also not a great idea. "Nothing frustrates a vet more than getting called at the end of office hours about a vomiting dog that has been vomiting since the night before," Dr. Charlie Rinehimer, associate professor of biology and veterinary technology at Northampton Community College, and practicing vet, reminds us. "Now he has to stay late, and keep his staff there also, which will translate into an increase in fees."

People who put off spaying their dogs at a young age will find that the operation done on an older animal will require more blood work and anesthesia monitoring and so will be more expensive.

Giving a good, honest history will also help keep costs down. "Admitting that you gave the dog a pile of leftover ham might save radiographs or ultrasounds to rule out blockage from a foreign body," Dr. Rinehimer notes. "Revealing the problem has actually been going on for a while will shift diagnosis strategy and may eliminate the need for drastic treatment."

Pet health insurance is becoming much more common in recent years and if the terms are fair, my opinion is that it's a step in the right direction. Most of the pet insurance companies are underwritten by human insurance companies and are structured in a similar way. Some cover preventive care and others are just major medical, but I've recently had conversations with insurance companies that want to take a more comprehensive approach— including behavioral and alternative medicine therapies among the services they will help underwrite. The best way to pick a company is to ask for a benefits schedule and see which plan best meets your needs.

Whether it is about financial arrangements or your dog's unique behavioral quirks, it's vital that you and your vet always keep an open line of communication going. I counsel my clients to keep detailed notes on their dog's physical and behavioral well-being between visits and throughout the year, paying special attention to any changes that have occurred since the last visit. Every time you speak with your vet, make sure to keep him updated on progress, both positive and negative. And don't forget that veterinarians want to hear the good news, too. In the words of Dr. Rinehimer, "Everyone is quick to call when things aren't going well, but few call to give positive feedback."

Finally, remember the famous adage "An ounce of prevention is worth a pound of cure." Keeping your dog in the best of health year-round is the surest way to stay out of your vet's office and avoid a large bill.

SPAYING AND NEUTERING

Fans of *The Price Is Right* may remember the way that the appropriately named Bob Barker closed out each episode: "Help control the pet population. Have your pet spayed or neutered!" Just like Bob, I'm a broken record when it comes to repeating this message: unless you are a professional breeder or have a well-researched and -planned strategy to breed or mate your pet, you should be spaying or neutering your dog—to help control animal overpopulation, and for the health benefits it will provide your pet.

The stage at which male dogs begin to mature sexually brings on a hormone rush that may lead to unpredictable behavior. Males that are physiologically ready, but not allowed to mate, become frustrated—creating pent-up energy that can lead to destructive behaviors. Males who are kept separated from females in heat may develop issues of dominance and aggression over your pack at home. Unspayed females, on the other hand, produce hormones when they are in heat that will attract undesired attention from any unsterilized male dog within sniffing distance. If you have an unspayed female puppy of six months or older, any chance encounter with an unneutered male could result in her becoming the canine equivalent of an unwed teenage mom.

Psychologically, sterilization curbs the unpredictable effects of the hormonal changes that occur in both male and female dogs. The nervous high-level energy that these hormones produce is eliminated, and dogs have less desire to wander and to scent-mark their territory. Aggression and anxiety brought on by the dog's hormonal cycle becomes a nonissue.

Many myths exist relating to health problems associated with early sterilization, such as uncontrollable weight gain and melancholy over the loss of sexual reproductive capabilities. A dog with a very high energy level caused by sexual hormones that calms down to a high or medium energy level after being spayed or neutered is in no danger of uncontrollable weight gain as long as the owner adjusts the diet and exercise to fit the new lifestyle. Weight gain in dogs is most often the result of overfeeding and underexercising, *not* sterilization. And do not fear that your dog will "mope" or grieve the loss of her reproductive ability. Remember, only humans live in the world of "should haves" and "what if's"! Dogs and other animals live in the moment, and if they have no hormones driving them to mate, that desire will simply no longer be present.

Contrary to the myths, sterilization can actually be a tremendous benefit to your dog's health.[3] Male dogs that are neutered run a much lower risk of prostate cancer, and spayed female dogs are less likely to develop uterine, ovarian, or breast cancers in later life. They will also avoid potentially fatal infections and false pregnancies.

Some studies have indicated that complications can arise from sterilization before the age of six months, but sterilization at or beyond that age will in the longer view yield a healthier, better-behaved pet. Your vet will let you know the optimum age to sterilize a dog or puppy. When that day comes, don't forget that it's *your* energy that will determine your dog's reaction to the operation itself. Make sure your dog or pup is in a relaxed, calm-submissive state before the procedure itself, because when he awakens from the anesthesia, he will be in the same state as when he went to sleep. In my opinion, a dog that seems depressed after a spaying or neutering is most often reacting to the owner's attitude about the event. Don't feel sorry for your dog—keep your attitude upbeat, calm and assertive. You are not taking something away from your dog; instead, you are giving him the gift of a life free of sexual frustration.

You Are What You Eat

When I began working with dogs as a new arrival to Los Angeles, I assumed most of what the television commercials told me was true: that I could find the finest nutrition in the world for my dogs on supermarket or pet supply store shelves. Once a week, I always managed to find the money to get them a large chunk of raw meat to enjoy, but beyond that, I didn't think very much about nutrition. All the trainers would talk about what they were feeding their dogs, so a lot of information was coming my way, but Dr. Palmquist at the Centinela Animal Hospital was the first to tell me about the different components of dog food and to watch out for those mysterious "animal by-products" on the labels. At that time I switched from a chicken by-product food to a lamb-and-rice-based food.

Today, I'm fortunate to have access to some of the best research in the world about the booming science of creating top-notch nutrition for animals. The most important lesson I have taken from this information is that, hands down, the key to your dog's good health starts with the right nutrition. The diet you feed your dog will have the greatest impact on his health. Your food choices may determine whether or not your best friend morphs into cranky old dog at age ten or the kind of spry, active senior that my pit bull Daddy has become!

In March 2007 pet owners across the country were horrified to learn that contaminated pet food originating from China was poisoning their beloved pets. Many pets were stricken ill or died as a direct result of eating tainted food. An investigation led the FDA and USDA to finger contaminated wheat gluten, specifically the toxin melamine, as the source of the sickness. A massive pet food recall followed, leading to several brands of both dog and cat food being taken off supermarket shelves. As a result of the FDA and USDA findings, the pet food manufacturer primarily responsible for the products has been inundated with lawsuits.

Long before the pet food recall of 2007, holistic vets like Dr. Paula Terifaj and Dr. Marty Goldstein had been championing the use of preservative-free, natural and organic food for companion animals. That's because scientific testing and in-depth investigations done by nonpartisan organizations such as the Animal Protection Institute (www.api4animals.org) have shown again and again that the commercial pet food industries do not have your dog's best interest at heart! Guidelines for pet food ingredients are not determined by the FDA, but by the Association of American Feed Control Officials. These AAFCO guidelines only ensure that the food you are buying meets a mathematical minimum of key nutrients. In one of her "30 Minute Vet Consult" manuals, *How to Feed Your Dog If You Flunked Rocket Science,* Paula Terifaj points out that these guidelines tell you nothing about the quality of the ingredients being used, whether the protein and carbohydrate sources have been tested for digestibility, or how well the nutrients will be absorbed by the intestines.[4]

Although we claim to love our pets as if they were our family members, the food we give them is often classified as "unfit for human consumption" and is even banned from human food manufacturing plants! The "meat by-products" listed on the label of that delicious-looking pet chow being served up in a million-dollar-budget television commercial may include "4-D" meat—meat from dead, dying, diseased, and disabled animals—often ravaged by cancerous tumors, worm-infested organs, and antibiotics and other more toxic drugs. Even more chilling is the fact that twenty states still allow the bodies of euthanized pets, shelter rejects, and zoo animals to be recycled as "meat by-products," which means they have been injected with a substance that medical authorities consider dangerous or deadly—even if absorbed indirectly after days or weeks. And the preservatives used to package these foodstuffs after the fact include chemicals made of plastics and rubber preservatives and are proven to cause diseases from liver damage to infertility to behavioral disorders.[5]

The truth is, dogs were not made by nature to eat out of cans, nor were they made to eat the same thing day in and day out. Cooking fresh food for your pets can circumvent all the potential health disasters lurking in commercial-grade pet food. Dr. Terifaj recommends simply combining and sautéing or boiling combinations of fresh proteins, carbohydrates, and vegetables. Most of my clients, however, have little time to cook for themselves, let alone their dogs. I recommend they turn to the select number of excellent natural, organic prepackaged pet foods created by smaller companies. You won't usually see these products on the shelves of your local supermarket or discount store, so seek out the specialty dog foods at pet supply stores or at natural food stores, and learn how to read the ingredients on pet food labels before you buy. The first three ingredients listed are critical, because they account for most of what your dog will be ingesting. Look for animal proteins listed as meat. Limit or avoid those with processed cheap grain products. Immediately reject any products with artificial preservatives, food dyes, and any meat or grain by-products. In the appendix of this book you will find many excellent resources and links for learning more about pet nutrition. Always check with your vet before you make any changes to your dog's diet.

In this land of abundance called America, obesity is a major problem—with humans and with dogs as well. In canines, it can lead to joint problems, skin problems, gland impaction, heart disease, and many other potentially life-threatening conditions. If you are following my exercise, discipline, and affection guidelines as well as serving your dog a moderate, nutritious diet, then you should be creating the balanced lifestyle he needs to prevent him from becoming overweight.

On the Front Lines Against Fleas

At the Dog Psychology Center, I learned the hard way that most over-the-counter remedies for fleas will not work. When you are treating fleas, you have to focus on three things: the pet, the house, and the yard. Sometimes if you address the house aggressively enough, it is possible to ignore the other two areas, but you should start by addressing all three.

The yard is the hardest area to treat, unless the dogs are kept in a pen outside. Cedar in a pen will help repel fleas, but beware: many dogs are allergic to cedar. There are also yard sprays, which will help reduce the number of fleas in the yard. If you have a full-sized grassy or wooded yard, it is often not a big part of the problem and can be ignored.

If your dogs spend much time inside the house, then that will usually be the front line of your battle with the fleas. The best solution is to apply boric acid to all surfaces the dog has been on. This includes everything: carpet, couches, and hardwood. Boric acid is available as 20 Mule Team Borax in the laundry aisle at the grocery store. Dr. Sherry Weaver of the Animal Hospital in Towne Lake, Georgia, prefers the Fleabusters brand, because it stays in the house longer. Boric acid is safe and effective, and it can last for years.

Prescription products such as Advantage, Top Spot, and Frontline kill almost all fleas within a day of application. Capstar, the newest product for fleas, will kill all the fleas on the dog within an hour. Other over-the-counter products, which contain older chemicals such as pyrethrins, will only kill a small percentage of the fleas. Home remedies such as brewer's yeast or garlic have been used for years to prevent fleas, although there has never been any proof that these actually work.

Remember, no matter what product you use on your dog, if there are still fleas in the environment, you will have a reinfestation. Do your research, use safe chemicals, treat all three areas, and you should be able to break the flea cycle in your home.

THE VACCINATION CONTROVERSY

When I first came to the United States, I didn't really have much knowledge about health care for pets. On my grandfather's farm in Mexico, we fed the dogs tortillas and milk and any scraps we could spare; they hunted on their own for squirrels, lizards, and iguanas. The dogs were scrawny and not very well groomed, but they were calm-submissive around humans, and even with no veterinary care to speak of, they usually lived about ten years. In my first stateside job as a groomer in San Diego, I was immediately impressed by the well-fed bodies and healthy, shiny coats on the dogs I cared for, so of course I assumed Americans had some magical secret for caring for their dogs' physical needs. After I opened the Dog Psychology Center in South Los Angeles and began rehabilitating dogs, I trusted the rules and guidelines I was given for vaccination. And at the time, I genuinely believed I was providing the best life possible for my dogs. Today, I look back and wonder if, even with all my good intentions and what I thought was the right information, I wasn't inadvertently harming them.

With the invention of the smallpox vaccine in 1796, routine vaccinations have become synonymous with good health, for both humans and animals. Vaccines work on the principle of intentionally infecting an organism with one kind of disease or infection (the antigen) to prevent another one (the pathogen). But as early as the mid-1980s, a few courageous veterinary researchers, spearheaded by hematologist Dr. Jean Dodds, began to speak up and question the conventional wisdom. In 1991, the prestigious *Journal of the American*

Veterinary Association sent out an alert to those in animal health care stating that not only is there no proof that all yearly vaccinations are necessary, but that in many cases, vaccines given at an early age can provide lifelong immunity and don't necessarily need to be repeated.[6] In July 1997, more than five hundred veterinarians, scientists, physicians, immunologists, and epidemiologists convened at the first Veterinary Vaccines and Diagnostics symposium and agreed that vaccine boosters should not be given more often than every three years.[7] After more than twenty-five years of research, Dr. Ronald Schultz, a veterinary immunologist and professor at the University of Wisconsin-Madison School of Veterinary Medicine, presented evidence that additional vaccines given after a dog's one-year birthday are probably unnecessary and possibly harmful.[8] But even as a growing amount of scientific research pointed again and again to the redundancy and possible adverse affects of yearly vaccinations, the veterinary community as a whole seemed to have been "vaccinated" against adopting new guidelines. In fact, nearly all of America's sixty-five thousand veterinarians still promote annual vaccinations.[9] Why?

According to Marty Goldstein, one of America's most respected holistic veterinarians, the manufacturing of animal vaccines is a multibillion-dollar business for the handful of multinational pharmaceutical corporations that have a corner on the market. "Initially, those companies may have responded to health epidemics in an admirable fashion. Over time, they've evolved as any business does, pushing all the products they can, vying for market share, and creating new markets, sometimes by creating a market for vaccines to fight mild diseases better addressed with treatment. And veterinarians, well intentioned as they may be, have shared in those profits."[10] Somewhere along the line, according to Dr. Jean Dodds, founder of Hemopet, an animal blood bank, "we stopped practicing medicine and started pushing vaccines and pills."[11]

MEETING DR. MARTY

When I appeared on the *Martha Stewart Show* in April 2006, Martha spoke to me of her love and attachment to her beloved chow chows, and her equally impressive devotion to her holistic veterinarian, Dr. Martin "Marty" Goldstein. I was intrigued, because for many years now, I have been gradually adding more and more "alternative" therapies such as massage and acupuncture to my dogs' health-care regimens, and Dr. Marty, a graduate of Cornell University's prestigious Veterinary College, offered a philosophy that seemed to mesh well with my own. To be honest, I think it's ironic that we call this kind of health care "alternative," when it actually has been used and proved effective over thousands and thousands of years, as opposed to Western medicine, which has only been around for a couple hundred.

Dr. Marty has a radio show on Sirius Satellite network called *Ask Martha's Vet,* and he contacted me about chatting with him on the air. Through that conversation we recognized in each other a shared passion for providing our animal companions with a lifestyle as close as possible to the one nature intended for them—both physically and psychologically. I was able to meet Dr. Marty in person after Daddy was treated for a canine transmissible venereal tumor in September of 2006. Although Daddy had passed through his chemotherapy with flying colors, had finally been neutered, and was declared cancer-free, I knew that the treatments he had undergone were lifesaving, but also very toxic to the body. When the *Dog Whisperer* show drove Daddy across country for some East Coast episodes, I used the opportunity to get an appointment at Dr. Marty's relaxing, comfortable Smith Ridge clinic in serene South Salem, New York. Dr. Marty, a wiry, athletic man with a twinkle in his eye and a wry sense of humor to complement his extensive intellect, examined Daddy and did a thorough blood workup. He then tailored a specific supplementation program just for

Daddy, including injectable homeopathic and anti-inflammatory vitamins. I believe Daddy's excellent health today is due in part to Dr. Marty's unique expertise.

While I was at Smith Ridge, Dr. Marty showed me the reams and reams of research he has gathered over the years, as well as photographs and case histories of animals that have been injured, diseased, and even killed by the very vaccines that are supposed to heal them. "I can't tell you how often a pet has been brought into our clinic with a history of telltale symptoms: fever, stiff or painful joints, lethargy, or lack of appetite," Dr. Marty writes in his excellent comprehensive 1999 guide, *The Nature of Animal Healing.* When Dr. Marty would offer a "guess" that the dog had been recently vaccinated, the owners would look at him as if he were a psychic. Just as often, Dr. Marty sees dogs and cats with chronic illnesses such as degenerative arthritis, enhanced allergies, oral ailments, kidney and liver failures, and even cancer. "Are the vaccines to blame? I can't prove that they are," Dr. Marty opines. "But when I began long ago to suspect the connection and changed my practice accordingly, an amazing thing often happened with those telltale symptoms. They began to go away."[12]

In 2003, the Canine Veterinary Task Force of the American Animal Hospital Association (AAHA) finally stepped up and faced the vaccination controversy head-on. The AAHA released an official report, amended in 2006, summarized in the following statements:

- No scientific evidence supports the recommendation made by drug companies that label their vaccines to be given annually.
- Overwhelming evidence indicates that vaccinations given after the age of six months can provide adequate protection for up to seven years and possibly for life.
- A strong recommendation was made to vaccinate no more often than every three years.[13]

Dr. Ronald Schultz and other experts extend those recommendations even further, pointing out that "no more often than" could also be interpreted to mean "never again." Schultz cites abundant research indicating that dogs properly immunized in puppyhood maintain lifetime immunity to hepatitis, distemper, and parvovirus. In fact, many vaccine critics charge that the "three-year interval" of the AAHA guidelines is an arbitrary number, perhaps chosen to appease worried veterinarians who fear lost vaccine revenues.[14] The revised 2006 AAHA Vaccination Guidelines divided vaccinations into three categories:

- Core: Vaccines that should be given to every dog
- Noncore: Optional vaccines that should be considered only if an individual dog's lifestyle or risk factors strongly warrant it
- Not Recommended: Vaccines not recommended by the AAHA under any circumstances

If you have connected with a veterinarian whose opinion you trust, then he or she should provide you with enough information and recommendations to make an informed decision about the vaccination schedule for your dog. One option offered by progressive veterinarians is antibody titer testing. A titer is a unit of measure, and an antibody titer shows approximately how much disease-fighting immunity is present in your dog's system at any given time. If your dog has plenty of antibodies in his blood, the titer level will be high—evidence that a vaccine is doing its job and your dog is enjoying a healthy level of immunity. A high titer is solid proof that your dog doesn't need a vaccine booster. But titer testing doesn't tell the whole story; a dog can show a low blood titer and still have good immunity. Still, Dr. Paula Terifaj calls titer testing "a step in the right direction" in the fight to curtail the practice of overvaccination.[15]

One area the new AAHA guidelines don't address is the vaccine

Core Vaccines	Distemper*
	Hepatitis (adenovirus-2)*
	Parvovirus*
	Rabies
	DHP—3 in 1 vaccine
Noncore Vaccines	Leptospirosis*
	Lyme*
	Bordetella (kennel cough)
	Parainfluenza
	May be considered on a regional basis where these diseases are known to be a true risk
Not Recommended	Adenovirus-1
	Coronavirus
	Giardia
	Crotalus atrox toxoid (rattlesnake)
	Pophyromonas (periodontal disease)

protocol for rabies. That's because rabies is the only core disease that can be transmitted to humans and thus is overseen by the Centers for Disease Control. Rabies is considered a serious health risk, and the fact that the handful of human cases reported every year are almost always the result of bites from rabid wildlife such as bats is good evidence that the rabies vaccine has done its job well in protecting pets and their owners. "Statistics prove that you are more likely to be hit by lightning than to contract rabies from the bite of a domestic dog," according to Dr. Paula Terifaj.[16] The law in most states requires rabies vaccination annually, although, as Dr. Marty says, "laws can change if enough logic and political clout are set against them. In New York, for example, the rabies vaccine was once an annual requirement; now it can be given once every three years."[17] If your vet is worried about giving your dog his mandated rabies vaccine for a valid medical reason—for instance, Dr. Marty cites a case of a ten-year-old dog named Maggie being treated for cancer and for whom he believed an unnecessary vaccine could be deadly—then he or she can mandate a titer to evaluate your dog's level of immunity to the rabies virus. The test results on Maggie showed her to have enough rabies immunity to last several lifetimes! These test results have no legal standing in most states,[18] but they can be helpful to you if you decide to challenge a state-mandated rabies booster. Dr. Terifaj suggests that your vet submit an official "letter of exemption" for your dog, stating clearly the medical conditions that put him at risk and providing any lab work, including titer results, to back up the challenge. Proactive owners and vets have saved many dogs from unnecessary and possibly harmful overvaccination using this method. Currently, Dr. Jean Dodds and Dr. Ronald Schultz have teamed up to develop and test five- and seven-year rabies vaccines. According to Dr. Dodds, "This is one of the most important projects in veterinary medicine. It will benefit all dogs by providing evidence that protection from rabies vaccination lasts at least five years, thereby avoiding unnecessary revaccination with its attendant risk of debilitating adverse reaction."[19]

A SPOONFUL OF SUGAR

"A spoonful of sugar helps the medicine go down," Disney's most famous magical nanny, Mary Poppins, warbled, and—metaphorically at least—the same applies to giving medication to your dog.

When an owner comes at a dog with an eyedropper or tablet or syringe, that dog has no way of knowing that the person is coming to help them. The only way the dog will perceive any kind of medication or grooming ritual as a positive is if the owner projects a positive, calm-assertive energy while giving it. Unfortunately, most of my clients share their all-too-human emotions of nervousness, worry, guilt, or tension when bringing medicines to their dogs. Then, when the dog shrinks away, barks, bites, growls, or shows any other sign of protest, the person compounds that negativity by adding frustrated and angry energy on top of it. No wonder the dog will come to associate anything to do with health care or grooming with a negative experience! Wouldn't you?

The most important thing to remember when giving medication to your dog is to approach it with a positive attitude. You are helping your dog! Don't feel sorry for him! If you have to go through a hands-on process, such as giving eardrops or clipping toenails, start with a walk to tire your dog out. Never give any kind of treatment to a dog in a high-energy state! Make sure you are relaxed as well. Next, create an association with a positive experience, such as a treat or a massage. If necessary, cover your dog's eyes to reduce any visual anxiety he might be having.

With ingestible medicine, remember rule number one: don't try to hide medication in your dog's regular food. Some dogs will become suspicious and will reject the food altogether. The clever ones will spit the pill out when they find it and you may not be the wiser. Instead, find a tasty treat that can surround the pill completely like soft cheese, peanut butter, or a cooked hot dog. If the medication can be given with food, offer the treat before feeding time when your dog is most hungry and likely to go for it. In rare cases, your vet will direct you to give the medicine on an empty stomach, and you may have to simply force it down. Once again, this takes a relaxed, tired dog in a calm-submissive state. Open the jaw, place the medication on the dog's tongue, and slide it backward over the base of his tongue. Unless you get the medication behind the tongue the dog will probably spit it out. Then follow the procedure with a massage or another reward that makes your dog feel relaxed and happy.

OUR VETS' SUGGESTIONS FOR GIVING MEDICATION

- Hide it in a treat—something soft and in one piece.
- If possible, choose the form of medicine—liquid or solid—that your dog takes better.
- Believe it or not, some dogs respond better to injections.
- Compounding pharmacies can flavor many medications into something more palatable.
- Always work with a relaxed, calm-submissive dog.
- Find a positive association for the experience such as massage, a treat, or a chew toy.
- Make sure your own energy is calm, assertive, and positive!

Vet Visit Blues

Betty is a wonderful, positive seventy-year-old grandmother who had been caring for Aussi, a dingo mix, for almost all of the dog's eight years. The two had become intensely bonded—especially during the time Aussi comforted Betty through two successful cancer treatments. The problem with Aussi was that she became violently defiant at the vet's office. After going through and failing with three vets in a row, Betty had yet to succeed in getting Aussi through even one routine checkup with blood work. In over five years, Aussi hadn't even had her nails clipped! Betty's daughter-in-law Dianne told me that Betty would start getting anxious the week before Aussi's vet visits. By the time the appointment arrived, Betty had worked herself into a worse state of anxiety than Aussi!

Since my area of expertise is behavior, not medicine, many of the cases I'm called in to handle involving vets usually have to do with a dog's anxiety about getting there. It makes sense for a dog that hasn't been properly prepared for a vet visit to have anxiety. After all, he is going into a new situation with strange humans who will want to touch him in unfamiliar ways. The scents in any vet's office can send off signals to a dog that there is something to fear behind the examining room door. That's because when dogs are afraid, they sometimes express their anal glands, and every dog knows exactly what that scent means. Think about it—that would be like asking a friend of yours who has no knowledge of horror movies to stand outside a theater where a slasher film is playing. Hearing the screams from inside, how could that person know that there really isn't murder and mayhem going on inside? In essence, it's your job as a responsible owner to let your dog know that "it's only a movie" inside—not a real threat to his safety.

The most crucial thing to remember is that your dog has no cognitive means of understanding what a veterinarian does, although he will immediately recognize positive, calm-assertive, healing energy. This is why your choice of a vet is so vital—especially a vet who is willing to meet with your dog before any medical work is done. A balanced dog is curious and naturally wants to hang out with new people who have good energy. If a dog meets his new vet in a relaxed, casual situation, then he'll begin his relationship with that person associating his or her scent with relaxation.

But being comfortable with the environment of the veterinary office is important, too. I always advise my clients to bring their dogs to the veterinary waiting room a few times before an exam is necessary, preferably at the end of a nice long walk. While the owner sits down in a chair, has a relaxing cup of coffee, and reads a magazine, the veterinary techs and assistants can give the dog water and a treat.

This allows the dog to become comfortable with the scents, the sounds, and the cast of characters of the vet's office while understanding that no harm will come to him when he's there. When you come back to the office for the real exam, you and your dog will already have the routine down pat!

Keep in mind that your attitude as the dog's pack leader is the most important factor in keeping him calm and collected in any new situation. Many owners worry, stress out, and anticipate the worst, long before they even leave the house for their dog's appointment. Your dog always mirrors your energies in these situations, and you can actually create the very situation you fear.

With Betty and Aussi, I first had to tackle Betty's worried, fearful energy, and to get her to see the huge role her own anxiety was playing in Aussi's stress. To get Betty in touch with her calm-assertive side, I asked her to hearken back to the state of mind she was in when she was fighting her own cancer. As I spoke these words, I could see her expression changing, from anxious and weak, to determined and strong. Instantly, she understood what she had been doing wrong. Next, I showed Betty how to give Aussi a good, proper "pack walk" before the vet appointment. As always, a dog that has been exercised is able to release any pent-up energy he may have developed during the day and is always more relaxed and receptive to unfamiliar circumstances. Bringing a dog into a stressful situation without walking him first is like taking a toddler who has eaten candy and skipped his nap into a fancy restaurant. By walking Aussi—and especially, by making the vet's office the destination of the walk—Betty calmed her down and also gave the dog a sense of purpose about where they were going.

At Dr. Gail Renehan's office, I helped Aussi get up on the examining table while Betty stood by. It was instantly clear to me that Aussi was not in an aggressive state—she was in a state of sheer panic.

Even before anything would happen, she would start to whine and scream as if she was being tortured. The humans around her would feel bad and get even more stressed, and the situation would escalate.

I had Betty in the exam room with Dr. Renehan and me, even though normally I would want to remove the owner so the dog does not use the owner's energy to gain more power. In this case, however, it was important for me that Betty witness the transformation. It took us a very long time to put a muzzle on Aussi—but I made Betty see the importance of staying calm and patient throughout the process, so Aussi knew the humans were not going to give up and back away, like they had in the past. It took work—but for the first time in eight years, Aussi got her blood work done, she got a rectal temperature, and she even got her nails clipped. The point was, we didn't give up. Betty got the message. "Today," she said afterward, "Aussi didn't win."

But of course, in the long run, Aussi did win, after all. She had taken care of Betty during Betty's medical treatments; now Betty was finally able to look out for her beloved dog's health. To ensure that Aussi's behavior at the vet continued to improve, I gave Betty the assignment of taking Aussi to the vet's office on a regular basis—not for any reason except to visit. The office staff would give her cookies, water, and attention; she'd get to know that environment as a place of warm, friendly associations. This would also help Betty get over her sense of dread every time an appointment was on the horizon, a dread she was infecting Aussi with, which only increased her anxiety.

I am happy to report that Betty's perseverance has worked. She followed my prescription of regular social visits to Dr. Renehan's office. When she finally did take Aussi to the vet again, Aussi submitted right away, without a struggle! Betty and Aussi are proof that an assertive pack leader can turn any negative into a positive.

PREPARING YOUR DOG FOR THE VET OR THE GROOMER

1. Introduce your dog to the vet and groomer ahead of time, if possible, in a relaxed, nonprofessional context. Let your dog check out this new person using the no-touch, no-talk, no-eye-contact method, until he seems at ease with him or her.

2. Take your dog to the location where he will be examined or groomed at least once in advance of the actual appointment. Arrive at the place at the end of a long walk, if possible. Let the assistants in the waiting room revive your dog with water and treats, while you rest and read a magazine. Your goal is to create an association between that environment and relaxation.

3. At home, make sure your dog is familiar with the ways he will be touched during a medical exam or grooming session. "Play doctor" a few times when your dog is tired and relaxed, creating a pleasant association for the tools and implements (clippers, blow dryers) as well as scents (alcohol smells, shampoo essences) he will encounter by providing massage, treats, and positive energy.

4. Exercise your dog before every visit! In addition, park a few blocks away and take a ten-minute or longer walk to the location.

5. Monitor your own energy before, during, and after the visit! You are the number one most important source for the way your dog interprets his world. If you are tense, he is going to be tense. Jog around the block, practice yoga, or

listen to soothing music before the visit—do whatever it takes so that your own energy remains calm and assertive at all times!

EMERGENCIES

When it comes to emergencies, calm-assertive energy is of even greater importance. If your dog has an unexpected accident or medical episode, he will be counting on you to make him feel safe. When owners are panicking, crying, and flooding the dog with their own anxieties and worst-case-scenario images, how can the dog expect to relax and accept treatment? Accidents can happen, and we must be prepared for them, both psychologically and physically. Psychologically, I advise my clients to pretend they are paramedics; professionals whose livelihood revolves around staying calm in the face of the very worst disasters. Use the power of your imagination to get you through the crisis period. Once your dog is safely in the hands of professionals, or after the immediate emergency has passed, call a friend or other family member, someone you trust and in front of whom you can share your deepest feelings. Only then are you allowed to collapse.

You are less likely to panic in the face of an emergency, however, if you are prepared. Consider learning pet CPR and pet first aid, classes for which are available in most areas. This training is very valuable and will pay off right when you need it most. You also should keep a special medicine kit just for your pet and have it well stocked with supplies.

YOUR DOG'S FIRST-AID KIT

Alcohol swabs

Cold pack

Eyedroppers

Flashlight

Gauze pads

Gloves

Paperwork

Contact info for your regular vet

Contact info and map/directions for a 24-hour emergency
    vet

Your dog's medical history

Styptic powder

Thermometer

Towel or blanket

Tweezers

PHYSICAL OR PSYCHOLOGICAL?

We only take cases for the *Dog Whisperer* series after the owners have assured us and signed a waiver stating that they have consulted with a vet and ruled out medical causes for their dog's behavior problem. Every now and then, however, I come across a case in which I have to ask myself, "Is there something physical or neurological going on here?" Usually, I can tell pretty quickly whether or not to refer the owners to a specialist, but it's important for all of us—professionals and owners alike—to remember that dogs can't verbally describe to us any physical strangeness or discomfort they are feeling. In fact, in

the animal kingdom, "admitting to" pain or weakness through behavior or body language is a good way to get yourself killed; therefore, dogs are more likely to mask their own physical discomfort
than to advertise it. It takes persistent observation on the part of all
family members to try to interpret their dog's physical and behavioral messages to make sure they're not actually cries for help.

A dog that begins to develop behavioral problems over a rela-
tively short period of time without a change in environment
should always be evaluated for an organic cause for the change
before you send him off to behavior boot camp. If your calm-
submissive dog suddenly begins to growl or snap or starts acting
weird, you need the help of your vet to determine if your dog is suffering from a medical problem. Arthritic dogs or any dog experiencing pain can start to show signs of aggression. Some older dogs
may start to lose touch with their surroundings as a result of hearing or vision loss. Seniors can also experience "senior moments"—
wandering around the house aimlessly, or they may begin to poop
and pee in the house. If the behavioral problem is coupled with a
change in eating or drinking habits, vomiting or diarrhea, inconti-
nence, or other physical changes such as rapid gain or loss in
weight or thinning hair coat, it's time to go in for a physical exam
and a blood and urine panel to rule out diseases such as diabetes,
hypothyroidism, or Addison's disease, to name a few. Dr. Charles
Rinehimer shared with me a case in which one of his nurses had a
previously sweet-tempered husky that, out of the blue, began snarl-
ing at her three-year-old son and showing dog aggression. She also
noted he was always ravenously hungry. A blood panel revealed he
had hypothyroidism. Once on thyroid meds, he returned to his
lovable old self.

HINTS FOR SEPARATING PHYSICAL FROM BEHAVIORAL ISSUES

Questions to ask:
- Have there been changes in the environment?
  Construction?
  New furniture?
  New pet?
  Person or pet who has died or moved away?
- When does the behavior occur? In what situation or with what particular stimulus?
- Is the behavior consistent or intermittent?

Rule out medical problems with a thorough exam and blood work; seek a specialist if needed.

CONSIDER THE ALTERNATIVES

As I've mentioned earlier, I think it's ironic that we consider solutions like herbal remedies, vitamins and other nutritional supplements, homeopathy, acupuncture, chiropractic, and massage to be "alternative" medicine. These are the treatments that were used with excellent results and few or no side effects for thousands of years before the first modern-age "pill" was even invented! Of course, modern medicines are responsible for saving the lives of many of our pets. Daddy underwent chemotherapy that saved his life. Medicines such as antibiotics and cortisone can bring our dogs back from the brink. But as Dr. Marty writes in *The Nature of Animal Healing,* "[d]rugs are essentially suppressive mechanisms. Typically, they suppress the symptoms of ill health that make you feel sick, rather than grapple with whatever might have provoked those symptoms in the first place."[20]

For long-term wellness, I am a big believer in remedies that treat the whole animal—body, mind, and spirit—rather than just the short-term problem. By giving dogs a lifetime of good nutrition and exercise for their bodies, plus discipline for their minds and affection for their spirits, we are allowing them to live as fulfilled, balanced dogs. A dog with a balanced spirit is a happy dog, and therefore a dog whose natural defenses are firing on all cylinders. To me, a dog balanced in body, mind, and spirit is much more likely to be able to avoid most disease and illness in the first place.

At the Dog Psychology Center, we try to provide everything the dogs need to fulfill the triangle of body-mind-spirit. Of course, we give the pack outdoor exercise—and lots of it! In addition to our daily walks and Rollerblade sessions, we play vigorous games of fetch in our own dog park. We offer pool games, obstacle courses, and as often as we can, we hike in the Santa Monica Mountains or run in the surf of the scenic beaches along the California coast. Sometimes we take the herding breeds to sheepherding class, or do agility work with the terrier breeds. Imagine what this kind of lifestyle does for a dog's mental as well as physical health, as opposed to the dog that lives a life indoors most of the day, with an occasional trip to the end of the street to pee and poop. Mealtime at the Center is a meaningful ritual, where we offer natural, fresh, tasty, and nutritious food. And for the older dogs, dogs with behavior problems, or dogs with any kind of chronic illness or physical issue, we provide homeopathic remedies, regular therapeutic massage, and acupuncture sessions a minimum of once every two weeks.

Perhaps you are reading this and thinking, "Well, of course Cesar is into all these far-out treatments. He lives in California, where everyone is practicing those wacky things." I can understand how those of you who have not been exposed to acupuncture, chiropractic therapy, or homeopathy might think of it as voodoo, so I encourage you to investigate it on your own. For a wide range of symptoms from chronic pain and arthritis, to lethargy and depression, to allergies and head colds, in the hands of the right practitioner, the medicine you call "alternative" today could become your effective, affordable, and side-effect-free option to pharmaceutical medications that make you sleepy, nauseous, or overweight. The truth is, the entire world seems to be coming back around to the usefulness of these methods. In Europe, nearly half of British doctors refer some of their patients to homeopaths. In France, almost every pharmacy boasts a homeopathic section.[21] Here in the United States, many mainstream insurance companies are now covering acupuncture and chiropractic sessions in their policies.

My own family benefits greatly from integrative medicine practices. Since Ilusion's role in our business is more intellectual, she does things like massage to help ease the stress in her mind so she can think freely and make clear decisions. Andre and Calvin are very involved in sports, so they have acupuncture to help relax their muscles and keep the positive energy flowing. Daddy gets acupuncture every two weeks for his arthritis; he also takes mushroom pills to help prevent cancer and eats an organic raw food diet. I take acupuncture because I have a really physical job; I'm up on my feet all day, I carry heavy weights, plus I'm exposed to a lot of different energies, including people who are upset or frustrated. The treatments keep me stress-free as well as neutral and centered. I would never encourage my own family to engage in a practice that I did not thoroughly research and find both safe and effective.

Just as when selecting a family physician or veterinarian, choosing an excellent homeopath, chiropractor, or acupuncturist is vital to the success of any therapy. Make sure you get plenty of references; investigate the doctor's education, experience, and licensing; and talk to current patients before you bring your family or your pets to any new practitioner. Interview the practitioner in advance, and make sure you agree with his or her energy, goals, and philosophy. And of course, make sure you discuss any alternative therapies with your family physician and/or veterinarian. Some homeopathic remedies may not be compatible with the pharmaceuticals your dog is already taking.

HEALING AND ENERGY

Anyone who has watched my show or read my books knows how important I consider the concept of energy to be when it comes to the way Mother Nature has created her world. Throughout humankind's history, nearly every system of medicine except modern Western medicine could be described as "vitalistic"; that is, they've operated on the principles that good physical and mental health depends on an equilibrium of the body, mind, and spirit, and that disease is caused by some sort of energy deficiency, blockage, or imbalance within one or more of those three elements. Acupuncture, which was invented by the Chinese as long ago as four thousand years, operates on the principle that energy circulates in the body through channels, which they call meridians. When a meridian is blocked, tiny acupuncture needles inserted at specific points along those meridians send a "charge" throughout the body, which opens up the blockage and allows the energy to flow freely again. In this way, the body can heal itself the way nature intended. In my experience, as well as the experience of many of the veterinarians with whom I consult on a regular basis, animals respond to this type of healing even better and more quickly than human beings often do. Perhaps it's because they don't have our Western intellectual skepticism to contend with, since no one has yet to demonstrate in a scientific way how acupuncture works. Happily, dogs aren't aware of this fact. They aren't looking for the graphs and charts of scientific evidence. They just feel the instant relief and relaxation.

Luna receives acupuncture

Lost and Lonely Luna

Luna was a one-and-a-half-year-old Lab mix with a debilitating fear of just about everything. Her owner, Abel Delgado, chose her from the pound for that very reason. "I went to the Pasadena Humane Society and there was this little dog about eighteen pounds, absolutely terrified in the back corner of a kennel. She was probably the most broken dog in the entire shelter. I thought, 'Wow, she really needs a lot of help.' I realize now she reminds me of what I was like when I was a kid." Although earlier in the book, I showed you how to avoid adopting animals with these kinds of acute issues, Abel is an example of the kind of person who knows what he was getting into. He made a conscious decision that he was going to do whatever it took to rehabilitate Luna. But after several months of trying everything he could think of to bring her out of her shell, Abel decided Luna and he needed professional help to accomplish the job. That's when he called me in.

Luna was definitely the worst case of fear anxiety that I have ever treated in my career. Although I can't know this for sure, I believe Luna was taken from her mother far too early. She wasn't addressing the world the way a dog does—nose, eyes, ears—she was all ears, eyes—never even using her nose. Loud noises such as a truck going by or children playing would terrify her, but then so would natural sounds such as birds singing and the wind. If my theory about Luna being weaned much too soon is true, then she is an example of how important it is that a pup be raised with its littermates and by its mother until two months of age. Luna simply had no idea how to be a dog!

In addition to socializing Luna with the pack and letting the other canines at my center teach her what being a dog is all about, I gradually exposed Luna to the various situations that used to intimidate her. I also decided she was a perfect candidate for the kind of natural healing that acupuncture can provide, since acupuncture—far more than massage or tranquilizers—has the ability to actually release stored trauma from the body. Before her first acupuncture session, Luna was wound up like a spring. She didn't seem to be able to let go of the tension in her body, even when she slept! Of course, I took her for an extra walk before the session, so we drained as much energy as we could. But the instant acupuncturist Dr. Audra MacCorkle placed the first needle into her forehead, Luna's tension seemed to escape her body like air leaving an overfilled balloon. Remember, acupuncture needles are very tiny, do not draw blood, and for most animals and people, don't hurt when they are inserted. By the end of her session, Luna was sound asleep, more relaxed than any of us had ever seen her before. If you are able to view this episode of the *Dog Whisperer* program, you can see the transformation take place on tape, right before your eyes.[22]

After two months at the Center, I took Luna to Abel at the

Harmony Project, where he conducts an orchestra of young inner-city musicians. For the first time in her life, Luna was able to relax and enjoy the music and the positive, healing presence of the wonderful and talented kids Abel gets to work with. Now, nearly a full year later, Abel says Luna is a brand-new, confident, and happy girl, finally able to enjoy life to the fullest. She still sees Dr. MacCorkle for massage, but Abel was so impressed with Luna's response to acupuncture that he got a referral and now gets treatments regularly himself. Of course, in most dogs, vigorous exercise alone will remove pent-up or negative energy. But for dogs like Luna and Gavin, a retired ATF (Alcohol, Tobacco, and Firearms) dog with a canine form of post-traumatic stress disorder, a treatment like acupuncture is the only surefire method I know for removing the toxic black ball of fear that keeps them from moving forward with their lives. Acupuncture, homeopathy, massage, and chiropractic work with the body and spirit, not against them. They allow the body to heal itself, from the inside out.

Of course, natural therapies require more dedication and personal attention than simply prescribing a pill. For example, if you put an older dog that has arthritis in a warm water bath with Epsom salts, let him relax, then give him a long therapeutic massage, it will be more effective and far less toxic to his liver than giving him a drug for the arthritis, but it will take much more time and attention from you. I believe this is an advantage, however, because when the treatments take longer, the animal also gets the benefit of his bond with you and whatever professional healer you might be working with. In nature, dogs lick each other to help heal each other's wounds, and sleep close together to share both bodily warmth and energy. It's in a dog's DNA to receive healing directly from another animal. And no energy is more important to your dog than the energy of those who love him the most—his human family.

8

Dogs and the Family Life Cycle

Helping Your Dog Survive the Ups and Downs of Family Life

Cesar working with children

"I think this marriage can be saved if I am absolutely convinced that Wendell will not hurt anyone." Tyler Shepodd's voice was low and serious as he confided in the *Dog Whisperer* director, Sue Ann Fincke, and our cameras. "If it doesn't work out, I understand that it could be the end of the relationship."

At the time this conversation took place, Tyler had just canceled the date of his wedding to his fiancée, Patricia Robbins. Though he was deeply in love with Patricia and she with him, theirs was definitely a case where love simply wasn't enough. The problem? Patricia's unpredictable Lab–pit bull mix, Wendell. A single nurse with a melting heart for all creatures in need, Patricia had rescued Wendell and added him to her "pack," then consisting of just her and her better-behaved chow mix, Ted. At first, Ted and Wendell fought constantly, but after a few years, a grudging friendship developed between the two. Not so between Wendell and Patricia's neighbors, who accused Wendell of chasing children and pets, and who had even taken Patricia to court for not being able to control him. When Patricia started dating Tyler, she put off introducing the man she thought might be "the one" to her dogs at home because of her nagging worries about Wendell's volatile temperament. But when Tyler popped the question, she knew she had no choice but to introduce him to her dogs. The meeting was a disaster, as she had foreseen—Wendell snapped at Tyler and cornered him in the kitchen. After several similarly violent incidents, Tyler laid down the law. Wendell simply could not be a part of their future family.

"If it was just Ted, she'd be living here, we'd be married by now. I just can't put my neighbors and myself at risk by having Wendell living here," Tyler admitted.

CAN THIS MARRIAGE BE SAVED?

Modern families are continually changing and adapting, but in most cases, a family or familial group starts with the commitment of two or more people, often in marriage. This commitment becomes the beginning of every family's life cycle. Although plenty has been written about stepparenting of children in blended families, not a lot of information is available about how to integrate a dog into a new couple's lifestyle. In my opinion, this time is crucial in a family's formation, and learning to share pack leadership of a dog can be an important first step toward creating a healthy permanent relationship.

Patricia and Tyler's case wasn't the only one where I've been called in to help when a dog was threatening to come between members of a new couple, but it certainly had all the earmarks of being one of the most serious. Wedding arrangements had been canceled, guests called and told to stay home, and Patricia's dress hung forlornly in her closet. During her interview with our director, Patricia sobbed constantly, and the taciturn Tyler seemed depressed and resigned. They were at an impasse, and no marriage counselors could help them. The pressure was on me as I sat down to hear their story.

The unhealthy dynamics were instantly clear: Tyler was fearful and distrustful of Wendell—especially since Wendell was a pit bull, a breed he was prejudiced against—and Patricia had created a "story" in her head that she had to give Wendell everything he wanted, because she was his protector. Wendell was reading all of these emotions, and they had combined to make him extremely powerful, dominant, and possessive. From the moment the consultation began, Wendell was crawling all over both Patricia and a very nervous Tyler, and he growled at me when I started to correct him. "You have a very possessive boyfriend," I told Patricia—and she knew I wasn't referring to Tyler! "If you were in control of your dog, he wouldn't disrespect anybody. What he's telling you right now is that you belong to him."

Like so many of my clients who have problem dogs, Patricia was completely unaware of how her own unresolved issues were being projected onto her dog, and in turn, onto her relationship with Tyler. I saw that her tears seemed out of proportion to the current situation, so I asked her to go back into her past and tell me what she was holding on to. Patricia wept again as she described being a child, witnessing dogs being kicked and abused in her family, and watching a dog die while tied to a post in the backyard while feeling helpless to do anything about it. I asked the reticent Tyler to be more supportive of Patricia as she lived through this horror again, while, at the same time, firmly requesting that Patricia please come out of her night-mare and join us here in the present! She was holding on to the past and making herself a victim—and dragging all the dogs and the peo-ple in her life down with her. I had to prove to her that the present could be different—and Wendell was going to help me.

Because Patricia had overprotected Wendell and kept him away from all other dogs except Ted, he had no social skills whatsoever. For-tunately, dogs are born to be social, and the ability to get along with other dogs is buried deep inside every one of them. I brought in two balanced pit bulls from my pack, Daddy and Preston, and then went to get Wendell from the laundry room. He threw a huge tantrum at first, but it only took minutes for him to release that toxic energy. When I brought him out to meet my dogs, Patricia started to panic, but as she saw Wendell beginning to relax while Daddy and Preston sniffed him, she too calmed down. By the end of the session in the backyard, Patri-cia was willing to admit, "There's possibilities." For her, that was a huge step forward, and I began to see that Wendell could be a very im-portant part of Patricia and Tyler's marriage. If the two of them could work together to help rehabilitate him, they would both be letting go of blocks that were also getting in the way of their human intimacy.

A week later, Patricia, Tyler, and Wendell came to the Dog Psychol-ogy Center to continue our work together. This time, I had a challenge for Tyler—to walk through my pack of thirty-seven dogs (includ-ing nine pit bulls!)—while remaining calm and assertive. Tyler did great—and I was able to show him that by mistrusting Wendell, he was contributing to Wendell's aggression toward him. Next, Patricia and Wendell joined us with the pack. Patricia was a wreck at first, but I counseled her to recall her experiences as a nurse, as well as a self-help workshop she once took where she was able to walk through fire. I saw a different side of Patricia that day—no less caring and gentle, but no longer the helpless victim she had played a week earlier. I coached both Tyler and Patricia as they walked Wendell through the Dog Psychology Center's rough-and-tumble industrial neighborhood. They were happily astounded to be able to pass by a gauntlet of unbalanced dogs—both behind fences and off-leash—and still keep Wendell next to them, happily calm and submissive. This was the day that the light-bulb really went off for both of them. Patricia apologized to both Tyler and Wendell for keeping them apart for so long and acknowledged how her fearfulness and negative energy had contributed to Wendell's behavior problems. Tyler was able to show a softer, less defensive side of himself to both Patricia and her dogs. "I think we can set a date again," Tyler affirmed, "and set this one in stone."

Before we make a commitment to another human being, it would be a wise thing for all of us to look closely at the relationships we have with our dogs, because our dogs are our mirrors. Any issues or problems we have with the animals that live with us will almost always be reflected in the relationships we have with the people

Wendell, Tyler, Patricia, and Ted

around us, too. Like Patricia, many of my clients tend to hold on to the past and project those ancient wounds onto those who surround them in the present. If you are unwilling to open your relationship with your dog to include your intended, then you have not totally accepted that person as a member of your pack, and you have some serious work to do before you tie the knot. Remember, when a dog is part of a family, everyone in the family has to play the role of equal pack leader. Look at your dog's behavior and ask yourself, "What part of myself am I still holding back? What issue from the past am I still holding on to?"

INTRODUCING YOUR DOG TO YOUR SIGNIFICANT OTHER

1. Include your dogs in your relationship from the beginning.

2. Introduce your dogs to your intended using the no-touch, no-talk, no-eye-contact method, and let them get to know him or her at their own pace. Both you and your potential partner or spouse should be familiar with the concept of calm-assertive energy.

3. Ease your significant other into the role of co—pack leader early in the relationship. Let him or her walk your dogs, together with you, then on his or her own, as frequently as possible.

4. Empower your partner with your dog. Don't take sides, and don't hoard the ownership of your dogs for yourself, because you'll risk making your partner the "outsider" in the pack.

5. Have frequent family meetings about the rules, bound-aries, and limitations you will both adhere to as the joint pack leaders of your home.

6. Don't bring your dogs into any human conflicts, or use them as buffers to your human intimacy.

A HOUSE DIVIDED—WHEN THE DOGS DON'T GET ALONG

"It's like having two kids from a different marriage, and you're fight-ing over the kids," Judi sighed. Judi Faye, a singer-actress, had met Burl Barer, a successful true-crime writer, over the Internet, and the two of them clicked as if they'd known each other all their lives. Both being mature, professional adults with productive independent lives and careers of their own, their five-month-long relationship shouldn't have faced any hurdles, but there was one, or rather two: Judi's seven-year-old pit bull, Tina, and Burl's two-year-old pit-bull, Isis. From the moment they met, the dogs wanted to kill each other, and time had only made the situation worse, not better. "We could split because of this. I hope not, but we could," Judi admits.

When I met Judi and Burl, it was clear that they were a great match and very attached to each other, and they definitely made each other laugh! One of the most interesting things that came up in the consul-tation was that Burl told me that, in his work, he deals with a lot of criminals with antisocial behavior. He explained that their brains don't work the same way that ours do, which makes them able to kill other human beings. I helped Burl see the parallel with dogs. When dogs are in an antisocial state, they don't have any "moral" problems with killing another being—a dog, a cat, or even a human. Doesn't matter how much we love them, or how much they love us. The best way to introduce two dogs with poor social skills that don't know each other is to walk them side by side, as a pack. It's best that they move forward together, and eventually surrender to each other. Never introduce two strange dogs head-on—that makes them gladiators. Eye contact between two dogs with aggressive tendencies is a likely way to provoke a fight. The nose should come first, in any dog-dog meeting.

"That's interesting," Burl mused. "Because whenever I meet with a sociopath, I always try to move to the side of him. It seems to calm him down." I could tell Burl's wheels were spinning and he was beginning to understand that dogs have a different psychology than humans. "Whatever it takes, if I have to approach my dog differently, I'm willing to do it," he said. "Whatever it takes to make this work."

I was glad Burl took that can-do attitude, because I had to tell him that, at the moment anyway, he was the source of Isis's red-zone imbalance. Isis's other issues, such as her separation anxiety and her unpredictable charging, told me that she was an insecure-dominant dog, and she was the one trying to hurt Tina, not the other way around. Burl's presence was empowering that behavior, so I asked him to wait outside while I gradually reintroduced Tina and Isis. Of course, since it was clear that Isis wanted to kill Tina, I made sure she was wearing a muzzle at all times. Though Isis kept trying to get to her rival, I manipulated Isis so Tina was able to smell her from the rear. Isis had never had rules, boundaries, or limitations, and she had never before had a human who had blocked her from trying to kill another dog *before* the attack began.

I strongly believe that the walk is not only our simplest but our best tool to begin solving most behavior problems. The way dogs in nature become a team and develop strong bonds is by walking together, so my next step was to get Isis and Tina to walk together as a pack. After I was comfortable that both of them were in a submissive state of mind, I passed the leash to Judi, to empower her to be the leader of these two female dogs. By the time Burl came into the picture, the two dogs already had two great human energies influencing them. I told Burl to relax, ignore, and imagine he was going to interview one of his subjects. When using his "professional" energy, Burl proved to have outstanding skills handling the dogs.

I gave Burl and Judi instructions to walk their dogs together as a pack every day; to remember their dogs were animals, not children; and to keep Isis's muzzle on for the time being, until they saw a consistent change in her energy. But what Burl and Judi ended up doing was what I encourage all my clients to do—to take my suggestions as foundations upon which to build their own solutions. Burl cleverly used the concept of nose-eyes-ears and his dog's natural curiosity to come up with a brilliant strategy: "I brought Isis into Judi's house, with Tina's scent all over the place, but I put Tina in another room. And I kept switching them. And I'd put each dog's scent on me and then play with the other. When Judi came back, both dogs met her at the door."

Burl's strategy was a sound one, especially since the couple had already begun desensitizing the dogs toward each other by walking together. Burl played on the fact that dogs aren't born to be aggressive, but they are born to be curious. By cleverly using scent as a motivator, he was able to make the dogs realize that they could all be one big happy family. "Now they have each other to play with when we go out," Judi bubbled. "When we come home, they're in the garage smoking cigarettes and playing cards," Burl added.

Two years later, Burl and Judi, Tina and Isis all share a house together in Van Nuys, California. "Nothing that really is important happens overnight," Judi told our crew. "You have to work at it, no matter what it is. And we cared enough about our dogs, and each other, to say okay, we have to do something."

I'm happy to say that Burl and Judi aren't the only happy endings in the romance department of the Dog Whisperer! Patricia and Tyler are

Judi and Burl watch as Cesar walks Tina and Isis

now Mr. and Mrs. Tyler Shepodd, and they currently are enjoying a loving and balanced life together with Ted and Wendell. "A lot has changed," says Patricia. "I was able to let go of so much. Today I put Tyler first. I trust him with the dogs, he's a great pack leader, and by trusting him, we've grown closer." "Thank you, Cesar, it's been great," adds Tyler. "We're getting better every day. We're learning every day."

POINTERS FOR BLENDED FAMILIES WITH DOGS

1. Empower each other as pack leaders for all dogs. As soon as possible, stop thinking of your pets as "my dog" and "her/his dog."
2. Make sure to introduce the dogs on neutral territory.
3. Don't let the dogs meet face-to-face. If they are calm, let

them meet each other by the smelling ritual. If they aren't balanced, walk them on either side of you until they relax and their body language is submissive.

4. Use the power of scent to get the dogs used to each other before they meet. Make sure the scent is associated with something positive, like food, exercise, or affection.

5. Keep rules consistent for all members of the pack.

6. Don't favor one dog over the other, and don't create a competition between the dog you came with and the dog your partner came with.

7. Remember, your dogs reflect your own energy! Don't drag the dogs into any conflict between humans.

THE BLESSED ARRIVAL: DOGS AND THE NEW BABY

Cosmo, a handsome, high-energy chow mix, was four years old when his owner, Armin Rahm, met his future wife, Victoria. The couple married after a whirlwind courtship and Victoria and her Lab mix, Boo, came to live in Armin's Southern California home. Everyone seemed to get along at first, and the newlyweds rejoiced when they discovered that Victoria was pregnant. But gradually, Cosmo's behavior began to change. It began with severe dog aggression on the walks. Whenever Cosmo saw another dog, he would immediately go into stalking mode, and it would be all Armin could do to hold him back. In the house, his behavior became more erratic toward Boo, and he was more rebellious than before. Two weeks before Victoria was due to deliver, the couple called me in. At this point, Cosmo had shown some aggression toward humans, and Victoria was understandably nervous about how Cosmos's new unpredictability would affect the new baby.

"It's just escalating at this point and I'm worried about bringing a child into this house with him not being consistent," Victoria told me. "On the walks, he's a terror." I asked Armin how he reacted when Cosmo misbehaved on the walks. "I'm in a calm state," he said—but Victoria was shaking her head no. I challenged him to come clean. "I guess at this point I'm frustrated," Armin sheepishly admitted. "That's good," I told him. "Don't hide who you are." The truth is, Cosmo already knew exactly how Armin was feeling. Another problem was that Armin was trying to reason with Cosmo *the name*, when in reality, Cosmo in his stalking mode was 100 percent Cosmo *the animal*. Armin needed to stop taking Cosmo's behavior so personally and begin to relate to him as animal-dog-chow-Cosmo, in that order.

The work ahead of me was clear. I had to make sure Cosmo and his owners were all balanced *before* the baby's arrival. Truth be told, Armin and Victoria were cutting things kind of close. I believe the time to deal with a dog's behavior problems is no less than nine months before you bring a new addition into your family.

It's vital to remember that infants can be especially vulnerable when there's an unbalanced dog in the house. Since babies smell different, sound different, and move differently from adult humans, a dog that's never before experienced a baby can find a new arrival strange and confusing. A dog may hear a crying baby and want to help by picking it up by the neck, the way it would a puppy. Or in the case of a dog with unaddressed aggression issues, a baby's small size and sudden movements may stimulate an unfulfilled prey drive. Often, new babies distract parents from paying attention to a dog that might have been an "only child" beforehand. Armin and Victoria admitted that Armin had been paying less attention to Cosmo during the time that his aggression had been escalating.

My first challenge was to help Victoria get over her fears, which were getting in the way of her being the awesome pack leader that I knew she could be. When my wife, Ilusion, was pregnant with my older son, Andre, she expressed all kinds of fears and "what-if's" about the baby being around my pack of rottweilers and pit bulls. It wasn't that her worries were unreasonable, but it was the uncertainty behind them that made her weak. I counseled her that whatever energy she was holding at the moment would become the energy of the baby when she held him in her arms. If she was afraid, the dogs would perceive the baby as being afraid, and that would make the baby weak. Ilusion learned how to walk through the pack with the proud energy of a pack leader, so that my infant sons would also be pack leaders by default. If I could offer the same help to Victoria and bring out the powerful pack leader inside of her, there would be no stopping her or her baby!

Victoria's walks with Cosmo went brilliantly, and she couldn't believe how her change in attitude instantly affected the dog's demeanor. But the source of the problem became clear once Armin took over. His knuckles grew white as he tightly gripped the leash, which he began forcefully jerking the moment he anticipated Cosmo's attack on the small dog I was walking. Of course, Cosmo reacted exactly as Armin feared he would. Dogs always agree with our state of mind, whether it is healthy or unstable. Armin's problem was that he was feeling bad about how Cosmo was behaving, and he was taking it very personally. He was also in denial about how much Cosmo's aggression frustrated and upset him. When I was able to point this out to him, the realization dawned. After a very successful session, I instructed the couple to leave the dogs with friends overnight before they brought the baby home, until I could return to show them how to properly introduce the dogs to the new arrival. I left them in peace to enjoy their last two quiet weeks before parenthood.

I was probably more excited than they were when I arrived at their home to meet new baby Lorelei, but first, I had to attend to business. I instructed Armin and Victoria to enter the room where the dogs were, but to create an invisible space around the baby, and

to send the dogs into the highest level of submission before they allowed them to get close. On a scale of one to ten excitement, the
dogs could not be any higher than level zero around the baby—they
had to know that "baby" means "be quiet, be gentle, and submit."
Another exercise I gave them to do was to place items of the baby's
clothing in areas of the house and watch closely how the dogs reacted to them. If they picked up those items with their teeth, that's
no good—they must correct that behavior. If they played with the
item or peed on it, that's no good, either. The goal was to condition
them to give space, respect, and submission for everything that belongs to Baby—to claim their space and create a protective bubble
around everything about her. I instructed the couple that, for the
first two weeks, the dogs should not be allowed to sniff the baby or
the baby's items from up close or to enter her room, in order to create that habit of respect. The dogs had to learn that the scent of
Lorelei meant a calm-submissive state of mind for them.

I returned to see how the new family was doing two weeks later,
at the end of their "homework" period. Mama Victoria was ecstatic
about how things were going. "It's more harmonious now. They're
mellow around her and they play, but they still kind of stay away."
"Both have given her the space. They seem to know that she's the
leader, or the coleader, with us," Armin added. Since the household
was adapting beautifully, I decided it was time to show the new parents how to incorporate the walk into their leadership rituals. By
putting Lorelei in her stroller and having the dogs follow behind, the
walk now became yet another way to communicate to the dogs that
the new baby was going to be their leader. That day, we made baby
Lorelei the youngest pack leader on the planet!

Recently, our crew returned to see how the family was doing two
years after I worked with them. I couldn't be more proud of the re-

sult. Cosmo's behavior problems have disappeared almost entirely, and if he ever does react to another dog on the street, the couple knows how to stop him in the moment and then move on. "It's not a big deal anymore," says Armin. Little Lorelei, now an adorable toddler, is embracing her role as pack leader and it's clear that the dogs follow her lead. In fact, her very first word was "Doggy!" And perhaps most wonderful of all, Victoria has discovered what a natural pack leader she is, and how much she loves working with dogs. She's used her maternity leave to volunteer for the Humane Society and is about to graduate from Animal Behavior College. "People don't understand that the people have to do the work, that it's not just someone coming into your house and magically clicking a button and making it all better," she says. "So I want to be out there to help people and let them know that these are the steps you have to take, and this is what you do." Victoria, I am so proud of you and your whole family. You truly have become a model "family pack."

Victoria, Armin, and Cesar work with Cosmo

The Crying Game

Even when we do our best to prepare our dogs for Baby's arrival, we must remember that they still will reflect our own energy back to us. If we're nervous, unsure, or frustrated, and project any of those negative energies, our own mood plus the strangeness of the new pack member can combine to create stress in a dog—particularly a dog that is anxious or dominant herself.

Before the birth of their daughter, Sophia Grace, Derek, and Stephanie Clay had enjoyed a happy, mellow life with their pack of three dogs—German shepherd mix Rocky, keeshond Zorro, and rottweiler Goliath. The couple were dog lovers and fans of *Dog Whisperer*—meaning they were devotees of the exercise, discipline, and affection formula. All their dogs got plenty of primal walking, and the couple did the right thing by preparing the dogs for the new baby in ways that I often recommend—by first bringing in a doll that cried; next, bringing in pieces of Sophia's clothes from the hospital so the dogs could be familiar with her scent. Though lower-energy Zorro and Goliath easily welcomed Sophia into the home, Rocky was another story. From the moment Sophia arrived, Rocky began a painful whining that wouldn't let up, no matter what the couple tried to do. Stephanie tried to describe the whining to me: "It's a mix of crying, yelping, whining, squeaking, and barking. I think the first week, he didn't let up once." The whining started when Sophia first came into the house, but it soon spilled over into their frequent pack walks and any rides they might take in the car. Every time the baby cried, Rocky's yelps would escalate to the point where he'd sometimes become hoarse. When Rocky's anxious outbursts started to affect the other two dogs, the couple went to their veterinarian, who prescribed tranquilizers for the dog—acepromazine, Clomicalm, Benadryl, and even Xanax—but the drugs were no help, either. "He started walking funny, but the medications didn't seem to help his nerves," Derek sighed. Both husband and wife were at their wit's end and had even discussed giving Rocky up for adoption.

"Rocky's our 'first child,'" Stephanie said, fighting back tears. "After seven years, I feel we owe him every option to try and solve this thing. I just want our whole family to be a family again. It just wouldn't feel whole without Rocky."

The day I came to visit the Clays, Rocky's anxiety was still sky high, though he had lost most of his voice from his constant whining. I had never come across a case like this before and was fascinated by the challenge. The pieces of the puzzle became clearer to me, however, when Stephanie attempted to show me how she put on all three dogs leashes when getting ready for a walk. Her body language was tense, she was flailing around everywhere, and her nervous energy was being transferred to the dogs—especially Rocky. "You're struggling," I pointed out to her. "Dogs will take advantage when people are struggling, especially if the dogs are already anxious." I asked the couple how Rocky had reacted when they first brought home the baby's scent. "It made him really anxious and excited," Derek responded. "He kept running all over the house, looking for the baby." The couple had missed that first opportunity to make sure Rocky was calm-submissive around the baby's scent. It was clear that Rocky was an anxious-dominant dog that felt his role should be helping with the baby somehow. In dog packs, everybody raises the puppies, and, lacking leadership, Rocky believed he was shirking his job.

When Rocky instantly submitted to my calm-assertive energy without so much as a correction, another piece of the puzzle became clear. The problem was not Rocky at all; it was Stephanie. The stress of being a new mother, sleepless nights up with the baby, and Rocky's crying had left her a bundle of frazzled nerves, and she was no longer providing any direction for the dogs' behavior. Rocky was trying to take over, and the other two more submissive dogs were looking to him for guidance. I worked extensively with Stephanie, making sure all the dogs were in a relaxed state before she started preparing for the walk. Next, I showed her how to put Rocky into the car—inviting him in, then asking him to lie down, making sure he was calm *before* she closed the door. "He needs direction from you," I told her. The same went for the sunroom, where she and Derek often put the dogs when things got too crazy inside the house. It's always important that dogs are relaxed and submissive anytime you shut a door on them, be it the car door, kennel door, or the door to your house. If you leave them in an anxious state, that's how they'll stay. I illustrated an advanced version of the exercise for the couple, which involved leaving the door open, yet keeping Rocky in the sunroom using energy alone. "You have to visualize what you want, not what you fear. Whatever you visualize will manifest itself." This last exercise was the "aha" moment that Stephanie needed to understand that it was *her* anxiety that had become the dogs', not the other way around.

"I'm visualizing it right now. We are going to be totally different, and we're a new dog and a new pack," Stephanie stated at the end of the day. "Now we'll all be able to work together and stay together. And be a whole family."

Four months later, the Clays sent my *Dog Whisperer* team a home video, in which all three humans—mom, dad, and baby—sat calmly on the couch, with a peaceful, relaxed Rocky beside them. Derek reported that they took Rocky sheepherding, to help drain some of his primal energy (energy he was expending on trying to care for the baby). "We have our whole family back," Stephanie gratefully reported. "Rocky has become the wonderful dog he was before."

In comparing these two cases of baby blues, it's interesting that Armin and Victoria's aggression problem with Cosmo forced them to learn how to create the proper atmosphere in their home *before* baby Lorelei's arrival. Derek and Stephanie, on the other hand, having no obvious problems with their dogs before the baby arrived, found themselves unprepared when faced with Rocky's mysterious whining. If you are expecting a baby, you should use the months ahead of time to make certain that you are solidly in place as your dog's pack leader, that you deal with any unresolved canine behavior issues, and that you practice fostering a calm, relaxed atmosphere at home.

PREPARING YOUR DOG FOR BABY

1. Evaluate the situation from the beginning. Are you absolutely certain that your dog sees you and your partner as pack leaders? Are you confident in your ability to manage your dog's behavior under any circumstances? If there is the slightest doubt in your mind, hold a family meeting and brainstorm about finding another, safer situation in which your dog can live.

2. Use the time you have before the baby arrives to work on taking your relationship with your dog to the next level. Practice leadership and communication using calm-assertive energy. Deal with any lingering issues such as separation anxiety, overexcitement, or possessiveness. Make sure everyone in the family is comfortable being a leader to your dog.

3. As the date of the new arrival draws closer, create new boundaries in your home around the places where the baby will be. Change your sleeping arrangements if necessary. Hard as it may be, gradually act a little bit cooler toward your dog, to wean her away from any dependency issues.

4. Rehearse setting boundaries around yourself while carrying a crying doll. If you have a close friend with a baby, invite her over and practice creating a protective "bubble" around her and the baby.

5. Practice walking with a stroller, making sure your dog stays behind it.

6. After the baby is born, bring home something with the baby's scent, and introduce it to your dog. Don't let the dog get too close to the item; let her sniff from just outside the "protective circle" you want to create around your baby. You are teaching the dog that the baby's scent is something around which she must be respectful. Introduce your dogs to the baby, not the other way around.

7. Bring the baby inside the house first, and then invite your dogs in. Don't let them too close at first—for the first few weeks, make sure they give the baby ample room.

8. Hold the baby with your calm-assertive energy. Since the baby is part of you and you are the pack leader, that automatically puts the baby in a leadership role as well.

9. Maintain clear boundaries around the baby with your dogs. As your newest family member grows, the dogs will automatically give her respect and space.

MIDDLE LIFE/LEAVING THE NEST

There's one phase of the family life cycle that is often downplayed, but that can have lasting repercussions for everybody involved. That's when the kids grow up and start becoming more independent, eventually leaving the nest as they embark on their own independent lives as adults. For some families, this transition flows smoothly; for others, it is a time of emotional upheaval. Teens can rebel and act out angrily as they try to assert their own will; parents can become resentful and deny their kids' growing need for autonomy. Ultimately, one parent or both can end up feeling depressed or rejected. Depending on the dynamics among the human members of the pack, this can also be a time when the role of the family dog undergoes a shift. In the many cases we've tackled during *Dog Whisperer*'s four seasons on the air (and the fifth season now in production), I've noticed a recurring pattern of cases with an "empty nest" dynamic to them. When parents or guardians of either gender begin to mourn the loss of their roles as caretakers and search for a new identity, they sometimes transfer all their nurturing energies to the family dog; often, with unwanted results.

WHAT A DRAG, DOG!

Compared with the usual single-issue empty nesters, Linda Jorgensen (formerly Linda Raffle), a youthful-looking middle-aged brunette, had several major life changes hit her almost all at once. First, her kids were all finally on their own, and though she missed them, Linda was proud of their character and independence. Second, she had recently retired from running a warehouse with over 130 employees. And third, Luke, her beloved basset hound of thirteen years, had passed away of old age. To fill the void in her home and her life, Linda adopted Leo, a basset hound puppy that was physically the clone of the recently departed Luke. But behavior-wise, it was a completely different story.

"When Luke was his age, my kids were around, so the time spent wasn't catering to a puppy, it was catering to my children, making them very independent and very responsible," Linda sighed, a lazy

Leo in her arms. "Which I haven't been able to do with this puppy. So in ten months, I've created this monster."

Even at his tender age, lethargic Leo was totally running Linda's life. Though she gave him constant attention and affection, he never obeyed her, and instead, used his low-energy behavior to manipulate her. Whenever Linda fired up her hair dryer while preparing to go out, Leo would become so depressed, he'd refuse to get off her bed, forcing Linda to carry him downstairs and lock him in the kitchen so she'd be able to leave. Whenever they went out on walks, Leo would run away from her and ignore her pleas to return home. The only way she was able to get him back to the house was to literally drag him down the street and carry him through the door. "It's getting harder and harder because now he's over fifty pounds," Linda told me. "I am so committed to doing what it takes to have a dog that lives in my house, because right now I'm living in his."

Leo being a drag

During our consultation, it became clear to me that Linda had humanized Leo to such an extent that, though she was a highly intelligent and powerful woman, she had completely ceased to see reality. When I asked her what discipline she used with Leo, she told me, "I've even threatened to take him down to the animal shelter and leave him overnight, so he can get a taste of how real dogs live. Then he can come back and behave himself."

"You know, it's a beautiful thing to have conversations with dogs, but they don't get it," I told her. "You need to make an agreement with yourself that it's okay to see Leo as animal-dog-breed-name, not just name, basset hound, human." "Child," Linda corrected me. At least she was being more honest now, so I got a little more honest with her. "You are in a different space now. You live alone, your kids are gone, and he's the perfect solution to fulfill that side of you, for you to fill up that empty space." Linda nodded in agreement. I continued: "So the psychology that you followed before, with your employees and your children, from your past life, that's what you need to follow now." I could see in Linda's eyes that I was getting through to her, so I jumped on the opportunity to do some hands-on rehabilitation while she was "in the zone."

I started by showing Linda how to get Leo to come into the kitchen on his own. By carrying him, she was conditioning his mind to believe that being carried was the only way to get into the kitchen, and by bringing him against his will, she was making the kitchen into a negative place. The key for Linda was not only guiding Leo gently to his place in the kitchen, but also changing her attitude and intention. She had to stop thinking of Leo as her helpless, needy "baby" and start communicating more assertively to Leo the animal, because what she wanted was the best thing for him, too.

Next, I showed Linda what she was doing wrong on the walk. Like so many of my first-time clients, she was letting Leo run the show, leaving the house in front of her and pulling her wherever he wanted to go. No wonder he wasn't coming back when she asked him to—she was telling him by her manner that *he* was the one who made the decisions! When taking Leo to play with Coco and Luigi, two dogs from my pack, I demonstrated to her how to keep control of the activity by giving it time limits. It turned out that Linda had a loud, assertive whistle that she used to employ when calling her kids home. This would now become her new method of telling Leo that playtime was over. Hearing Linda whistle gave me chills, she sounded so powerful! Because Linda had been a confident mother and a self-assured boss, she caught on to the concept of calm-assertive energy right away. All I had to do was help her see that her unconscious reactions to her own empty nest were motivating her behaviors. "I went from being a full-time mom to home alone," Linda recounted. "So I took all that and put it on Leo as my new baby. But Leo's a dog."

The case of Linda and her lethargic Leo was a piece of cake, not only because Linda was already proficient in being a leader, but because Leo was only ten months old and still looking for direction. Linda called me for help at a perfect time in both their lives, before she and her dog were more ingrained in their habits. Three years later, Linda reports that Leo is no longer a drag, is perfect on his walks, and has been cured of all the issues we tackled on the show. He does have one last quirk, however—chewing on toilet paper. I'm confident that Linda will solve that issue on her own!

Cases in which the owner's issues are not quite as clear, and in which the dog's behavior has escalated much further, can require more intensive methods of rehab.

CHIP VICIOUS

Min-pin Chip was seven and a half years old when his owners, the Packs, finally called me in to help them. The Pack family consisted of mom Lisa, dad Tom, and teenagers Steven (fifteen) and Natalie (eighteen). They'd had Chip since he was a puppy and told me that Chip's behavior started escalating from nervous barking to vicious biting when he was around two years old. He would lunge at or attack and try to bite any stranger to the family, from service people, to the mail carrier, to friends and neighbors. For the next five years, the family allowed the aggressive behavior to continue unchecked—mostly because Lisa, the mom, refused to give Chip any discipline whatsoever. She even allowed Chip to start attacking her kids. "I'm always nervous around Chip," Natalie, the Packs' willowy older daughter, admitted. "Chip's bitten me a lot. Probably fifty times, he's bitten me. Even yesterday, he probably bit me, I don't even remember." "He bites hard," added fifteen-year-old Steven Pack. "He bit my lip in two places, and I had to get stitches. There was a lot of blood."

Any of my regular fans know that I don't agree with any parent who puts her dog before her kids—especially her kids' safety. But Lisa Pack went one step further than that; she actually put Chip ahead of her husband! "There have been many occasions when I've said, 'Lisa, I don't think we can keep him. I'm worried about the liability here,'" Tom Pack confided. "We could lose everything. But my wife has told me on a number of occasions that I go first." "I do love the dog," Lisa responded. "I have no intention of giving him up."

Lisa was clearly the weakest link in the Pack family, and the source behind Chip's aggressive instability, but she finally made the commitment to reach out for help, after an incident where Chip got a little too vicious toward a baby in a stroller. The upside-down family dynamics continued to reveal themselves during the consultation. "He will attack the kids, but not us," Lisa told me. "Especially not me." "He worships her," Tom chimed in. I asked the family what the consequences would be if Chip bit one of the kids. Natalie shook her head. "I always say, 'Mom, you've got to punish him,'" she said. "But she says, 'Oh no, he's my little sweetie, I don't want to be mean to him, I don't want to yell at him.'" "But what about you guys?" I asked the kids. "What happens if you do something wrong?" "Grounding!" Steven cried out. "Privileges taken away," added Natalie. "But nothing happens to Chip?" I asked Lisa. She laughed nervously. "You know what my wife always says?" Tom added, as the kids both chimed in. "Chip is the only one in this house that gives me unconditional love."

The scene continued to play out like a drug or alcohol intervention session. Three family members knew the problem was Lisa, and faced with the truth, she finally caved in and let go of her denial. She was eager to learn to play the role of pack leader, so we headed back to the house to go hands on. I was able to show Lisa how I took dominance away from Chip by calmly and assertively standing my ground with him. However, on a walk with Sonny, a golden retriever from my pack, Chip staged a totally unprovoked attack, showing me that he really lacked all social skills, with dogs as well as with people. The Packs agreed to let me have Chip at the Dog Psychology Center for two weeks, to teach him how to interact socially with others of his kind.

It took Chip a few days to learn how to fit into the pack without aggression, but once he got the message, he adapted quickly. As part of his rehab, I brought in my wife, Ilusion, to stand in as a female pack leader for him. Since Lisa had conditioned him to see all women as weak, Ilusion used all her calm-assertive skills to mentor Chip in his new behaviors.

Finally, the Packs arrived to take Chip home. I was amazed—I truly saw a changed Lisa. Her eyes were brighter, her posture was better, and she walked right through the pack and took charge of Chip right away. It's so gratifying to me when someone is willing to come out of denial for the sake not only of the dog, but also of the whole pack. When everyone does what's best for the entire pack, then a family can truly begin to grow as a unit.

Recently I was at a book signing for the *Dog Whisperer Ultimate Episode Guide* at the Torrance Borders, when who should walk in front of me but Tom and Lisa Pack. The couple told me that Chip has become a welcome and productive member of their family due to Lisa's consistent commitment to staying calm and assertive at all times. During the shooting of the segment, I realized that Lisa had gravitated to Chip for comfort since her kids began creeping closer to real independence. Chip could always be the helpless baby that Lisa was able to care for, even if he did hate everyone else. She had created a bubble around the two of them to shield her from change, though it was really hurting Chip and her family. I am extremely proud of Lisa for stepping up to the plate and taking the pack-leader challenge. It takes a lot of courage to let go of denial and admit the truth about yourself and how your behavior is affecting your family, and that is exactly what Lisa Pack did.

THE OTHER WOMAN

I definitely don't want to give the impression that this kind of life crisis happens only to women. Usually the parent or guardian who has put the most energy into the caretaking of the kids is the one who struggles more as they become teens and leave home, but that's not always the case. New issues can emerge later in life, well after the children are out on their own. In the case of Malcolm and Judi Sitkoff, after kids, grandkids, and forty years of marriage, Malcolm started turning to another woman—a five-year-old bichon frise named Snowflake.

"They say love is very close to hate," Judi sighed. "If it were up to me, Snowflake would be gone." Malcolm disagreed. "Snowflake and I are good for each other. We both like to walk. We're each other's therapy."

When I sat down with the feuding couple during the consultation, I was absolutely stunned when Judi told me that she hadn't slept in her own bed for over a year. Snowflake would attack her every time she tried to get into bed, and Malcolm would actually allow it! Judi had moved to a depressing recliner in the downstairs TV room. I could see right away that Malcolm was the source of the problem, which he denied. The excuse he gave for not making Snowflake get off was, "She won't do it. I can't get her off. I've taken her off several times and she always comes back." "Because you don't mean it!" I told him. "The only way animals don't listen is when the human doesn't mean it." Judi jumped in, reminding Malcolm that many years ago, they had had a German shepherd that would lie on their bed during the day, but jump off the minute she heard Malcolm's truck pull into the driveway. Why? "Because Malcolm didn't allow dogs on the bed." I was stumped again. "How come you don't practice that now?" "Because that dog was huge. This dog is little." Malcolm was in such deep denial, he didn't even see how completely illogical that argument was!

Judi was being terrorized by the family dog and was getting no support at all from her husband; the wife's and the dog's roles seemed to be totally reversed. The pecking order in that house was Snowflake, then Malcolm, with Judi way at the bottom! I had to make Malcolm and Judi into a team again, so they'd both be pack leaders and Snowflake would be the follower. Still, the whole situation totally confused me. Why had Malcolm bonded more with a little white dog than he had with his own wife of forty years?

Malcolm gave us part of that answer when, while we were working in the bedroom, he admitted that he liked to think of Snowflake as "his" dog and his dog alone. "I never had a dog that was mine. When I was a kid, I always had to share my dog with everybody else. And this dog really is *my* dog." This is a huge mistake that I've seen made over and over in my clients, and in some of the examples that I've shared in this book. By dividing a household into more than one "pack," you are creating an antisocial dog. Dogs want to be part of a family or a pack. They don't want the daily stress of living in a place where half the household becomes rivals or enemies.

Another piece of the puzzle fell into place when, following a hunch, I asked Malcolm if he was harboring any anger toward Judi. Reluctantly, he admitted to me that there had been an unresolved personal issue between them for years. It had been kept at bay when the kids were at home, but now that it was just the two of them, it became an anger that simmered on the back burner and had never been dealt with. Malcolm was still furious at Judi for something that had happened years before, but instead of working it out with her, he was using Snowflake to indirectly express his rage. In my opinion, this is one of the cruelest things we can do to our dogs—saddle them with our own emotional baggage. We humans aren't able to be balanced when we have unfinished business gnawing away at us—how can we expect dogs to handle our burdens if we can't carry them ourselves?

I worked with Malcolm and Judi for a few hours, teaching them both how to own their own space when it came to the bed, and trying to get through to Malcolm that he needed to empower Judi so she could pass through her fears and move forward. I taught both Malcolm and Judi how to correct Snowflake firmly and without emotion. Then I gave them one very specific homework assignment: at the end of two weeks' time, I wanted Judi to be back, fearlessly sleeping in her own bed.

When I returned two weeks later, the couple accused me of drugging their dog. "She's a completely different dog," said Judi. "She listens to us and everything. Did you give her a pill?" "No," I answered, "I gave you guys the pill." What I did for the couple was give them an outside perspective on what was happening in their household, with their dog, and in their marriage. They needed to get back on track and work as a team again. The result was not only a happier wife—but a more peaceful, balanced Snowflake as well.

EMPTY NEST/MIDLIFE DOG DOS AND DON'TS

1. DO remember that your dog's behavior is always, in some way, a mirror of your own. If your dog has bad behavior that escalates, take a closer look at any changing situations in your own life or your family dynamic that could have set her off.

2. DO be honest with yourself. If necessary, consult a therapist or a good friend whose opinion and candor you trust. Ask them if they see you "acting out" or compensating for your changing life circumstances in any way.

3. DON'T let a dog take priority over your human family members, and *never* let a dog get away with hurting your partner, spouse, or children.

4. DON'T let a dog remain bonded only to one member of the family, while targeting the rest. This means you are not a pack. Make an effort to bring everyone into the family pack dynamic.

5. DON'T saddle your dog with all your emotional, spiritual, and psychological baggage. Your dog is attuned to all your emotions, but she doesn't have a degree in human psychology. It's not fair to the dog to expect her to fulfill all our human needs.

6. DON'T make your dog your "needy baby." Respect her autonomy as an animal and build her self-esteem; do not erode it by being an overly protective "parent."

BREAKING UP IS HARD TO DO

"My dog, Layla, was just taken out of my home by my husband who I've recently separated with. He has taken her from me and given her away. He thought that if he couldn't take care of Layla that he didn't want me to have her, either. My heart is broken and I miss her so much. I have asked people for advice and everyone says she's just a dog, get another one. But I want to know if Layla and I have rights and what those rights are. I am capable of caring for her and her needs. Can anyone help me get my Layla back?"

"I used to share two dogs with an ex-boyfriend, and I always took care of them, paid for everything, and they are both listed and licensed under my name. Since our split I gave my ex a chance to prove that we could still share the dogs. He failed because he has no time and no responsibility, and their living conditions worsened. I decided that I would not bring them back to his home to visit and they are now living with me full-time. I am curious to know, what are the chances of him trying to get my dogs and winning?"

We found these two heartfelt pleas among others online on New York's Divorce and Family Law blog, and they reflect an issue that's hard to avoid these days. It's a harsh statistic, but every year in the United States, about 49 percent of marriages end in divorce.[1] I'm not a mathematician, but since approximately 59.5 percent of American families have dogs,[2] that would have to mean that a whole lot of divorcing families have to deal with the tough question of who gets to keep custody of their beloved pet. A few years back, the idea of custody battles over dogs was something that many lawyers and judges barely took seriously. The basic attitude was, "It's just a dog, what's the big deal?" But the news that Americans consider dogs to be important members of their families has finally reached the legal system. According to the *Christian Science Monitor,* dozens of law schools across the country—including Harvard, Georgetown, and Yale—now offer animal law classes, including seminars on pet custody issues, and at least two California firms specialize in animal law.[3] Not only that, but the San Francisco–based Animal Legal Defense Fund, a maverick nonprofit 501(c)(3) charitable organization of litigators dedicated to protecting the rights and advancing the causes of animals through the legal system, has filed amicus ("friend of the court") briefs in over thirty different national divorce cases, urging the judge to throw away the time-honored tradition of treating companion animals as property and instead, considering the pet's interest first.

EMERGENCY BREAKUP TIPS

- Find a qualified attorney to advise you. If possible, seek one who's informed about animal law.
- Remember that animals are considered property in the eyes of the law.
- Collect all receipts and records to present if you are asked to provide a proof of purchase or adoption.
- If possible, provide receipts for veterinary care, grooming, dog training classes, food, and anything else to prove your investment in the dog.
- Collect statements from friends or neighbors to back up your claim that you spent time and energy caring for the dog.
- Consider mediation or arbitration, which may provide you with a better forum to plead your case.[4]

INNOCENT VICTIMS

What concerns me most about the issue of dogs and divorce is that, like children, dogs can end up being innocent pawns of a couple's anger at each other during this very turbulent time. I've witnessed real people's craziness during this time reflected in their dogs' unbalanced behavior. Dogs bearing witness to a breakup often show aggression where they never had before; normally outgoing dogs can turn extremely anxious and fearful; and happy-go-lucky dogs can sink into the throes of depression, refusing food and losing interest in the things they once reveled in. The tense, toxic environment of many divorcing households can infect dogs in the same ways that it does children, and putting dogs in the middle of a tug-of-war custody battle can only make that worse.

If you are reading this book, then I know you consider your dogs far more than just household property items to be divvied up at the end of a relationship. Many modern couples, and certainly my clients, consider their dogs to be their children, and imagine parting from them to be just as wrenching. Considering the human children's needs first can be one solution to this dilemma. Children often bond more deeply than adults to family pets. In fact, at least one recent study shows that dogs can greatly help children overcome the pain they feel during a divorce.[5] At the Institute for Psychology at the University of Bonn, Germany, Dr. Tanja Hoff and Dr. Reinhold Bergler interviewed 75 children of divorce and their mothers with dogs, and compared them with 75 divorced mothers and children without dogs. A year after the divorce, the mothers of children with dogs reported significantly less aggressive behavior toward self and others, less destruction like vandalism, less irritability, and less need to be the center of attention to their children, compared with the dog-free families. The children themselves described the dogs as a living companion indispensable in the crisis (95 percent); a companion for unquestioning, loving attention (88 percent); a companion to whom you can tell your problems, anger, and rage (85 percent); an important help when worried (84 percent); a retreat free from conflict when parents quarrel (77 percent); and a considerable help when overcoming loneliness in a broken home (77 percent). This study and practical experience lead me to encourage divorcing parents to consider assigning dogs to the home where the children will spend the most time.

But there's an important distinction to be made between the toll a divorce takes on children and on pets. Unlike humans, dogs live in the moment. Although a child will be affected by a divorce for the rest of his or her life, dogs, if properly moved to a new location and a new pack, can happily adjust and move forward without any psychological damage as long as we give them the opportunity. That's why shared custody arrangements, where members of a couple switch off caring for the dog, aren't really for the dogs—they are for the humans. However, if a couple can refrain from putting the dog in the middle, then in my opinion, shared custody is a great idea. When you find humans who have each put 100 percent into the dog's life, then both partners deserve to be with the pet because they have invested, body, mind, and heart in that dog.

That's the fair thing to do, the honest thing to do, and good karma, because each is not trying to hurt the other through the dog. If each member of a couple gives the dog the proper exercise, discipline, and affection and they stick to a clear custody routine, going back and forth from two familiar places can be a fun adventure for the animal. With proper calm-assertive energy and consistency, a smooth-running custody arrangement can give divorcing humans the comfort they need and also be a great thing for dogs.

Some couples who have more than one dog tend to simply split up the pack. This is a solution that may seem fair for the humans, but remember, in nature, dogs don't separate from their pack members unless one of them dies. Other reasons the pack might break up could be when one member becomes a liability to the group's survival, through illness, weakness, or another type of instability. A dog might also leave or be forced out after a power struggle, or if the pack becomes too large for the available resources. Dogs don't understand when a pack breaks up for no clear reason, and divorce doesn't exist in the animal world. Breaking up two or more dogs that have bonded as a pack can be traumatic to them, unless you wean them away from the group. Since a couple breaking up usually knows in advance when they will no longer live together, they can separate their dogs first for a day, then two days, then a week, until they begin to understand that they are moving to a new pack. For the first week or so, they may be confused and disoriented, but eventually they will adapt to the new situation.

When divorcing humans use dogs as weapons against each other, then the dog can end up with the human who is not as invested in fulfilling her life. If this is the case, then the dog will "miss" the person who really offered her balance. This can be manifested in depression, lethargy, anxiety, or other unstable behaviors. This is why I hope any couple or group that is splitting up remembers that no matter what the law says, a dog is less a possession than a living, feeling being that can adapt to any new situation, but only if the human leadership remains unflagging, even in the most turbulent of times.

The most important thing to remember about your dog during any kind of breakup, divorce, or family upheaval is that your emotions will be mirrored in your dog's behavior. Learning how to calm yourself and project a relaxed and assertive energy around your dog will not only be a wonderful thing for her benefit, it can also be excellent therapy for you. Doing the right thing for your dog during this time can truly be a win-win proposition during an otherwise stressful life transition.

The Golden Years

Once of the things I love most about my culture in Mexico is that our families keep our seniors with us. We care for them, value their company, and always give them the respect and attention that their age and experience deserve. Since I've been in America I've seen that the elderly here are often left alone to fend for themselves, right when they need their families the most. Often, seniors in America say they feel separate, isolated, and lonely. The result? Only in America do you have people like Leona Helmsley leaving entire fortunes to their dogs after they pass. Why do they do this? Because the dog gave them so much in their later years, fulfilling them more than even their own children and grandchildren. Because we share the pack instinct with dogs—that is, the need to bond and form family ties— seniors can get a sense of family that they crave and miss from dogs. Therefore, to some humans, leaving money is the only way they believe they can say thank you to a dog for all the joy and love she gave them through their later years.

Seniors with dogs need to remember that dogs don't care about money. They care about leadership. Just because you are sixty-five, seventy-five, eighty-five, or ninety-five years old doesn't mean your dog doesn't need to be fulfilled every day and know that she is safe because you are the one in charge. Once you have accomplished leadership through giving your dog exercise, discipline, and affection, that dog will willingly fulfill all your needs for companionship and family. But don't use your AARP card as an excuse to punch out! Sorry, but there are no "golden age discounts" for leadership.

When people reach the stage of their golden years, they often are ready to slow down and enjoy the simple things in life. A dog is an amazing resource for seeing the world through the eyes of a being that celebrates every single moment on this earth. Dogs can offer seniors companionship, peacefulness, and a 100 percent appreciation and acceptance. Dogs take joy from life every day, right up until the moment they die. Canine companions also contribute to our social well-being. Several documented studies suggest that pet ownership offers benefits to both physical and psychological health for older people, especially male owners.[6]

When I am called in to help a senior dog owner, most often I arrive to find a dog that has far too much energy for its owner. Sometimes, family members will give a puppy to a senior relative, thinking they are giving the person a purpose in life and something to nurture. This may be true, but as we've seen, puppies are a lot of work. They also have an abundance of energy. In a dog pack, seniors often avoid the puppies or push them away when their energy is highest. My rule of thumb—that you should always adopt a dog with the same or lower energy than you have—is especially important when choosing a dog for a senior.

"DROP IT, SUGAR!"

Peacefully retired, with a large home in an upscale mobile home park, Lynda and Ray Forman decided to adopt Sugar, a three-month-old beagle. From her first day home, Sugar was a terror, biting and possessing anything in sight. Lynda thought the dog would provide needed companionship and comfort to her husband, who suffers from MS and is wheelchair ridden, but where Ray was concerned, Sugar proved to be anything but sweet. She would terrorize him, grabbing his cups, newspapers, and television remote and destroying them with her teeth. She wasn't much better when the Formans' two grandchildren, Carly and Sam, would come to visit. Sugar took a liking to their clothing, sometimes ripping it right off their bodies and biting them. Lynda's arms and hands were covered with bites from Sugar that looked like tattoos. The dog that was supposed to bring joy to their golden years had become the Formans' worst nightmare. "She's 90 percent bad and 10 percent love," Lynda told me.

Of course, the Formans' first mistake was to adopt a young dog with a high energy level, when really all they wanted was peace and quiet. But I could immediately see that Sugar was acting out of frustration and anxiety, not to mention complete and utter boredom. Although they were walking her about an hour a day—Ray on his motorized scooter and Lynda on foot—it wasn't a proper walk. Sugar would be pulling the whole time and tracking, not migrating or paying attention to her pack leaders. Lynda's second and probably biggest mistake was to use treats to "negotiate" behavior with Sugar, instead of using them to reward good behavior. If Lynda wanted something Sugar had in her mouth, she would bribe her with a treat in order to get her to drop it. This had become a vicious cycle. In nature, dogs don't bribe or negotiate with one another. The only currency they use to negotiate is *energy*.

This may have looked like an extreme case to the family involved, but I could see that the problem wasn't Sugar at all; it was Lynda. I addressed myself mostly to her during the consultation, because she was the backbone of the family and needed to muster all her strength to become a real leader to Sugar. Additionally, Ray felt that because he was handicapped, he couldn't exert leadership at all. I explained to him that most of the connection between humans and dogs doesn't come from a human's physical strength; it comes from the strength of his or her energy. Service dogs don't care that their owners are physically challenged, but they do need their owners to share calm-assertive energy and leadership. That goes for any seniors who are afraid that their physical frailties will prevent them from projecting strength. In my opinion, leadership is 99.9 percent in the mind. When I asked young Carly and Sam, the grandkids, what they had learned from the consultation, Carly got it right away. "Sugar's not the boss of us. We have to be the boss of Sugar."

Fortunately, Sugar obliged us by behaving at her worst, running around the living room and grabbing at everything from a newspaper to the remote to a water bottle. I began by "claiming" all the objects she usually claimed, in the same way a dominant dog would. At first, I had to use a firm touch for her to get the message, but after only two very mild physical corrections, all I needed was to project "claiming" energy with her for her to stay away from the objects that were now "mine." I even upped the ante by putting a jar of her favorite treats right in front of her and asking her to wait ten minutes until I gave one to her. When Sugar responded to me with relaxation and calm submission, I rewarded her with chicken and affection. Lynda could see that she had been rewarding Sugar before she earned it! "This is the kind of dog I want . . . that I wanted all along!" Lynda exclaimed, after she had also succeeded in claiming the same objects from Sugar.

Even though Sugar seemed like a super-high-energy dog when she was frustrated, she was still only a puppy at eleven months. I predicted she would grow up to have a medium to high energy level, but the good thing was, Lynda and Ray had every tool they needed to be two seniors with a young dog. Ray had his scooter, and as soon as I showed him the correct way to use it with Sugar, it was clear that she would get great workouts by riding alongside him. Lynda had a three-wheeled bike with a basket that she sometimes used to visit some of her friends in the mobile home park. I instructed her to ride with Sugar next to her every morning, so Sugar would get two vigorous workouts every day to help fulfill her primal needs and drain her energy. If Ray and Lynda followed through, they would succeed in being two retirees who could actually keep up with their young, energetic dog. Their granddaughter, Carly, had the best energy in the household, and she would play the role of a member of the younger generation teaching her elders. The Formans could turn this case around if they asserted their leadership and made sure that Sugar's needs as a growing dog were fulfilled.

Nearly three years later, the Formans report that Sugar has made amazing progress—and so have they. If she lapses into mischievous behavior, all they have to say is "Drop it, Sugar!" and she complies. They've been consistent with her exercise, and it's gotten them outside more, too. A dog can be the best medicine in the world for senior citizens, if they understand how to keep that dog balanced.

Cesar shows Ray how to "walk" Sugar

SUCCESS STORY

Two Seniors, One Rottie—Helen and John Lawce and Patches

Patches

On March 17, 2007, my husband, John, and I adopted Patches, an eighty-five-pound, ten-month-old female cross between an Australian shepherd and a rottweiler. We were really not looking for another dog. We have two teenage sibling Aussies, Rocky and Bird, and a rescue border collie, Cass, who was six years old then. I just happened to stop by the Humane Society and saw that she had just arrived that day from another shelter where they were unable to find her a home. We went back, made sure Cass approved, and took Patches home that night, just at closing time for the shelter.

Well, as Cesar might have told us, her energy levels were a little high for two sixty-something-year-olds. Patches was completely untrained, undisciplined, and crashed furniture wherever she went. She pulled like a mule on the leash. When we would try to take her collar to move her, say off a couch, she would grab our hand in her mouth and give us a warning look. We took her to the vet for a check on the third day and she did the same to the vet. We finally got a muzzle on her and got the exam done.

O . . . kay. Luckily, we had started watching the first season of *Dog Whisperer* on DVD from the library. John had been a horse trainer, following the methods of John Lyons and Monte Roberts, so Cesar's methods seemed like a similar approach toward dogs, and we liked them.

We went home and started with some basic discipline. No attention if she barged in. No food until she was calm, submissive, and sitting down. We taught her to back up four feet and sit before she could eat, claiming her dish and teaching her to respond to a command. Later the backing-up trick worked well when she started to barge toward elderly guests. We put a collar on her high on her neck and started walks, in the backyard as well as around the neighborhood, because we have four goats in back, and we did not want her chasing them. We kept her on the leash in back for a month to get her used to the goats, but she still had a predator stare when she was looking at our old goat, Doinkie. We had to correct her a lot every day for that stare. One morning when she started to charge, John put her quietly down on the straw and used the hold Cesar shows to keep her down until she submitted. After that, she never ever showed any tendency to chase another goat. The goats immediately sensed the change in her and were no longer spooked by her.

We then thought of getting her a treadmill, as Cesar suggests, to drain off some of her energy. She loves it! It does not tire her, but it calms her down immensely. We also got her a backpack, and she carries the water for all four dogs and the two humans when we go out walking.

She has turned into the most wonderful dog we have ever had. She is so intelligent, loving, and now, willing to please. I think that we would never have succeeded with this dog without Cesar, even though we have had countless dogs and felt we were their pack leaders. She was just more dog than we had ever had, and having always had stock dogs, we were not really sure how to treat a "power breed," as Cesar calls rotties. If I could speak to Cesar, I would say, "Thank you so much for helping us fit this fantastic dog into our pack, and showing us how to do it calmly and lovingly." I would also say that in practicing being calm and assertive, I am actually a better person in general and can handle situations at work that I would not have been able to do before Cesar. Bless him and his pack, and all his family and volunteers.

OLDER HUMAN, OLDER DOG

If you are a senior, to avoid struggling with a dog that has a higher energy than you have, I strongly encourage you to look into the possibility of adopting an older dog. Older dogs and older humans are humming on the same frequency. They still want to enjoy every day of their wonderful lives, but they want to do it at a slower, more relaxed pace. There are many advantages to adopting an older dog.

Older dogs are house-trained, and they won't destroy your possessions because of teething like a puppy or adolescent. They tend to have lower energy levels, even if they were high-energy dogs in their heyday, so they require less vigorous exercise in order to stay balanced. They are often as quick to learn as younger dogs, because they are more relaxed and better able to focus. They are accustomed to living in a human world on a human schedule, and they have a lifetime of practice in adapting to new circumstances and fitting into a new pack. Daddy, my trusty pit bull sidekick, is fourteen years old now. He's got arthritis and had a bout with cancer, but he's still as happy and relaxed as ever, and as willing to join in my efforts to help other dogs to become balanced.

Despite their many advantages, older dogs in shelters are usually the first dogs to be euthanized. Cute young pups will be snapped up right away because of their adorable antics and winsome faces, but dogs older than nine years are passed over time and time again. As hard as it is for me to believe, some people actually get rid of their dogs when they get older! They don't want to deal with their health issues or simply can't afford the vet bills. A wonderful organization, the Senior Dogs Project, is dedicated to working with rescue organizations to promote the cause of older dog adoptions and to educate the public about the plight of older dogs and the joys of owning them. Their website (www.srdogs.com) can provide you with links to organizations with senior dogs for adoption, as well as health-care tips and other useful resources.

When is a dog considered a senior? Technically, dogs hit the final stage of their life cycle at about eight or nine years of age, but that doesn't mean they will show their age by then. Just like humans, a well-cared for, balanced dog will stay youthful longer. Size and breed can also contribute to how old a dog acts or feels. Many dogs today live active lives until fourteen to eighteen years of age! Researchers have recently challenged that old saw claiming seven human years equal one year of dog life and have come up with some more accurate estimates.[7]

There are some practical things to consider if you are considering adopting an older dog. First, make sure you have the resources to

A DOG'S AGE IN HUMAN YEARS

Age	Up to 20 lbs.	21-50 lbs.	51-90 lbs.	Over 90 lbs.
5	36	37	40	42
6	40	42	45	49
7	44	47	50	56
8	48	51	55	64
9	52	56	61	71
10	56	60	66	78
11	60	65	72	86
12	64	69	77	93
13	68	74	82	101
14	72	78	88	108
15	76	83	93	115
16	80	87	99	123
17	84	92	104	
18	88	96	109	
19	92	101	115	
20	96	105	120	

Chart developed by Fred Metzger, DVM (metzgeranimal.com).

cover any necessary medical bills that might arise. Consider taking out pet insurance. Just like humans, older dogs can have minor health issues and aches and pains that you'll need to keep on top of, such as thyroid problems, bladder control issues, bone problems, or skin growths. Most of these are minor issues that, if properly treated by a veterinarian, won't greatly affect your dog's quality of life, or your own.

Before you bring a senior dog home, make sure the house is "senior friendly," which means clear of obvious obstacles to the dog's getting around, with food and water dishes in an easy-to-find spot. Find out as much as you can about the dog's previous life—what kind of food she was eating, how much exercise she was getting, and what her sleeping and waking schedules were—so that you can make any necessary changes as gradually as possible. The Senior Dogs Project provides an excellent list of tips for keeping on top of your older dog's physical and psychological health.

THE TEN MOST IMPORTANT TIPS FOR KEEPING YOUR OLDER DOG HEALTHY

1. Establish a relationship with the best veterinarian you can find. For older dogs, it is advisable to make an appointment with the vet every six months. Your vet should be someone whom you trust and with whom you feel very comfortable.
2. Become informed about the conditions common to older dogs and the therapies used for them. Be alert to symptoms, bring them to your vet's attention promptly, and be prepared to discuss treatment options.
3. Feed your older dog the best food you can afford; consider feeding her a home-prepared diet and two small meals daily rather than one large one.

4. Don't overfeed your dog. Obesity will create health problems and shorten her life.

5. Consider the use of dietary supplements such as glucosamine/chondroitin for arthritis.

6. Give your senior dog adequate exercise, but adjust it to her changing abilities.

7. Attend to your dog's dental health. Brush her teeth daily and have them cleaned professionally whenever your vet advises it.

8. Tell your vet you wish to have your dog vaccinated only once every three years, as currently advised by the major veterinary colleges.

9. Be diligent in controlling fleas and ticks, and keep your dog and her environment scrupulously clean.

10. Make your senior dog as much a part of your life as possible, and do all you can to keep her interested, active, happy, and comfortable.[8]

The Mortality Question

I believe that an elderly person who adopts an older dog is doing a great service to dogs and to the world, but I understand that seniors often hold back on making this choice because they don't want to go through the pain of bonding with a dog only to lose her in three or four years. It is always true that dogs have a shorter life span than we do, something we'll deal with in Chapter 11. But I believe the joys of helping an older dog far outweigh the grief of losing her. You may only have your dog for three years, but those can be the best years of both your lives! After an older dog passes away, once you are through the grieving process, you have an opportunity to help another dog that needs you. Reaching out to an older dog is a way that seniors can continue to contribute to the world and spread good karma, while getting unconditional love and companionship in return.

Death of a Family Member

GREYFRIARS BOBBY.
DIED 14TH JAN 1872.
AGED 16 YEARS.
LET HIS LOYALTY & DEVOTION
BE A LESSON TO US ALL.

INSCRIPTION ON BOBBY'S GRAVE, EDINBURGH, SCOTLAND

The statue of a scruffy Skye terrier is located at the corner of Candlemaker Row and George IV Bridge in the scenic city of Edinburgh, Scotland, and it's been a tourist attraction since its dedication, 135 years ago.[9] The story of the little dog it depicts has inspired songs, poems, books, and even movies. As the legend goes, "Greyfriars Bobby" was the inseparable companion of John Gray, a night watchman for the Edinburgh police department. When Gray died of tuberculosis in 1858, Bobby spent the next fourteen years of his life sleeping on his master's grave at Greyfriar's Kirkyard. The city council members of Edinburgh were so moved by the dog's unshakable loyalty that they disregarded their own law, which decreed ownerless dogs to be destroyed, and they made Bobby a mascot for the city. Even today, Bobby's story is passed down by word of mouth as a classic example of a bond between dogs and humans that even transcended death. Much more recently, in November 2007, a Colorado man went out for a ride on his ATV with his two golden retrievers and was missing for three weeks. A hundred-person manhunt discovered the man, dead from exposure, patiently guarded by his two dogs, who—though emaciated and dehydrated—hadn't left their owner's side since his collapse.[10] There are countless other examples of the fierce ties of devotion that connect us with our canine companions.

Though these are both beautiful examples of one of my favorite qualities of dogs—their amazing loyalty—they are also examples of what can happen to dogs when they lose their pack leaders and no one, animal or human, steps in to fill the void. Humans tend to see these stories from an emotional-spiritual point of view, but for a dog, waiting for a pack leader that has passed is an instinctual thing. I witnessed many similar situations while growing up Mexico. A dog would become attached to an old farmer; when the farmer died, the family would bury him and then forget about the dog. In the dog's mind, he sees the body going in there—"That's the body of the guy I always follow. When the guy went into his house, I waited for him outside. When he went into the cantina, I waited for him outside. This is what I know—whenever he goes somewhere, I have to wait for him. No one is giving me any new direction, and the one who gives me direction just went into that hole. So I will be loyal to my pack leader and wait for him here until someone gives me a better plan." As romantic as these tales seem to us, waiting for a pack leader who will never come back is obviously detrimental to any dog's quality of life.

Dogs can teach us so much about death because they don't worry about death's coming, as we do. Dogs are highly emotional beings, and their bonds to their pack members are the most important things in their lives. They show powerful, deep grief when they lose another dog or a person. This grief can take the form of loss of appetite, sleeping more than usual, sluggishness, and lack of energy. Some dogs may wander around the house, trying to reconcile the lingering scent of their loved one with the fact that the person or dog is not there anymore. This can go on for several weeks, but it's perfectly normal. If the members of the human pack deal with their own mourning in a healthy way, the dog will eventually move through the grief process and find its balance once again. Dogs always want to go back to balance, if only we would let them! More often, it's the humans in the household who have trouble moving through the mourning phase, and we project our own trouble coping onto our animals, which see death as a process, not a tragedy. This doesn't mean you should hide your grief from your dog— remember, you can't lie to her—but do give her room to move through her own emotions in her own time. Let her be *your* teacher and coach in learning to embrace and accept the cycle of life—even if that includes the end of the cycle, death.

An animal's grief may be even more severe if the person or animal that passed away was the dog's pack leader. In nature, if a pack leader dies, the pack will mourn and have some confusion for a short while, but right away a new pack leader steps up to the plate and takes charge. Number two will move up to number one, and the rest of the dogs' positions will adjust accordingly. There is never a void in leadership. If a dog's human pack leader passes, the dog will naturally be looking to someone else in the pack for direction. If I pass and nobody tells Daddy what to do, of course he's going to be going through this kind of process (in dog terms): "So what's up now, guys? All my life I've been challenged every day and now that he's not here, what's going to happen to the pack? You're all so sad.

I'm sad. But I'm still here. What do I do with myself?" That's why, in a family situation, it's so essential that all the humans in the home be able to step in and play the role of pack leader to all the dogs, so they don't feel a huge gap in the leadership role left by the person or animal that has gone. In my family, Ilusion, Calvin, and Andre are all leaders to our dogs, because a dog left without a leader will be disoriented, confused, and depressed and may step in to fill whatever voids in leadership he senses. As we've seen, that can be the starting point for a behavior problem or issue that may have never existed before.

Clients and fans often ask me if it's important for a dog to be at a burial, or to experience the body of a person or animal that's passed. If the member of the family—human or animal—who passed was ill beforehand, chances are the dog probably knew the person was going to die long before the other humans did. Dogs' amazing sense of smell detects cancer, liver failure, and all kinds of illnesses and disease. They are amazingly intuitive. If there is an accident, or something occurs so that, in the dog's mind, the pack member just leaves and never comes back, I think it can be beneficial to a dog to smell a body, or something from the body, to get closure. Dogs know the scent of death right away, but they understand and accept it without question. Moving on is part of their journey. To move on is what dogs know best.

I believe the very best way to help a dog when a close human—or animal—passes is to give her direction immediately. Don't feel sorry for her or lie around and share your own misery. Instead, take her for a long walk. Put her in the swimming pool to change her state of mind. Take her for a hike to a place she's never been before, or take her running on the beach. A new challenge can change a dog's life. Once a dog has new direction, then the brain gets programmed: "Okay, this is my life now. The moment." Of course, let her move through her grief in her own time. But while you are both honoring the dead, don't forget about the living.

HELPING YOUR DOG DEAL WITH LOSS

1. Expect some symptoms of grief, like loss of appetite, lethargy, and mild depression. These could last for days, weeks, or months.
2. Do not deny your own grief, but do what you can to work through your emotions in a healthy way. Remember, your dog is a mirror of your own energy and emotions.
3. Don't feel sorry for your dog, but continue to provide your strong and consistent leadership.
4. Provide your dog with clear direction, every day. Don't alter her schedule or routine if at all possible.
5. Give your dog new challenges, new environments, and new adventures as soon as possible. Dogs want to celebrate life, not dwell on death!

9

Ms. Pack Leader

Women and the Power of the Pack,
from Ilusion Wilson Millan

My husband doesn't usually recommend giving pets as gifts, but on his last birthday, some neighbors of ours gave him a tiny three-month-old Chihuahua-terrier mix. Like our household really needs another dog! In addition to the twenty to forty dogs living at the Center at any given time, right now at our home in California's Santa Clarita Valley, we've also got pit bulls Daddy and Junior, Coco the Chihuahua, and Sid the French bulldog. When certain dogs Cesar is rehabilitating need special care, they, too, join our family for as long as the process takes—Gavin, the ATF dog, lived with us for nearly two months. But the Millan family has never been known to turn down a dog in need—or, for that matter, a particularly cute dog. And Cesar's birthday dog, Minnie, was heartbreakingly cute. While Cesar makes sure we always act as a "pack" in our family, with everyone caring for and acting as co–pack leader to every dog, we all have dogs that we're particularly close to. For Cesar, it's Daddy and Junior. For Calvin, it's Coco. And when I first met Minnie, I knew she was the one for me.

Cesar often says we get the dogs we need, not necessarily the dogs we want. That's definitely true of Minnie and me. Minnie may weigh only five pounds soaking wet, but she's got my heart wrapped around her little paw. She is my weakness, the daughter I never had. She fills up a void in me; she's like a blank slate onto which I can project everything I'm not getting from my husband, my sons, and my job. My relationship with Minnie epitomizes the most common weaknesses I see in many of Cesar's female clients as they struggle to get control over their own dogs. This is what we all have in common: we are all giving pieces of our power away. At home, in the workplace, and with our dogs, the women of the world are shedding pieces of our innate power like a dog's winter coat. We mistakenly think we are being generous by doing this—after all, we usually give our power away to the people we love—but the fact is, we are really limiting our ability to be strong, effective pack leaders. That's what our loved ones really need! Though Cesar and I are known for our good-natured squabbling, both he and I agree on one thing—if more women were pack leaders in the world, it would be a much safer, saner place.

In the books and blogs Cesar writes, when he does television interviews, and especially, when he gives his three- to four-hour seminars around the country, he often jokes that he learned how to rehabilitate dogs because his wife rehabilitated him. Today, I laugh right along with him, but for many years, this wasn't a joke at all to me. It was my life. At the risk of tarnishing his own image, Cesar suggested I share "my side" of our story here, as a way to open up his readers to a different point of view about pack leadership.

HE'S THE ONE

I met Cesar at an ice-skating rink when I was sixteen. He had been casually dating a girlfriend of mine, and she couldn't stop talking about this Mexican guy who was really smart and loved dogs. I was going around the rink one last time when I looked up and saw this incredibly handsome young man standing at the entrance to the rink. I thought I heard a voice say, "He's the one," and I turned around, expecting to see my friend there. To my shock, she was nowhere in sight. There were plenty of times in the years to come when I would come to regret listening to that voice, but today, after nearly fifteen years of marriage, I can truly say that the voice was right on the money. Cesar and I were each other's destiny.

When I first starting dating Cesar, he spoke very little English. He had a job washing limos and was training dogs on the side. He was actually "training" them back then: sit, come, stay, the whole deal. He was always trying out new methods and still developing his theories about why so many dogs in America had behavior issues. I learned early that to love him was to love his dogs. I remember asking him early on, "Where do you hang out? I mean, what do you for fun?" He said, "I play with my dogs." That was his fun. "And if you want to be with me, you gotta hang out with my dogs." He said that to me very clearly. I didn't realize at the time how his dogs were truly his passion. All I knew was that there was something about this man that made me feel calm, safe, and comfortable.

We married when I was eighteen after I learned I was pregnant with Andre. Neither one of us was really ready for it. I was just coming into my own as an "independent woman," and I had all kinds of dreams about the "freedom" I deserved in life. Cesar had just been in America for a little while and didn't want anything to get in the way of his goals and ambitions. One thing about the way he was raised in Mexico, however—his family gave him a strong sense of honor. He truly believed the only honorable thing to do was to get married and make a home for our child. As for me, I was in love with Cesar and felt that if I just gave him enough unconditional love and adoration, everything would work out. This is the fairy tale women are taught. We come to believe that we can save the world by sacrificing our own needs to love.

The one thing I remember about the year I was pregnant with Andre was that, Cesar was almost always with his dogs. We were living in his "bachelor pad" studio apartment, and we had very little money. I worked as a cashier, which got more difficult as my pregnancy advanced because I had to stand all day long. Aside from work, I was alone much of the time, except I did have one constant companion that first year of our marriage. His name was Morgan. He was a Chinese pug that Cesar was training and taking care of, and he was the one I used to talk to when I was down. It was incredibly lonely. When Andre was born, Cesar obviously adored his new son and was proud of him, but he was never at home. I felt I was just someone to cook and clean and run errands for him. And of course, he complained about that! It's true that, as a housekeeper, I'm no Martha Stewart. Although I'm a phenomenal cook, I get very disorganized and messy when I'm under stress. And I felt stressed and overwhelmed the entire first two years of our marriage.

The straw finally broke for me just after Andre's first birthday. Cesar was just going it alone in his business for the first time. He was still trying a lot of different methods or techniques to see what worked best. He just kept saying, "These dogs; I train them but they don't need that." He was saying that training was a kind of "a cover-up" for what the dogs were going through. That was the time when he started reading everything he could get his hands on and came across Leon F. Whitney's *Dog Psychology* and Bruce Fogle's *The Dog's Mind*. He was obsessed. And right when his obsession was at its height, I got sick. According to Chinese medicine, the gallbladder expands due to anger, and healer Louise Hay relates gallbladder disorders to bitterness and hard thoughts. I must have been suppressing an enormous amount of anger and bitterness because my gallbladder ruptured. While I was in the hospital, something inside me just cried out, "Enough."

RULES, BOUNDARIES, AND LIMITATIONS

I spent three weeks after my surgery recuperating at my mother's house. Chinese medicine also calls the gallbladder the seat of determination and decision, the place where courage originates. Although I was terrified, I finally got up my courage and told Cesar that I was leaving him. I said I would take Andre and he could be free to pursue his passion, his dogs. He was shocked. "What do you mean, you're leaving me? What do you mean, you're moving on?" But I had made up my mind. I was twenty years old. My son needed his mother healthy, and one thing I was sure of—I wanted to live.

Three months into our separation, Cesar called me and begged me to come back. He said, "We have a son together. Don't you care about our son?" And I said, "You know, Cesar, if you really want this to work, you're going to have to start acting like you want this to work." I told him I wanted to go to counseling to work on myself— because I wasn't putting all the blame on Cesar. I knew I had to do a lot of self-examination to understand how I'd let myself get into the situation I was in. But I also insisted we do marriage counseling together before I would come back. And to Cesar's credit, he said he would go, too. People marvel at how I was able to get a Mexican man into marriage counseling, but the truth was, Cesar truly believed the problem was with me, and that the counselor would simply point that out and we'd be done with it! By the way, it's not a coincidence that this is exactly the same time that Cesar started incorporating the concept of "rules, boundaries, and limitations" into his theories of dog rehabilitation. I had just given him a set of rules, boundaries, and limitations for the first time in our relationship!

So there we were, the first day at the counseling place. I'll never forget our amazing counselor, Wilma. She was a tall, beautiful black woman who was the essence of feminine power. She always carried herself with dignity, and you never ever heard her say anything negative. She used to say, "If I'm not having a great day right now, I've got the whole day to work up to that." She sat on the couch and said, "Ilusion, you really need to tell Cesar what it is that you want from him. Be loving about it, but say what you need to say." So I took a deep breath and said, "You know, honey, I really want you to listen to me and pay attention to me because I feel like you don't care about me. I feel like all you care about are your dogs and your work." Cesar just sat there, nodding his head, but not really taking anything in. Wilma finally said to Cesar, "Don't you hear her, Cesar? She needs affection from you! She needs you to tell her that you love her, that you care about her. She wants to share her life with you!" As she spoke, I noticed Cesar had picked up a notepad he had brought with him and he was scribbling on it madly. Suddenly, he looked up and said, "It's just like with dogs!" "What?" I cried. "You're calling me a dog?"

Luckily, Wilma saw what was really happening and she calmed me down. "Let him talk," she told me. Cesar turned the piece of paper around to show three circles. "Dogs need exercise, discipline, and affection to be fulfilled. What Ilusion is saying is, it's just like dogs, except she needs affection first!" I'm sitting there saying, "Cesar, this is about us! Not your dogs! We're trying to save our marriage here!" Fortunately, Wilma helped me understand that this moment was actually a breakthrough. It was Cesar's way into understanding human relationships for the first time in his life. Wilma explained to me that Cesar had been raised in a different culture, one that didn't even acknowledge that women had needs, let alone rights. In fact, Cesar later observed that dogs here in America get far more affection than women do in Mexico. Wilma taught me to be patient with Cesar and give him the room to change on his own. Her insights helped save my marriage and helped bring our family to where it is today. Although it didn't happen overnight, by creating a metaphor that he could relate to, Cesar took the first steps toward becoming a truly committed husband and father.

Anyone who meets and gets to know Cesar today can't imagine him being anything like the man I just described. And there's a reason for that: he's absolutely not that man anymore. If anyone tells you people can't change, tell them to come talk to me. My husband truly did the hard and sometimes painful work and transformed himself from the inside out. One of the things that Cesar learned in therapy was that deep inside, all his life he had harbored a secret anger about the way his father treated his mother. Cesar is a man with a deep sense of honor and fairness, and even as a boy, he knew that when it came to the attitude toward women that he saw around him, something was very unfair in his family, and even in his culture. He had really hated the fact that he wasn't allowed to be sensitive as a boy and was ridiculed when he cried or showed tenderness toward animals.

Once Cesar felt safe enough to open up and own all those feelings, he was able to become the man I'm proud and grateful to be married to today. He truly sees me as his equal partner in our family and business life, and he is always thinking about my needs. During the day, he often picks up the phone to call me just to tell me I'm in his thoughts, and he is always spontaneously surprising me with things, from flowers to gifts, to simply coming home and telling me how lucky he is to have me in his life. I believe in miracles, and our relationship is one of them.

MAKING THE WORLD TURN

Wilma taught me a lot about Cesar, but also about myself. She used to say, "Ilusion, women are the engines that make the world turn." Or as Cesar (today, the world's most unlikely feminist) would say, women are the pack leaders of the world. People ask why so many of my husband's clients are female. No, it's not because they think he's sexy, and I don't for a minute believe it's because women aren't as "good" with dogs as men are. The answer, I believe, is that women are the ones who are driven by our natures to fight to the death to hold the pack together. We are the ones who are willing to work on a relationship—whether it is man/woman, parent/child, or owner/dog—and do whatever it takes to fix the problem. In many of the cases Cesar tackles, the problem with the dog is affecting the whole family, but it's the woman in the family who finally convinces everyone else to go outside and seek help.

This determination to fight for the pack is our strength, but it can also be our weakness. Like me, many women are blindsided by the fact that you can't love a person—or a dog—out of their problem or out of their issues. You have to find what Cesar would call the calm-assertive energy within yourself first. You need to love yourself enough to create boundaries and limits for yourself, because if you can't do it for yourself, how can you create them in a relationship that will help you flourish? Relationships are supposed to make us stronger and happier, but we can't become happier by loving someone who's not stable. That goes for pets, kids, and husbands.

Raising Kids and Dogs

As a mom, I see many parallels between raising healthy, balanced kids and raising healthy, balanced dogs. In very basic terms, we have to lead them. They both look to us for guidance. Both our boys are works in progress, but I'm proud of them. They are truly unique individuals, but they are who they are because their dad and I set loving rules, boundaries, and limitations and always follow through. Cesar and I have come to believe in the power of the pack when it comes to family life; and we always notice that when things begin to descend into chaos, it's because we are not all working together. When we come together as a family, everything goes so much more smoothly. I would advise any women with families and dogs out there to remember that in a pack, everybody pitches in together for the really important tasks. One of those tasks is raising a dog or a puppy. If you find yourself the only one caring for a dog that everybody claimed to want, it's time for a family meeting where you put the cards on the table and say, "Look guys, I'm not going to be the only one doing this. If you don't help out, then this dog is going to have to be placed in a home where the whole family cares about it." As Cesar says, owning a dog is supposed to bring a family together. Don't let your family miss the opportunity in sharing in this wonderful responsibility.

Minnie and Me

This brings me back around to my relationship with Minnie, who is a little bit skittish and sometimes gets territorial and insecure-dominant around our front door. When I provide the kind of solid loving but firm leadership to her that I do to my sons, she never acts out. But one particular day, I was sitting around in our upstairs family room with a friend. I had put Minnie into an adorable little pink dress that makes her little butt look so cute when she walks, and my friend and I were petting her and cooing to her and treating her like a little princess—everything Cesar counsels us not to do! Suddenly, the doorbell rang and Minnie went bananas with her insecure-dominant barking. Before I knew what was happening, she tore down the stairs and if I hadn't got there in time, she might actually have bitten our bookkeeper, Kathleen. Kathleen (of Kathleen and Nikki, one of Cesar's success stories) is a dear friend, and I don't want her to be hurt. I don't want her to quit being my bookkeeper, either. Nor do I want Cesar to come home to the headline "Dog Whisperer's Chihuahua Mauls Bookkeeper!" As cute as Minnie is in her little pink dress, I couldn't relinquish my pack leader role at that moment. I had to correct her and follow through, waiting until she calmed down.

More important, however, I also had to acknowledge my part in Minnie's bad behavior. As women, we have to realize that certain loving emotions that we share with our dogs can be perceived by them as "soft energy" or weakness. What happens then is the dogs feel they have to compensate and take care of us. They actually have to overextend who they are as a dog, to try to make sense of what they perceive is an imbalance. I've seen on so many occasions how dogs end up taking the place of a leader when they really don't want to lead. And because they don't want to lead, they end up developing some weird neurosis like, say, running away from the toaster. That's a very codependent relationship where the only real codependent is the human.

From an eighteen-year-old pregnant teenager who was afraid to tell her macho husband "no," I've grown into a thirty-two-year-old mom married to a wonderful man who is a true partner to her in every sense of the word. Who would've guessed it would be the same man? I work side by side with Cesar, managing his businesses and, in my all-too-rare free time, volunteering with troubled kids at K9s for Kids, which is a true passion of mine. This change happened for me because I chose to face the obstacles in my path rather than run away from them. And I really think it all began with my setting those first rules, boundaries, and limitations for Cesar. The voice I heard in the skating rink was right, Cesar was the one—but not in the way I expected. By standing up for myself, I not only saved my marrige to the most wonderful, unique man in the universe, I also began to accept and acknowledge the power that I believe all women have within us. The good news is, you don't have to rehabilitate a husband to become a pack leader! You can just start with a dog.

Through our sometimes turbulent but always exciting fifteen-year marriage, Cesar has learned to put the pack first—the family pack, that is. As a woman and a mom, my lesson was somewhat different. To be fully present for my pack, I learned that I must set my rules, boundaries, and limitations and hold firm to my own personal power. I'm no good to anyone—husband, kids, or dogs—when I let it go.

10

PACK LEADERS—THE NEXT GENERATION

A Kid's Perspective, from Andre and Calvin Millan

Andre, Ilusion, Cesar, and Calvin with puppies

As my wife, Ilusion, has just shared with you, she rehabilitated me just in time to become a devoted husband and father. At the time of this writing, our sons, Calvin and Andre, are nine and thirteen, respectively. They are both growing up to be fantastic human beings. Andre is really coming into his own these days; he was a husky, slightly insecure boy in elementary school, but his love for sports has turned him into a middle-school athletic star. His confidence has skyrocketed as a result. Unfailingly honest and courteous to a fault, always respectful and trustworthy, Andre has the most positive attitude toward life and a gentle energy and is just about the most loyal friend any person could ever have. Calvin is a bundle of energy; he's very much like I was at his age. Just like me, he instinctively walks into a pack of dogs and communicates "leader" to them. He has a hilarious sense of humor and cracks us up all the time. He relishes being the center of attention. Right now, his passion is comic books—he loves to read and collect them and spends hours writing and illustrating his own. He seems to be going through a "question authority" stage these days, which is driving us both a little crazy—especially since we were both rebellious kids in our own ways, and we're seeing all our own weaknesses reflected in him.

I always tell my sons, "I have raised many dogs, but you are my only sons. I may make some mistakes, but I want you know I am giving 110 percent to being your father." Sometimes that doesn't make me very popular when I give them rules, boundaries, and limitations . . . but I tell them, my goal is to raise them to be good husbands and good dog owners. I was born a good dog owner; as you have read, I had to work very hard at becoming a good husband. Anything else our boys do, be it college, career, travel—whatever—is up to them. But as long as they are good husbands and good dog owners, I know they will be able to honorably handle any challenge life gives them.

I can't imagine raising kids without dogs in the household. It simply wouldn't occur to me. Reams of recent research continue to pour in, attesting to the many benefits of dog ownership for both adults and kids.[1] For example, some programs help kids with reading disabilities by having them read to special Reading Education Assistance Dogs (R.E.A.D.). The program creators noted that reading skills, including stuttering, improved.[2] Some pediatric experts believe that, contrary to the conventional wisdom, owning a dog can actually reduce allergies in children.[3] American Psychiatric Institute studies show that petting an animal can reduce anxiety and tension in both adults and kids and can make social situations easier as well and can raise self-esteem.[4] I know from my own family's experiences that owning dogs makes children much more responsible, disciplined, and conscientious at an early age.

At our home and at the Center, Calvin and Andre both participate fully in the care and feeding of all our dogs. I believe that kids with pets, especially dogs, develop a better sense of empathy for the people and animals around them. They learn how to care for another living being and how to put another's well-being before their own. Learning how to see the world through a dog's eyes opens the door to all the miracles that Mother Nature has to offer and keeps kids in touch with the instinctual side of themselves, the side that our modern society so often neglects to nurture. Because I realize our sons have much wisdom of their own to share with the world, instead of writing a chapter about kids and dogs from a grown-up point of view, I asked them to tell you in their own words what their experiences growing up around so many dogs have been like. I also suggested they give other kids some inside tips about the dos and don'ts of dog ownership.

Wisdom from Calvin

When my dad first introduced me to the pack, I think I was about three years old. Maybe I was younger. I don't remember very much about it. I think there was a bunch of German shepherds there then. I do remember that one of the first things he taught me was how to walk through the pack. Just walk on through; don't be afraid. They can tell if you're unsure and they may growl. Don't give any affection, no touch, no talk, no eye contact. Eye contact means aggression. If they bump against you, just stay as strong as you can without being all stiff, and just keep on moving.

Whenever I walk through a pack of dogs, even if it's forty or fifty dogs, I just really want to pet them. I can't help it. But my dad taught me I can't pet them when I first come in because they are in their excited mode. My dad taught me that a dog's growling is a very, very bad sign. That's, like, the top thing dogs should not do around kids. The second thing is, they shouldn't be too hyper. He showed me how the dogs have to be in the middle. I can only pet 'em or play with them when they're in balance.

At the Center, my dad also taught us how to feed the dogs. You gather the food and you put it in the dish with your hands and you mix it up well. Then you call the dogs, and my dad has a special way of holding the plate up in the air. And he holds the plate up until the dogs sit back and look at him and then he holds it up again, so he makes them wait. Then when they're sitting down, he puts the dish down and he does it to every dog except for Daddy, because Daddy is pretty old now and gets special food. Daddy gets this raw meat, and it's cold so we have it in the freezer.

The most important thing I tell kids my age about dogs is that if you see a strange dog, you *must* ask a parent or a teacher or another adult if you can pet the dog before touching him. Do *not* just go ahead and pet him, because you may get bit!

Most people don't know this about dogs, but dogs can be like medicine. After I slept with Coco for like a week, I slept better and so did he. There are dogs that can go into hospitals and actually make people feel better.

I love all animals and I want to bring them all home from the pet

Calvin and Ewok

store, but my dad is pretty much all dogs all the time. Every sentence includes dogs. I'm into dogs, but I'm more into comic books now. I'm making comic books about my dad and how dogs communicate. I'm just a comic nerd. But I am really good with dogs. I really did rehabilitate one dog all on my own. That was Coco, my Chihuahua. It was like love at first sight when I met Coco, but then they told me that Coco had been very mean and would just bite anything he could find. Especially kids. But I wasn't afraid of him or scared of him. I just said, "Hey, Coco, you're just so cute," and I played with him and told him what to do and he did it. He was always waggin' his tail with me. And after a few months being my dog, he didn't bite people anymore. Now I have my own website, www.CesarMillanKids.com. It's called "Ask Calvin," where I give kids advice about dogs, answer questions, and there are games to play there, too.

WISDOM FROM ANDRE

I love my family. My family is athletic, playful, trustworthy, respect-ful, calm, assertive. There is just no way on earth my family would ever not have a dog. Everybody has dogs—my cousins, my uncles, my grandparents, everybody. A dog makes you feel secure, okay, like everything's all right. You know he's going to protect you from any-thing. Everything about dogs is awesome—the way they look, the way they play, the way they have the energy to connect to humans, and to other species, too.

I think my dad took me to the Center for the first time just a cou-ple weeks after I was born. Whenever it was, I can still remember all these dogs just surrounding me looking at me. The energy from all those dogs was amazing. When I had got all my shots and stuff, I

Andre with Daddy

would crawl around there and I became addicted to this dog named Tupac. He was a pit bull and I think he had been abused or something. Everywhere I went, he went. Everywhere he went, I went. We had a really good time until he was adopted out, when I was about six.

After that, I was really attached to a pack of rotties. There were about six or seven of them and it was like they kind of raised me. Whatever I did, they did. Whatever they did, I'd do. We went to the mountains together, the beach, everywhere. There was this one rottie whose name was Kane. And whatever Kane did, the other dogs followed, and his partner in crime was Snoop. They were really protective of me; it was like having a gang of huge bodyguards around all the time. Rest in peace to all of them.

The very first thing my dad taught me about dogs was about puppies. He said that everybody loves puppies, but the first thing you cannot do is go and scream, "Oh my God, I love that!" Instead he taught me to be respectful, use nose, eyes, and ears, and do not touch, don't talk, just observe. The next thing he taught me was exercise, discipline, affection. Exercise is, like, walk the dogs. You *cannot not* walk your dogs, period. End of story. Discipline is, don't let them get out of order. Affection, give it to them when it's earned. He also taught me about energy. Don't have excited energy around dogs, just calm, assertive energy. Calm-assertive energy is a state of mind kind of thing. It's a state where you cannot be angry, frustrated, scared, nervous, excited—just be cool. It's just breathe and relax. All your emotions are in neutral. When you first meet a dog, ignore it, don't think about it. Let it come to you. Once it comes to you, if it starts licking you, it's okay to touch. That's part of the discipline. That's letting him know you're in charge.

At home, everybody takes care of the dogs. My brother has to clean and dust, mop up under the wee-wee pads. I have to feed the dogs, give 'em baths, and make sure they have water. Oh, and I also have to walk the dogs. The most dogs I've ever walked at once is ten dogs. No lie. I did it on the Rollerblades. Believe it or not, it's not scary at all, it's just keeping all the dogs in a calm-submissive state of mind. It all happened one day because I was helping my dad down at the Center, and after we went around the block once, all the dogs were looking at me instead of my dad, so my dad wanted to see what they would do. He said, "Okay, you can take the dogs." But I had all the fast dogs. It was pretty intense. With the fast dogs on Roller-blades, you really have to know how to stop. What was amazing is, we made this sweet, perfect curve turn, but then at one point I went over a curb and I had to jump—the dogs were still pulling and I was riding in the air. It was like flying. When I landed I said stop, and they stopped. But I had to press down hard on the brakes. It was pretty cool. I think even my dad was impressed. Anyway, I'd like to work up to twenty dogs someday. Ten was just so awesome.

I don't think most kids understand how to be around dogs. They are just looking to get bit. Absolutely do not approach a dog just 'cause you think it's a nice dog. Just ignore it. Let it come to you. If it comes to you, let him smell, let him sniff, once he's done you can touch him, if he lets you. If he lets you, he submits right there. If he doesn't like you, he'll probably back up four feet, with an "I don't care about you" look. So then you have to leave him alone.

I know parents are always asking, "When is my kid gonna be ready to handle a dog?" Ask your kids, "Are you *really* ready?" Because if they're not ready for the responsibilities but just want the dog because they want it, then it's never going to work and you'll have to give it back.

But some kids, you can tell they really are ready by all their other behaviors. If they're respectful, trustworthy, and honest and have calm-assertive energy. That means you've got your life in balance. To me, that means a kid who knows how to work when it's time to work, and play when it's time to play. They know the difference. That's how I like to live my life.

The dog I'm totally addicted to now is named Apollo. He's a rottie and this really cute girl rescued him, but he was way aggressive toward people and they were going to put him to sleep, like the next day. But the girl brought him down to PETCO when the *Dog Whisperer* producers were there looking for stories for the show and she was crying. It was really sad. The show's producers said, "Whatever you do, do *not* put him to sleep; just hold on, let Cesar meet him." So my dad went and got him and brought him to the Center. One night he brought him to our house. They were in the garage and I came in. My dad said, "Andre, watch out, this is a mean dog, he's human aggressive." But to me, that guy was like the coolest thing I've ever seen in my life. The moment he saw me, Apollo came running and jumped toward me and starting licking me; it was just awesome. My dad's like, "Andre, you're gonna get bit." I go, "What are you talking about? He's licking me, stop worrying." My dad was kind of shocked. He said, "Wow, he really likes your energy." It was, like, as soon as I walked in, Apollo sensed, "Hey, this guy is a good guy." Apollo used to attack all men, no exceptions. But my dad says I have a different kind of energy, a gentler energy or something. I think my dad actually learned from me on this one, which made me feel really good.

I followed all my dad's rules with Apollo. Exercise: I walked him around, solo. Discipline: I fed him, made him wait for the food, then affection after. That's when I'd play with him, like we'd go jump in the pool. Apollo has really changed. He's turning out to be just such a good dog.

Someday, I would like to follow my dad, or lead into my dad's place. I don't want to be exactly like him—not like I'll be the Dog Whisperer, I would also have other activities like playing soccer. But I definitely want to help people and dogs. It's just such an excellent feeling. I really want to show other people what is the right thing to do for the dogs.

ANDRE AND CALVIN'S TOP TEN
TIPS FOR KIDS

1. Never approach any strange dog.
2. Never pet a dog, no matter how cute, unless the owner or a responsible adult tells you it's okay.
3. Practice the no-touch, no talk, no-eye contact rule when you first meet a dog. If she licks you, she likes you.
4. Don't run away from a growling dog—she'll only chase after you. Stay calm, hold your ground, don't look at her, and wait for help.
5. Don't play with a dog that's overexcited. Playful energy is good, hyper energy is bad.
6. Make sure you're really ready to be responsible before asking your parents for a dog. It's a lot of work.
7. Walk your dog every day!
8. Pitch in with the whole family to take care of your dog when it comes to feeding, cleaning up, and health care. Your dog will appreciate it.
9. Give your dog exercise, discipline, and then affection. No skipping straight to affection, no matter how much you may want to!
10. Practice calm-assertive energy. That means stay cool, balanced, and positive around your dog. (This helps in school when you're taking a test, too.)

Andre and Apollo: The Epilogue

In our family, we have met hundreds and hundreds of dogs, and many times people want to leave their dogs with me. Just like clockwork, my kids fall in love with every single new dog that comes into the Center or our home. Andre was always asking me when he could have his own dog. Now, I've explained that dogs living in a family should never be treated as belonging to only one person—they should always be part of a pack and must respect all the humans in the family as pack leaders. But it's only natural that certain energies are drawn to one another, like Coco was to Calvin, like Minnie was to Ilusion, and like Daddy was to me. Calvin was only five or six years of age when Coco the Chihuahua came into our lives and he ended up rehabilitating Coco, but Andre had not had that opportunity until Apollo. Andre is only thirteen years of age, but he is very mature. He has shown me how much he cares for animals and how respectful he is of them, and he knows not to blame them for anything that happens; that is a must. I was there at the moment that Andre and Apollo met in the garage and it was like one of those magical moments—like they had met somewhere else before. The connection between them was instant, and it was beautiful. Apollo gave the leadership to Andre right away, and Andre took it as if they had known each other for a million years.

Now, Apollo still needs some help. He still has issues with trust, especially with men. But I know that Apollo trusts Andre 100 percent, and I will always be there to supervise both of them, so I have no doubt that by working together, we will complete Apollo's rehabilitation and he will become the perfect, balanced family dog, able to be around anyone safely. So I made the decision to give Apollo to Andre as his forever dog.

When the big day came, I decided to surprise him. I waited out on the patio with Apollo and called to Andre to come down. When I told him, he just cried out, "Oh my God! Finally!" His face must have hurt, he was smiling so hard. And Apollo, who was right there, must have known what was going on, too, because right at the moment when I said, "Okay, buddy, this is your dog," Apollo licked Andre's face and then just rolled right over, belly up, as if to say, "I'm yours!" I reminded Andre of what a big responsibility it is to have a dog, especially a powerful breed dog. Andre is thirteen now, but Apollo is still young, so when Andre is twenty-three—in college, or in his own business, or whatever he wants to do—Apollo will likely still be right there by his side.

Our family has certain rituals that we follow when we have things we want to express or to change or to promise to one another. One of the things we do is write things down, to give them even more meaning. So I wrote up this pledge for Andre. "I, Andre Millan, promise to Apollo, to use my wisdom about dogs in the direction of balance and love." That, to me, is exercise, discipline, and affection forever. And I will make sure he will do it—I am still Andre's pack leader!

"This is definitely the best day ever, Dad," Andre kept saying, over and over.

I am so very proud of both our sons.

11

MOVING ON AND LETTING GO

How to Say Good-bye to Your Best Friend

Daddy looks to the future

My pit bull Daddy and I, we have each other's backs. We have been there for each other for fourteen years now—in fact, Daddy was with me the day Calvin was born. Daddy knows what I'm thinking and feeling all the time, and I know what he's thinking and feeling. Daddy has an enormous amount of wisdom and life experience, and he is incredibly observant about everything going on around us. He alerts me to important things all the time—when a dog's energy is bad and he doesn't want to be around that dog, or when a person's energy is negative and I should try to avoid him or her. He never fails to remind me to pull myself together when I'm starting to get out of balance. When we're away from each other, I know we both feel like something in our life is missing. Others who have cared for Daddy when I travel tell me that even though he's happy and takes part in his usual activities, he also spends time every day burying his nose in my clothes and playing with toys that I have handled. Whenever we reunite, it is a celebration for both of us.

Aging with Grace

The reality, of course, is that Daddy is a dog and I am a human. Being a healthy Hispanic male, my expected life span is at least seventy-seven years. Being a healthy pit bull, Daddy's expected life span is supposed to be between ten and fourteen years. That's a pretty big difference. Now, Daddy is fourteen, and he is in excellent health. You could say he is definitely aging gracefully, and I have every reason to believe that he's got at least a few good more years left in him. But there is no doubt that he is starting to show signs of his age. Because he has exercised every day of his life, his body is still in very good shape. He might have lost a little bit of the muscle tone he used to have, but that's normal. Where you really see the age is in his energy level. He's slowing down. When we walk with the pack, he can't keep up with the younger dogs anymore. He still wants to walk and even to run, but he has to do it at a more leisurely pace. When he does try to keep up, it definitely stresses him out because of his arthritis, so I must find ways for him to walk where he won't feel the pressure to match the younger dogs' pace. He tires so much more easily these days. When we go to different places, I see that he wants to sleep when we return to the car, when before he always liked to sit up and look out the window at every new thing passing us by. Where he used to leap up into the back of the car, now he puts his front paws up and I help him lift up his rear. Daddy pants more often, when he's tired or when he's hot. Things that normally didn't make him stressed before now sometimes stress him out.

To combat these normal symptoms of aging, I give Daddy acupuncture every two weeks, which helps release the stress from his body so that it doesn't build up. I make sure he gets plenty of exercise, because exercise relieves stress and keeps the body young, but it has to be gentler exercise than before. Instead of giving Daddy drugs for his arthritis, I use homeopathic remedies, massages, and salt baths, which are all pleasant experiences for him. I give him many opportunities to swim, which he loves and which is really good for his muscles and joints. And of course, being a new "grandfather" to Junior brings that good youthful energy that always cheers him up. Junior is another kind of natural remedy for Daddy's old age.

Because of advances in modern veterinary medicine, as well as the relative comforts provided by domestication itself, American dogs are living longer than nature actually designed them to live. In the wild, canines die from injury, or starvation, or critical illness, rarely from old age. As harsh as it might seem, wild canids that become ill or feeble are likely to be banished, left behind, or even killed by the rest of the pack.

Living with us, dogs don't have a lifestyle that depends on their making life-and-death decisions for survival every day. As they age, they contract the same kind of ailments and infirmities that we humans suffer from. Typical signs of old age include becoming tired easily, disoriented, and socially withdrawn or irritable, as well as changes in elimination, sleeping, and waking patterns.[1] Measurements of the brains of older dogs have shown that they secrete more stress-related hormones, even when they're resting. Technically, the ultimate cause of death is an excess of these hormones, called glucocorticoids.[2] This is why natural stress-relieving remedies such as acupuncture, massage, and gentle exercise like swimming are so important to Daddy's routine. Pushing a senior dog too hard with the same kind of vigorous exercise that he used to enjoy can put unwanted stress on both the dog's body and his mind. Since mental stimulation improves brain function and actually grows more connections within the brain at any age, making sure you keep challenging your elderly dog's mind is another way to delay the negative effects of aging—in fact, I know from many personal experiences that you can absolutely teach an old dog new tricks! In his book *Natural Dog Care*, Dr. Bruce Fogle suggests this checklist for maintaining the health of your elderly dog:[3]

Provide frequent short walks rather than one long one.

Groom more often. It helps circulation.

Feed smaller meals more frequently.

Provide your dog with soft bedding if he has calluses.

Take your dog out after every meal, just before bedtime, and first thing each morning.

Watch your dog's weight. She will be healthier if she is kept trim.

Provide warmth and comfort for sleeping and resting.

Change the diet according to your dog's medical needs.

LIFE CYCLE, PART THREE

I do everything just listed and more for my friend Daddy to help him enjoy every single day of his golden years to the fullest. But there's one thing I cannot do for him, or for me, and that is to stop the clock. This is the hard fact about our love affair with dogs—we eventually have to come to grips with the reality of life without them.

When I was growing up in Mexico, I saw a lot of birth and I saw a lot of death. That's just the way it is on a farm. The cycle of life is all around you, and you have a chance to become more comfortable with it. In modern urban America, I've observed that everybody loves the first two parts of the life cycle, birth and life, but they don't want anything to do with the third part. They don't even want to say it. I have seen people running away from death, denying it, pretending it doesn't exist, or, at the very least, refusing to admit that it could ever affect *their* lives. When death does eventually touch them—because eventually, it does touch all of us—these people are shocked. They don't know what to do. They either keep running away, blocking the pain with drugs or alcohol or whatever else they can find, or they break down totally. But death is something we must accept and surrender to, not run and hide from. I believe it is so important to teach our children about death whenever we have the opportunity—not to make a big deal out of it, but to help them understand that this is part of what it means to be a living being on the planet. Death is something we share with elephants, with ants, with horses, with whales, with fleas, and of course, with dogs. When it comes to the end of life, we are all in the same boat. My grandfather (who lived to be 105) taught me that our existence here on earth is made up of three parts—birth, life, and death. All three are natural and all three are beautiful. People have different religious, spiritual, and scientific beliefs about death, but I was taught that all living things have a soul and that when we die, the soul leaves the body and continues on in another form. This is a belief that my wife shares, and we have passed it on to our kids. Of course, no one can prove what happens after death, but our own spirituality is a great comfort to us.

The general attitude in Mexico, at least the way I was raised, was "Your dog died? Get another one!" Because I had such an inborn affinity for dogs, I don't think I ever bought into that way of thinking, but it wasn't until I came to America, met my wife, and learned how to open up the emotional/spiritual side of me to the full range of all my feelings, that I really understood the deep pain that comes from losing one's best friend. All the dogs in my first pack of rottweilers eventually died of cancer. Before I came to the United States, I didn't even know dogs could get cancer. Each of my rotties died in my arms, looking into my eyes as if to say, "It's okay, I trust you, I love you for giving me such a great life." Of course, it was excruciating to go through. And of course, I cried afterward, and then I went inward and became very quiet. Ilusion came to know that when I am grieving, I am always quiet, and she always respects that and gives me whatever space I need. Living in America, I have learned to let my feelings out and to experience them to the fullest, even the dark ones. But the reality is, I have a wife and kids. I have a pack of dogs. All of them need me. If I am honest with my feelings and move through them, no matter how painful they are, then I can come out the other side and be there again for my family and my pack. If I hold on to those feelings, then they will become toxic. Then I am not there for anyone, not even myself. I am certainly no good to either of my packs, human or canine. That makes me a selfish person.

If your elderly dog is sick or in pain, I believe he will tell you when it's time to let him go. We have access to such amazing medical technology nowadays that we can use painkillers to put a "bandage" on a dying dog for extended periods of time, but who are we really doing it for? The dog? Or ourselves? Remember Jack Sabato, Virginia Madsen's son, from the first story in this book? Jack was only eleven years old, but he had wisdom beyond his years when it came to the life cycle. He and his mother had been keeping their thirteen-year-old shepherd mix, Dixie, alive on pain meds for a long time, unsure whether or not it would be doing the right thing to euthanize her because of her illness. Jack described to me the moment when he believed Dixie was trying to tell him that she was really ready to leave. "Dixie looked at me in a way that I've never seen. She looked at me, like, spiritually. And I knew it was time for her to go, because I could tell she was in pain." I, too, have seen this look in a dog's eyes. It is the most trusting look in the world. The dog is telling you, "I trust you to do the right thing for me, even if it causes you pain."

BREAKING THE NEWS

For families with children, it is up to the parents to decide how to break the news that a beloved member of the family has passed or is going to pass shortly. A friend of mine was recently telling me about how his parents told him his dog Smoky "went away to a farm." I've heard that story so many times from people; I guess America must have thousands of acres of farmland out there with millions of old family dogs—and cats!—running around on them. In all seriousness, though parents tell these white lies with the genuine good intentions of sparing their children pain, I have heard from dozens of adults who, even in their forties and fifties, remember feeling that there was something "off" about the story at the time. When they learned the truth, they were left with a feeling of anger and betrayal that has stayed with them to this day. Children have an inborn sense of fairness, and they expect a certain level of honesty from their parents about the most important things in life. The death of a pet is one of those very important things. This is an opportunity for a true teaching moment between parents and children. It is an opportunity to strengthen the parent-child bond, to share a common vulnerability, and to make the pack stronger by coming together at a very important juncture in the life cycle.

When a pet dies in my family, I am going to be the one to break the news. I will gather the family together and let everybody talk about his and her feelings. There will probably be tears, and there will also be questions. Ilusion and I will try our best to answer our boys' questions with honesty and integrity. If we are going to have to euthanize the dog, I will ask our boys whether or not they would like to be a part of it. If they tell me no, in a reasoned, mature way, I will respect their wishes. But if I hear them answer weakly, like they are trying to avoid or hide from reality, I will want to talk with them more about it and help them deal with their feelings better. I don't believe it's right for us to let our children run away from pain. It's only from going through the painful things in life that we gain wisdom.

When I have to euthanize any of the dogs I have loved and raised, I always decide to make their last days the best days we have ever shared together. I will take the dog out into nature to her favorite place in the world, whether it is the beach, or the mountains, or the forest. We'll do whatever it is I know she loves to do, and I will joke, and laugh, and I will do my best not to let it enter my mind that this is her last day. I will not poison the energy between us with sad thoughts. There will be time for sadness later, once she is gone. But I want her to have the experience of a perfect day with me so she knows I did everything I could to make her life complete. When we go to the clinic, I will make sure she is tired and relaxed in a beautiful state of mind. And though I may be dying inside, I will focus on all our happy days as I look into her eyes and say good-bye for the last time.

HEALTHY GRIEF

Most of the animal species on this earth experience grief at the loss of a mate or pack member. Herds of elephants grieve; they even have an elaborate mourning ritual not unlike our own funerals.[4] Whales and dolphins grieve; female dolphins have carried around the dead body of a lost infant for days on end after the pup's passing. But no animal grieves more deeply than humans. That is because we experience the past and the future in vivid detail. Our imaginations are so powerful, what we conjure in our minds can become a kind of reality. When we grieve, we obsess over the past that will never be again, and we imagine a future empty because we've lost the one we love. The truth is, healthy grief moves through all these emotions in a gradual process, and eventually passes through the other side. For human beings, there is no completion date for grief. It can last as little as a few weeks, or as long as several years. Some people who never succeed in working through the process end up making grief a permanent part of their personalities. A good rule of thumb is that the more we share our feelings, the more smoothly we pass through them. In America, grief over the loss of a pet is accepted as a very real and serious issue. Many excellent resources are available, some of which appear in the appendix of this book, to help people through the mourning process. I urge you and your family to take full advantage of any of these Internet sites, books, and grief counseling programs in order to move forward and heal your heart after you have lost a beloved dog or pet.

Animals can teach us much about grieving. When a pack of dogs loses a member, there will be sadness, lethargy, and confusion as the group comes to grips with the reality of not having that dog around anymore. All the dogs bond together to get through this phase. Eventually, within a few days or weeks, the group reorganizes and moves forward again, until the universe brings the pack a new member to take the place of their lost friend. Once the pack is in balance again, everything returns to normal.

One very unhealthy way to handle grief is to immediately go out and get a "replacement" dog to fill up the empty space that the lost companion has left behind. To me, this is totally against the order of Mother Nature. In nature, no living thing is instantly replaceable. Moving on after a death is an organic process, not something that can be "fixed." Yet many parents rush out to buy a new puppy for a child when he is still crying over his lost companion. When you bring a dog—adult or puppy—into a household that is heavy with the weight of mourning, you are bringing that animal into a toxic situation. The energy of the pack is weak, and the dog will immediately sense instability. That's when most dogs will move in to try to fill the leadership position, and when most issues arise. Make sure you have cleared your home of pain before you bring a new member into your pack. You want to be bringing home a new dog from a position of strength, not weakness. That is the only way you will be able to fulfill that dog's life.

MOVING FORWARD

My cowriter, Melissa, recently attended her college reunion, where a cherished classmate of hers—a devoted and loving mother of two little girls—told her that she'd never get a dog for her kids. "I never want to put them through the pain of losing a dog," she said. "I couldn't bear to see them go through that." Obviously, this woman wanted only the best for her daughters, but by protecting them from the reality of a dog's death, I wonder if she may be holding them back from experiencing one of the most joyful experiences on this planet—dog ownership. Instead of loving and losing a dog and then saying, "I'll never put myself through that pain again," think of the unselfish way your dog lived his life, and make the decision to honor his memory in every new day of your own existence. You can honor a lost dog by talking about him with your family, telling funny stories around the kitchen table, passing photographs around, looking at home movies and videos, and using your powerful human memory to bring him back to life again. You can make a memorial for him by creating a scrapbook or webpage with pictures, stories, and poems, or if you are really ambitious, you can write a whole memoir, like John Grogan did in *Marley and Me*.

To my mind, the very best thing you could ever do to honor your dog's memory is, when you are truly ready and back to your old self again, to bring another dog or another animal into your life. Millions of dogs and cats desperately need homes, and now you have the wonderful lessons your first dog taught you to pass on to them. Don't try to make the new dog into your old dog, because every animal is different. Appreciate the new dog for who he is in his own right, but take advantage of all the great experiences you had with your departed pet and the education he has given you. If a dog could think and talk in human language, this is what I believe he would write in his last will and testament: "Never forget me, and all the incredible times we shared. Now go forth and celebrate life the way I did—honestly, fairly, and unselfishly—by sharing your love again with another dog in need. This is what you can do every day to thank me for the time I spent with you, and to honor my memory."

As for Daddy, I always say, "Daddy and I will be together for one hundred years." Is it a joke? Yes. I do recognize that our time together will eventually have an end, and it could well be sooner rather than later. As painful as it is, I do think about it. I don't avoid it or deny it; I talk through my feelings with those I love. I know when the time comes, I will be fully prepared to do whatever is best for Daddy and not selfishly just think about myself. But I also don't obsess over a future without Daddy in it. I am not going to let anything in the world take away from all the wonderful days we do have together. Remember, we humans are the only species on earth who dread the coming end of the life cycle. Dogs live in the moment, and they celebrate every moment, right up until the last. For everything they give to us, we owe it to them to make every moment of their lives peaceful, fulfilled, and joyful.

RESOURCES AND FURTHER READING

Resources

CHAPTER 1: A MATCH MADE IN HEAVEN

Humane Society of the United States
www.hsus.org
    Information on adopting a pet and resources for responsible pet owner-ship; also a solid resource for checking a breeder's track record.

The American Kennel Club
www.akc.org
    Provides information and resources on breeds and breeders.

General Animal Welfare Resources

American Society for the Prevention of Cruelty to Animals
www.aspca.org

World Society for the Protection of Animals
www.wspa-usa.org

Best Friends Animal Society
www.bestfriends.org

Where to find a pet:

Petfinder
www.petfinder.com
    Lists over 200,000 adoptable animals in shelters across the United States.

Pets911
www.pets911.com
   Network of animal rescue organizations and services across the country.

Dogster
www.dogster.com
   Online community of dog enthusiasts with a search feature for finding adoptable dogs in your area.

CHAPTER 2: GIMME SHELTER

National Animal Control Association
www.nacanet.org

City of Los Angeles shelter locations:
http://animalcare.lacounty.gov/locationByCity.asp

Bassett Hound Rescue
www.daphneyland.com

   For more information from the Humane Society on finding the right breeder, visit the link below for a downloadable brochure and checklist.
http://www.hsus.org/pets/pet_adoption_information/how_to_find_a_good_dog_breeder/download_or_order_the_flyer_on_how_to_find_a_good_dog_breeder.html

CHAPTER 3: THE HOMECOMING

Mastering Leadership Series
http://www.cesarmillaninc.com/products/dvds.php
   The DVDs in this series are a great source of information for all dog owners.

CHAPTER 4: RAISING THE PERFECT PUP

Fogle, Bruce. *The Dog's Mind: Understanding Your Dog's Behavior*. New York: Macmillan, 1992.

Rutherford, Clarice, and David H. Neil. *How to Raise a Puppy You Can Live With* (4th ed.). Loveland, Colorado: Alpine Publishing, 2005.

Scott, John Paul, and John L. Fuller. *Genetics and the Social Behavior of the Dog.* Chicago: University of Chicago Press, 1965.

The Monks of New Skete. *The Art of Raising a Puppy.* New York: Little, Brown and Company, 1991.

Chapter 5: Rules of the House

International Association of Canine Professionals
www.dogpro.org
    Great source to turn to when you need professional training assistance with your dog.

Chapter 6: Away from It All

Where can I find information on traveling with my pet?

http://www.airlines.org/customerservice/passengers/Air+Travel+for+Your+Pet.htm
    Great source on air travel for pet owners.

Pet Friendly Travel.com
http://www.petfriendlytravel.com/
    Lists information and more on pet-friendly destinations.

How do I find someone to watch my pet while I'm away?

The National Association of Professional Pet Sitters
http://www.petsitters.org/
    Organization for professional pet sitters includes excellent information for the public.

Pet Sitters International
http://www.petsit.com/
    International pet sitting service.

The American Boarding Kennels Association
http://www.petcareservices.org/
   Nonprofit trade association for pet care services businesses in the United States and around the world.

CHAPTER 7: AN OUNCE OF PREVENTION

Fogle, Bruce. *Natural Dog Care.* London: Dorling Kindersley Ltd., 1999.

Goldstein, Martin. *The Nature of Animal Healing.* New York: Ballantine Books, 1999.

Terifaj, Paula. *How to Feed Your Dog If You Flunked Rocket Science.* Palm Springs: Bulldog Press, 2007.

Terifaj, Paula. *How to Protect Your Dog from a Vaccine Junkie.* Palm Springs: Bulldog Press, 2007.

   In 2006, the AAHA (American Animal Hospital Association) revised its guidelines for the use of vaccines in dogs. For more information, please see the following website:
American Animal Hospital Association (2008). 2006 AAHA Canine Vaccine Guidelines Revised. Retrieved May 5, 2008 from
http://aahanet.org/PublicDocuments/VaccineGuidelines06Revised.pdf.
   For more information on Jean Dodds's revised vaccine protocols, please visit *http://www.itsfortheanimals.com/DODDS-CHG-VACC-PROTOCOLS.HTM.*

Where can I find information on pet insurance?

   A good website to compare what companies have to offer is *www.petinsurancereview.com.*
   For those considering pet health insurance, AAHA offers the following suggestions:

   1. Be sure you understand what the policy covers. Some policies (but not all) cover some preventive care, such as vaccinations, but there may be additional cost for this coverage.

2. Understand the exclusions. Almost all policies exclude preexisting conditions and some exclude hereditary conditions. Some may exclude certain conditions unique to certain breeds.

3. Almost all policies have a deductible and a copay requirement. Some pay according to a set schedule of "usual and customary fees," whereas others pay based on the actual incurred expense. Be sure you understand how expenses will be reimbursed.

4. Ask whether or not the policy allows you to seek care from a veterinarian of your own choosing or whether you must go to a veterinarian who participates in the company's network of providers. When faced with a pet's serious illness, most pet owners want to be able to obtain care from their regular veterinarian.

5. Speak with your veterinarian or someone on his or her practice team. Although veterinarians do not sell insurance, chances are they have had experience with the policy you are considering and can provide helpful advice.

(*The Cost of Compassion: Frequently Asked Questions About the Cost of Veterinary Health Care*, 1997, AAHA Press.)

Where can I get information on spaying or neutering my dog?

http://www.americanhumane.org/site/PageServer?pagename=pa_care_issues_spay_neuter
Excellent source of information on spaying or neutering your pet; also includes insight to health benefits of pet sterilization.

SPAY/USA
www.spayusa.org or *1-800-248-SPAY (7729)*

What holistic options are available to my dog?

American Holistic Veterinary Medical Association
www.ahvma.org

International Veterinary Acupuncture Society
www.ivas.org

American Veterinary Chiropractic Association
www.animalchiropractic.org

Dr. Marty Goldstein, DVM
www.drmarty.com

Fleabusters
www.fleabuster.com

Where can I find information on pet first aid and CPR?

Pet Tech
www.pettech.net
    Provides information on finding a pet first-aid and CPR instructor in your area.

The American Red Cross
http://www.redcross.org/news/hs/firstaid/010801petfirstaid.html
    Article with information and further resources on pet first aid and CPR.

American Animal Hospital Association
http://www.healthypet.com/library_view.aspx?ID=81&sid=1
    Tips and information on first aid for your pet.

CHAPTER 8: DOGS AND THE FAMILY LIFE CYCLE

Animal Legal Defense Fund
www.ALDF.org

Nonprofit group dedicated to protecting the lives of and advancing the interests of animals through the legal system.

Senior Dogs Project
www.srdogs.com
Provides links to organizations with senior dogs for adoption, as well as health tips about caring for an aging canine and other useful resources.

www.metzgeranimal.com
The website of Metzger Animal Hospital of Pennsylvania provides a wide range of useful information on canine health, especially relating to older dogs.

CHAPTER 9: MS. PACK LEADER

Cesar and Ilusion Millan Foundation
www.millanfoundation.org
National nonprofit foundation designed to aid and support the rescue, rehabilitation, and placement of abused and abandoned dogs.

k9 Connection
www.k9connection.org
Nonprofit organization that mentors high-risk youth with the help of dogs.

CHAPTER 10: PACK LEADERS—THE NEXT GENERATION

R.E.A.D. Program
www.therapyanimals.org/read/
Aims to improve the literacy skills of children through the assistance of dogs.

CHAPTER 11: MOVING ON AND LETTING GO

Delta Society
www.deltasociety.org
Nonprofit group that aims to improve human health through service and therapy animals.

Association for Pet Loss & Bereavement
www.aplb.org
    Wonderful source of pet-loss support.

American Veterinary Medical Association
http://www.avma.org/careforanimals/animatedjourneys/goodbyefriend/plhotlines.asp
    Grief counseling and pet-loss support.

International Association of Pet Cemeteries
www.iaopc.com
    Nonprofit organization that provides information for the final arrangements of your pet.

Humane Society of the United States
http://www.hsus.org/pets/pet_care/coping_with_the_death_of_your_pet/

Further Reading

Fogle, Bruce. *The Dog's Mind: Understanding Your Dog's Behavior.* New York: Macmillan, 1992.

Fogle, Bruce. *Natural Dog Care.* London: Dorling Kindersley Ltd., 1999.

Goldstein, Martin. *The Nature of Animal Healing.* New York: Ballantine Books, 1999.

Rutherford, Clarice, and David H. Neil. *How to Raise a Puppy You Can Live With* (4th ed.). Loveland, Colorado: Alpine Publishing, 2005.

Scott, John Paul, and John L. Fuller. *Genetics and the Social Behavior of the Dog.* Chicago: University of Chicago Press, 1965.

Terifaj, Paula. *How to Feed Your Dog If You Flunked Rocket Science.* Palm Springs: Bulldog Press, 2007.

Terifaj, Paula. *How to Protect Your Dog from a Vaccine Junkie.* Palm Springs: Bulldog Press, 2007.

The Monks of New Skete. *The Art of Raising a Puppy.* New York: Little, Brown and Company, 1991.

NOTES

CHAPTER 1: A MATCH MADE IN HEAVEN

1. Janet M. Scarlett, "Reasons for Relinquishment of Companion Animals in U.S. Animal Shelters: Selected Health and Personal Issues," National Council on Pet Population Study and Policy, January 1999, http://www.petpopulation.org/research_reasons.html.
2. American Kennel Club, *Facts and Stats,* March 2008, http://www.akc.org/press_center/facts_stats.cfm?page=8.

CHAPTER 2: GIMME SHELTER

1. The Humane Society of the United States, *The Crisis of Pet Overpopulation,* 4 May 2007, http://www.hsus.org/pets/issues_affecting_our_pets/pet_overpopulation_and_ownership_statistics/the_crisis_of_pet_overpopulation.html. Every year, between six and eight million dogs and cats enter U.S. shelters; some three to four million of these animals are euthanized because there are not enough homes for them.

CHAPTER 4: RAISING THE PERFECT PUP

1. Dogs' life spans vary according to their size: smaller breeds have longer life spans (twelve years or more) than larger breeds (approximately ten years). The Humane Society of the United States, *Dog Profile,* http://www.hsus.org/animals_in_research/species_used_in_research/dog.html.
2. http://www.scienceclarified.com/Ca-Ch/Canines.html.
3. John Paul Scott and John L. Fuller, *Genetics and the Social Behavior of the Dog,* Chicago: University of Chicago Press, 1965, 94–95.
4. Clarice Rutherford and David H. Neil, *How to Raise a Puppy You Can Live With* (4th ed.), Loveland, Colorado: Alpine Publishing, 2005: 13–25.
5. Bruce Fogle, *The Dog's Mind: Understanding Your Dog's Behavior,* New York: Macmillan, 1992, 71–72.
6. Clarice Rutherford and David H. Neil, *How to Raise a Puppy You Can Live With* (4th ed.), Loveland, Colorado: Alpine Publishing, 2005.

7. Ibid., 136–46.
8. In 2006, the AAHA (American Animal Hospital Association) revised its guidelines for the use of vaccines in dogs. The chart listed is a basic summary of those results. See American Animal Hospital Association, 2006 AAHA Canine Vaccine Guidelines Revised, 5 May 2008, http://aahanet.org/PublicDocuments/VaccineGuidelines06Revised.pdf.

CHAPTER 5: RULES OF THE HOUSE

1. For more in-depth notes on how to fulfill your dog's breed, see *Be the Pack Leader*, 125–66.

CHAPTER 6: AWAY FROM IT ALL

1. http://www.ifly.com/san-francisco-international/traveling-with-pets.
2. The Humane Society of the United States, *Choosing a Pet Sitter*, http://www.hsus.org/pets/pet_care/choosing_a_pet_sitter/.

CHAPTER 7: AN OUNCE OF PREVENTION

1. U.S. Department of Labor Bureau of Labor Statistics, *Occupational Outlook Handbook, Veterinarians*, http://www.bls.gov/oco/ocos076.htm.
2. http://www.healthypet.com/faq_view.aspx?id=67.
3. The American Humane Association, *Why Spay or Neuter Your Pet?*, http://www.americanhumane.org/site/PageServer?pagename=pa_care_issues_spay_neuter.
4. Paula Terifaj, *How to Feed Your Dog If You Flunked Rocket Science*, Palm Springs: Bulldog Press, 2007, 10.
5. Martin Goldstein, *The Nature of Animal Healing*, New York: Ballantine Books, 1999, 47–53.
6. Paula Terifaj, *How to Protect Your Dog from a Vaccine Junkie*, Palm Springs: Bulldog Press, 2007, 9–12
7. Martin Goldstein, *The Nature of Animal Healing*, New York: Ballantine Books, 1999, 96.
8. University of Wisconsin-Madison News, "Schultz: Dog Vaccines May Not Be Necessary," 14 March 2003, http://www.news.wisc.edu/ 8413.
9. Martin Goldstein, *The Nature of Animal Healing*, New York: Ballantine Books, 1999, 96.

10. Ibid., 79–80.

11. Ibid., 80; for more information on Jean Dodds's revised vaccine protocols, see http://www.itsfortheanimals.com/DODDS-CHG-VACC-PROTOCOLS.HTM

12. Ibid., 71.

13. *Journal of the American Animal Hospital Association*, Vol. 39 (March/April 2003).

14. Paula Terifaj, *How to Protect Your Dog from a Vaccine Junkie*, Palm Springs: Bulldog Press, 2007, 16–20.

15. Ibid., 37–38.

16. Ibid., 29.

17. Martin Goldstein, *The Nature of Animal Healing*, New York: Ballantine Books, 1999, 98.

18. Ibid., 98–99.

19. Paula Terifaj, *How to Protect Your Dog from a Vaccine Junkie*, Palm Springs: Bulldog Press, 2007, 32. For further information, visit http://www.theholisticvet.com/RabiesChallenge.html.

20. Martin Goldstein, *The Nature of Animal Healing*, New York: Ballantine Books, 1999, 14.

21. Ibid., 136.

22. *The Dog Whisperer with Cesar Millan*, Episode 403, originally aired Oct. 5, 2007.

CHAPTER 8: DOGS AND THE FAMILY LIFE CYCLE

1. http://www.nationmaster.com/graph/peo_div_rat-people-divorce-rate, 2004.

2. Elizabeth Weise, "We Really Love—and Spend On—Our Pets," *USA Today*, December 10, 2007, http://www.usatoday.com/life/lifestyle/2007-12-10-pet-survey_N.htm.

3. Danna Harmon, "A Fiercer Battle in Today's Divorces: Who'll Get the Pooch?" *Christian Science Monitor*, 26 Jan. 2004, http://www.csmonitor.com/2004/0126/p11s01-lihc.html.

4. See the Animal Legal Defense Fund website (www.ALDF.org) for more suggestions and guidelines.

5. The Delta Society, *The Positive Influence of Dogs on Children in Divorce Crises from the Mother's Perspective*, http://www.deltasociety.org/AnimalsHealthFamilies Influence.htm.

6. June McNicholas and Glyn M. Collis, Department of Psychology, University of Warwick. Research supported by PFMA and SCAS. Presentation from the 10th International Conference on Human-Animal Interactions, People and Animals: A Timeless Relationship, Glasgow, Scotland, October 6–9, 2004.

7. Chart developed by Fred L. Metzger, DVM, State College, PA.

8. The Senior Dogs Project, *The Ten Most Important Tips for Keeping Your Older Dog Healthy,* http://www.srdogs.com/Pages/care.tips.html.

9. Historic-UK.com, *Man's Best Friend—Greyfriars Bobby,* http://www.historic -uk.com/HistoryUK/Scotland-History/GreyfriarsBob.htm. William Brody sculpted the statue from life, and it was unveiled without ceremony in November 1873, opposite Greyfriars Kirkyard. And it is with that sculpture that Scotland's capital city will always remember its most famous and faithful dog.

10. Matt Van Hoven, "Dogs Stay with Owner for 3 Weeks After Death," 6 Nov. 2007, http://www.zootoo.com/petnews/dogsstaywithownerfor3weeks afte.

CHAPTER 10: PACK LEADERS—THE NEXT GENERATION

1. Shannon Emmanuel, "How Dogs Can Benefit Children," 15 Sept. 2005, http://www.articlecity.com/articles/pets_and_animals/article_61.shtml.

2. http://www.therapyanimals.org/read/.

3. http://www.pawsitiveinteraction.com/pdf/Release_Summit_2004.pdf.

4. Sandra B. Barker and Kathryn S. Dawson, "The Effects of Animal-Assisted Therapy on Anxiety Rating of Hospitalized Psychiatric Patients," *Psychiatric Services,* June 1998, http://psychservices.psychiatryonline.org/cgi/content/ full/49/6/79/.

CHAPTER 11: MOVING ON AND LETTING GO

1. Bruce Fogle, *Natural Dog Care,* London: Dorling Kindersley Ltd., 1999, 20.

2. Ibid., 21.

3. Ibid., 21.

4. PBS, *Nature,* "What Is the Depth of Elephant Emotions?" http://www .pbs.org/wnet/nature/unforgettable/emotions.html.

ILLUSTRATION CREDITS

INDEX

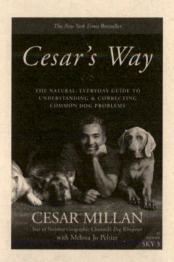

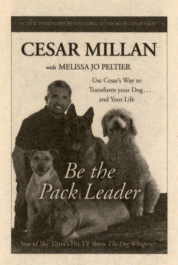

Now in paperback

Bestselling author Cesar Millan takes his principles of dog psychology a step further, showing you how to develop the calm-assertive energy of a successful pack leader and use it to improve your dog's life – and your own.

£7.99 Paperback   ISBN: 978 0 340 97645 6